# CHILDREN, FAMILY AND THE STATE

## A Critical Introduction

Rob Creasy and Fiona Corby

P

First published in Great Britain in 2023 by

Policy Press, an imprint of
Bristol University Press
University of Bristol
1–9 Old Park Hill
Bristol
BS2 8BB
UK
t: +44 (0)117 374 6645
e: bup-info@bristol.ac.uk

Details of international sales and distribution partners are available at policy.bristoluniversitypress.co.uk

British Library Cataloguing in Publication Data
A catalogue record for this book is available from the British Library

ISBN 978-1-4473-6894-6 hardcover
ISBN 978-1-4473-6895-3 paperback
ISBN 978-1-4473-6896-0 ePub
ISBN 978-1-4473-6897-7 ePdf

Cover design: Nicky Borowiec
Front cover image: istock/MHJ

# Contents

| | | |
|---|---|---|
| **1** | **Introduction** | **1** |
| | 1.1 Why read this book | 1 |
| | 1.2 Bronfenbrenner's socio-ecological model | 3 |
| | 1.3 Piaget and Vygotsky | 4 |
| | 1.4 How does society influence children's development? | 4 |
| | | |
| **2** | **The family** | **9** |
| | 2.1 What is a family? | 9 |
| | 2.2 Seeing the things we do for love as a script to be followed | 12 |
| | 2.3 How have relationships changed? | 14 |
| | 2.4 Does reflexivity mean that we project manage our own lives? | 16 |
| | 2.5 How discourse makes us believe the way families behave is natural | 17 |
| | 2.6 How does discourse have power? | 21 |
| | 2.7 How state governance draws upon discourse | 23 |
| | 2.8 How might you use this chapter? | 24 |
| | | |
| **3** | **Parenting and failing families** | **29** |
| | 3.1 How does the state regulate families? | 29 |
| | 3.2 Is it the case that what parents do is more important than who parents are? | 31 |
| | 3.3 Does social class influence parenting? | 34 |
| | 3.4 Should the state help parents? | 35 |
| | 3.5 What do we mean by failing or troubled families? | 37 |
| | 3.6 Can failing families be seen as part of an underclass? | 41 |
| | 3.7 Murray and the start of concerns | 44 |
| | 3.8 Being critical and using this chapter | 47 |
| | | |
| **4** | **The state** | **51** |
| | 4.1 Why is the state relevant to studying children and families? | 51 |
| | 4.2 Can the state do things that individuals cannot? | 53 |
| | 4.3 How values shape what the state does | 54 |
| | 4.4 What do we mean by the state? | 57 |
| | 4.5 How the state can regulate the context of your life | 59 |
| | 4.6 Should we give up personal freedoms and let the state have more power? | 62 |
| | 4.7 Considering the power of the state | 64 |
| | 4.8 Rights, and some arguments for restricting or removing them | 65 |
| | 4.9 Removing rights because of who, or what, you are | 69 |
| | 4.10 Democracy and populism | 73 |
| | 4.11 Making use of this chapter in an assignment | 75 |

| | | |
|---|---|---|
| **5** | **The relevance of political ideologies** | **79** |
| | 5.1 What do we mean by political ideologies? | 79 |
| | 5.2 Making sense of Left and Right in politics | 81 |
| | 5.3 Neoliberalism: individuals, free markets and inequality | 84 |
| | 5.4 Neoconservatism: morals, culture wars and nationalism | 89 |
| | 5.5 Social democracy: equal opportunities, social inclusion and the Third Way | 93 |
| | 5.6 Communitarianism | 96 |
| | 5.7 Social and cultural capital | 98 |
| | 5.8 What you can do with this chapter to make your assignments stronger | 102 |
| | | |
| **6** | **Welfare, policy and the family** | **107** |
| | 6.1 How is ideology put into practice? | 107 |
| | 6.2 How does ideology underpin welfare? | 110 |
| | 6.3 How have ideas about the family shaped welfare services? | 111 |
| | 6.4 Deserving, undeserving and the problem of need | 114 |
| | 6.5 How can we ensure that welfare only goes to the deserving? | 116 |
| | 6.6 How the state shapes family life | 118 |
| | 6.7 So what? | 119 |
| | | |
| **7** | **Wellbeing** | **123** |
| | 7.1 What do we mean by wellbeing? | 123 |
| | 7.2 Does wellbeing represent individualisation? | 125 |
| | 7.3 Inequality and wellbeing | 127 |
| | 7.4 The key ideas that really should be in an essay | 129 |
| | | |
| **8** | **Vulnerable children** | **131** |
| | 8.1 A discourse of children as naturally vulnerable | 131 |
| | 8.2 Policy and need | 133 |
| | 8.3 What is the social context of vulnerability? | 134 |
| | 8.4 What might you use in an essay out of this chapter? | 136 |
| | | |
| **9** | **Resilience** | **139** |
| | 9.1 Why is resilience important? | 139 |
| | 9.2 What do we mean by resilience? | 140 |
| | 9.3 Can parents help to develop resilience? | 142 |
| | 9.4 Why we need adversity | 142 |
| | 9.5 What can I do with this? | 144 |
| | | |
| **10** | **Risk** | **147** |
| | 10.1 Children, risk and resilience | 147 |
| | 10.2 The move towards individual responsibility, reflexivity and choice | 151 |
| | 10.3 Are we protecting children when we remove all risks? | 153 |
| | 10.4 Where do I fit this in? | 155 |

# Contents

**11    Safeguarding**                                                                   **157**
   11.1   How culture and values define a child in need and a child        157
        being harmed
   11.2   Should we keep all children and young people safe?                 161
   11.3   Sex, technology and risk                                           162
   11.4   The social and political context                                    165
   11.5   Making use of this in assignments                                   168

**12    Life-chances, inequalities and social mobility**                                 **171**
   12.1   How life-chances explain social inequalities                       171
   12.2   How life-choices explain social inequalities                       173
   12.3   What social inequalities, and what is wrong with inequality?        175
   12.4   What can the state do about inequalities?                           178
   12.5   Why is in-work poverty important?                                   181
   12.6   Why housing matters to children                                     185
   12.7   Is social mobility important for children?                          190
   12.8   Using this chapter                                                  194

**13    What, there's no conclusion?**                                                   **199**
   13.1   So what?                                                           199

References                                                                                201
Index                                                                                     221

# 1

# Introduction

This chapter will help you to understand:

- how this book will help you in your studies;
- why Bronfenbrenner is useful in understanding children and families.

## 1.1 Why read this book

This book is aimed at students studying issues relating to children and families. The aim of the book is to introduce and explain a range of key issues and concepts that are central to contemporary society alongside offering a critical introduction to the relationship between children, families and the state. It also aims to provide some guidance to students on how to use what you have read when writing academic assignments and provide some questions that should help you think about relevant issues and develop critical thinking.

### Study tip

Occasionally students say to us that they have been told that 'our opinions don't count, or don't matter'. Rubbish, of course they do. What doesn't count, however, are opinions that are unsupported and that's why it is important to read.

To explain, you may often cover issues in class and in assignments that you do have opinions about but being a student means providing evidence to support your opinions.

You get evidence from the reading that you do. So, it is perfectly acceptable to have opinions but unless you can support them, they will carry very little weight.

So, the solution is that you read extensively and that you always link your opinions to the reading that you have done.

Take guidance as to what to read from your tutors. Always treat recommended readings as per reading lists or handouts as being the most useful (as well as this book!).

There are other books relating to childhood and families, but we often feel that many of them either take knowledge of political ideas and ideologies for granted or underplay the complexity and scope of politics and policy in relation to how these impact upon the lived experiences of children and families. For anyone studying childhood or families a consideration of the state may not always seem so obvious. We accept that students rarely enrol to study childhood and/or families with a view to studying politics, social policy or social theory. However, we would argue that without a consideration of these three issues, it is possible to end up with a somewhat incomplete understanding of the contemporary context of concerns in relation to children and families.

To this end we have not only attempted to make sense of the context of childhood and families, but we have also sought to interrogate some contemporary concerns. When we say context, we are talking about the place of childhood and families within society and how the state, through legislation and policy, does much to shape that context and, in doing so, can be seen to regulate childhood and families.

Throughout the book, though, we have focused upon offering a critical perspective of contemporary issues. This is relevant to undergraduate studies as we are aware, through our own teaching, that students often lose marks in assignments for not being critical enough. As such we will pick out what it means to be critical throughout the book and demonstrate that being critical is concerned with identifying weakness in arguments rather than presenting one author which says one thing followed by another author who says something else. In some ways the nature of the education that students experience before higher education (HE) contributes to a lack of criticality. The focus on results in the compulsory and the further education sectors has created students who are preoccupied with the content of assignments and on what they often term 'getting it right' (Creasy, 2018).

Studying in HE is not the same. Very often you have to focus much more on what you do with content. Higher marks do not come from having the right content. Higher marks come from using it more effectively, by being logical and structured and by writing in clear and concise ways.

---

**Study tip**

When it comes to politics and policy it is not at all unusual to find contradictions or to find that words are being used in ways which seem a little slippery.

Describing a social concept as slippery is useful because many concepts can be hard to pin down.

When studying social science, you have to get used to this, and recognise the complexity of many of the things we tend to take for granted in life. You need to accept concepts as being potentially slippery in that an absolute, or definite, description can sometimes be a bit elusive, or maybe even impossible.

---

We hope to be able to demonstrate that contradictions and slippery words are nothing to be alarmed about. Overall, we also hope to be able to develop a broader understanding of childhood and families by showing how politics and policy, as well as practice, shape the context of our lives. In doing so we cannot claim to be entirely original. One theoretical approach that is very relevant to this book and which most students of childhood will have encountered is that presented by Bronfenbrenner.

## 1.2 Bronfenbrenner's socio-ecological model

Many students reading this will have encountered Urie Bronfenbrenner (1979) previously as his work has been very influential within 21st-century Britain. Bronfenbrenner's socio-ecological model provides an excellent example of how we might develop a broad understanding of issues relating to children and families. It also provides an example of how you can frame your understanding of them and of how you can frame what you what write about them.

---

### Study tip

The idea of framing is very useful. It is an approach which can help you be more effective as a student in how it provides a focus for your work.

So, when we say framing, we explain something in a way that keeps the focus within one particular area, we don't go out of the frame. This keeps our work focused.

Usually, it refers to either adopting a particular theoretical approach to explain something or it focuses on one particular issue.

In this section we use the work of Bronfenbrenner to frame an understanding of children's lives.

In considering Bronfenbrenner we are able to provide an approach that will demonstrate that an understanding of the state is important if we are to study children and families.

---

Bronfenbrenner's work is often presented as being a socio-ecological model. Ecology is about the environment and what we are doing here is thinking about the environment that the child lives in. At the same time children live in an environment where the relationships between people are important. If we accept that relationships are important then we can also see that relationships are a social phenomenon, so now it makes sense if we see Bronfenbrenner's model referred to as a socio-ecological model. Bronfenbrenner's model is based on social relationships and how social behaviours and services combine to create the environment in which the child lives.

## 1.3 Piaget and Vygotsky

Bronfenbrenner's work is useful for illustrating how ideas can be seen as being shaped by the social context. So, Bronfenbrenner is concerned with children's development and draws on the work of Vygotsky to move away from the typical psychological model of development that has been the dominant position in western countries for quite some time. For example, pick up any book entitled Child Development and it will invariably be focused on psychology. Usually, psychological theories focus on the child as an individual, something that fits very well with western ideas about individualism. Vygotsky was Russian and you can see his ideas as having been influenced by the more collective concerns of socialism that had become dominant in Russia a little before Vygotsky was writing. So, in Vygotsky's approach, the social experiences of children take on greater significance than their individual psychology. This can be seen in the difference in the position taken by Vygotsky, who develops a social-constructionist approach compared to Piaget.

### Note

The simplest way of seeing the difference between the Piagetian and the Vygotskyan approaches is that for Piaget the child is like a little scientist, whereas for Vygotsky the child is more like a little apprentice.

The little scientist explores their own world as an individual and makes sense of it as they do so. As they do this they develop. However, as they explore their surroundings, their world, they are constrained for a large part by the fact that, for Piaget, they go through stages of development. This underpins the 'ages and stages' approach to child development.

As an apprentice they learn about their world in the company of others and are guided by those who are more knowledgeable. Grasping this is essential to make sense of Piaget and Vygotsky. Be clear about what the differences are but accept that this is a simplified version.

Now consider the culture in which each of these theoretical approaches was developed; both were working around the same time. Piaget was working in Europe, where ideas about individualism were dominant. Vygotsky was working in Russia, where ideas about being part of society were dominant. When we think about it like this we can start to see how our ideas are shaped by our social and cultural experiences.

As such, in adopting a Vygotskyan approach, Bronfenbrenner considers what contributes to the social and cultural aspects of how a child develops. He presents a range of influences that are very often illustrated as a set of Russian dolls or, more usually, as concentric circles, where the child is at the centre.

## 1.4 How does society influence children's development?

In taking the typical representation of Bronfenbrenner's model as being a set of concentric circles with the child at the centre, what we see is that the immediate concern is the child's world: the micro-system of families, schools and day-care settings. The child's peer group would be here. However, these settings are not independent of each other so changes in one micro-factor may affect the child in another. Consider how the relationships between families and schools have been seen as important for some time (Hughes et al, 1994; Whalley and Centre, 2007; Knowles and Holmstrom, 2013; Siraj and Mayo, 2014). Now consider that not all families are supportive of the work that schools do. What this means is that a child in a family that we could call school-resistant may experience school very differently to a child living in a family that is school-supportive.

We can also see that a child is affected by settings which they are not involved in, exo-systems such as the parent's workplace. So, if parents have to work long hours or have a job that involves shift work, we might think about how this could impact on children. The next factors in Bronfenbrenner's model reflect the broader elements of society and culture such as government policies, values and religious practices. There is also an additional system, the chronosystem. The chronosystem represents change over time. This is important, and we can confidently say that for older adults, their experience of childhood will have been different to the typical 18–21-year-old student's experience of childhood now because society has changed over time.

Bronfenbrenner is relevant to this book because of the way in which he points to a range of factors that are shaped by politics and policy which in turn shape the lived experiences of children and families. He demonstrates the value of being critical in how he presents a theoretical model for understanding the context of children's development which recognises the limitations of many psychological theories. Bronfenbrenner also shaped practice in that he was very much involved in policy programmes which directly affect children's lives. This is the link to the state! Bronfenbrenner's work was the basis for the Head Start programme in the US and was instrumental in shifting the focus away from the child in isolation, which psychological theories are often guilty of, to consider children's position within families, communities and society.

The Head Start programme focused upon families and communities which experience disadvantage. The policy was based upon evidence which demonstrated that children from deprived backgrounds performed less well at school. The aim was to level the playing field. In the UK, the Labour government from 1997 to 2010 drew from the success of Head Start in the US and introduced a similar policy programme which they called Sure Start. Sure Start was also aimed at overcoming the disadvantage that is typically experienced in poorer communities.

However, although Sure Start was successful as a policy approach (Anning and Ball, 2008; Lewis et al, 2011; Donetto and Maben, 2015; Hall et al, 2015), policy changes introduced by the Coalition and Conservative governments since 2010 effectively closed it down. It is worth noting that the Conservative government of 2019 onwards proposed to reintroduce a limited number of Family Hubs which will reflect the Sure Start type of family centre from 2022 (DfE and Ford, 2021).

In considering Bronfenbrenner then we can demonstrate why a consideration of the state is necessary if we are to understand the lives of children and families. If we consider Sure Start as an example of a state-run programme, we can see why it is that any consideration of children and families also needs to consider the role of the state. This is because the experiences of childhood and children's lives, and their futures, can be seen as being shaped by the state. If we take a simple view of Bronfenbrenner's basic model, children's development takes place within families, and this influences issues relating to how they develop by shaping their experiences and opportunities. At the same time the position of families is influenced by a range of issues relating to the state, such as the extent of support that is provided to families or in respect of policies which shape the economic position of different families.

A particular focus within Chapter 3 will be a concern with what in the UK has often been referred to as failing families, or alternatively, troubled or even troublesome families. Such families are seen as presenting a problem not only for the communities in which they live but also for themselves. Think about this in relation to how children develop. Phrases such as 'I blame the parents' or 'The apple never falls far from the tree' suggest not only that children will only learn from their parents, but that they will grow up to be increasingly like their parents. So, this argument suggests that if parents engage in behaviours that can be considered to be problematic then we can expect their children to also engage in similar behaviours. Well, that's the idea.

---

### Pause for reflection

Can you identify weaknesses with claims that children will grow up to be like their parents?

It is not difficult to pick holes in this idea and this is what we mean by being critical. This is not to say that children do not learn from their parents nor is it to say that they won't adopt some of their parents' habits or ways, but as a student you must always be careful not to fall into the trap of being deterministic.

When we say 'I blame the parents' we are saying that children have no free will, no agency. In sociology, agency refers to our capacity to make our own decisions and act on them.

---

The argument that children will be just like their parents also suggests that children are only influenced by their parents and that is clearly not the case. Children are not only subject to socialisation from their parents; they are also subject to a range of socialising influences such as from their peers, or their experiences at school and the influence of the media. Bronfenbrenner's socio-ecological model reflects this aspect of children's lives and gets us to think about the range of factors and settings which shape the context within which children develop. To reiterate what Bronfenbrenner is saying, this takes place against a more general backdrop of social, cultural and economic factors which are all significantly shaped by the state.

As an example, read the book *Chavs* (Jones, 2016). Focus on how Jones describes and discusses the changes that families in Ashington, Northumberland, have experienced since the decline of the mining industry. Many families in Ashington included men who worked in mining. That work has now gone, and though some may have found other jobs many struggled to secure work and some of these families may have come to be reliant on state benefits. Other sectors of the economy have also seen a decline in numbers working in that region of the UK. Jones is referring to changes in the 1980s, but O'Hara and Thomas (2014) also demonstrate how the range of actions carried out by the government since 2010, that came to be known as austerity, has affected the context of life in Britain.

This includes the way that the government set about reducing the size of the public sector, which involved making many thousands of workers redundant. Charlesworth (2000) provides a similar account to that of Jones, of another once-industrial town, Rotherham, to illustrate the changes that have been brought about by the decline of industry in the UK. This is usually referred to as deindustrialisation. In one sense we can accept that work does change, that industries do decline for many reasons. However, in the UK this did not just happen; the state had a part to play in the change.

Deindustrialisation refers to the decline of industry within a country's economy and the move towards a focus on services (Greenstein, 2019). One thing that Greenstein notes is that service-sector jobs are often associated with lower wages. Industrial workers had generally earned higher wages than service-sector workers. Deindustrialisation within the UK has taken place over a long time (Nettleingham, 2019) but the mining industry declined very quickly and this rapid decline led to real social problems as a consequence of large numbers of men in particular becoming unemployed at the same time, often in areas where alternative employment was scarce (Strangleman, 2018).

---

**Study tip**

It always helps to put your studies in the context of your own life and the lives of people around you. So ask your parents and grandparents, aunts and uncles, about their lives and experiences.

The issue of work, and changes to work, may have passed you by so consider what work people do in the area in which you live. Has this changed over time: for example, have some industries closed? Can you see how this has changed roles in families, such as men not being the main earner, or women working full time?

---

This seems to be moving away from a concern with children and families. However, one thing that you should always ask as a student is 'So what?'. This is a good time to ask that question. So what? Why is this relevant to children, families and the state? It is relevant because we could say that deindustrialisation was a government strategy. The Conservative government of the 1980s, led by Margaret Thatcher, introduced policies and acted in ways which actively contributed to deindustrialisation. The families in Jones' study or in Rotherham as per Charlesworth's study can be seen to be much poorer than they had been before deindustrialisation, and this has inevitably had an impact upon their children.

We can also say then that if we are looking at the lives of these families, and the children who live in them, they have been shaped to some extent by the actions that were taken by the state. So now we have two examples of the ways in which the state has had an impact upon the lives of children and families within this chapter. Firstly, in respect of services that are provided to support them such as welfare support or service provision such as Sure Start Children's Centres. Secondly, by pursuing economic and industrial strategies which can advantage or disadvantage families. Other examples will be covered throughout the book, but all will be demonstrated to have an impact upon the context of childhood and families.

## Further thoughts

Consider how we come to see things as normal or natural. This might be because of what we have been taught or because of the everyday sayings that we hear.

For example, consider how we often see the natural world as competitive and hierarchical. This draws on Darwin's ideas about the survival of the fittest and reinforces ideas about individualism. But compare this to Peter Kropotkin's arguments. Kropotkin was trying to find evidence to support Darwin's theory but instead of conflict and competition in the natural world he saw animals working together for mutual benefit.

Kropotkin is not as well known as Darwin in the west, but might that be because Darwin fits more comfortably with individualism? So, as you read through the book keep thinking why it is that we believe what we do.

## Further reading

Read about Bronfenbrenner's socio-ecological model and make sure that you are clear as to why it is both social and ecological.

# 2

# The family

This chapter will help you to understand:

- how we can define the family;
- how the family practices approach can be useful in your studies;
- what discourse is.

## 2.1 What is a family?

Defining the family is not so easy yet it is something that we very often take for granted (Frost, 2011; Steel et al, 2012). In this book we are less concerned with how we might explain what the family does and more concerned with considering what we mean by the family and the ways in which the family is impacted upon by actions that are taken by the state. In this way we will consider how the family is shaped. We are also concerned with what this means for children. This sees us considering the ways in which social policies are able to shape family life or experiences. Because of this it is important to come up with a workable definition or model of what we mean by the family.

We can see how the concept or idea of the family is firmly embedded within UK culture but once we start to try to pin it down we run into problems. We can point to the idea of the nuclear family as an adult couple with children and compare this to an extended family, the same adult couple with children who are in a close relationship with other relatives such as grandparents, aunts and cousins. Although the idea of the nuclear family and the extended family are in everyday use, they have real limitations in explaining what a family is because there is simply so much diversity.

Although the nuclear family comprised of a heterosexual couple with 2.4 children features very strongly in ideas about families, we know from our everyday experiences that many families do not look like this. As such, it is possible to identify single-parent families, reconstituted families, same-sex families and others, and in doing so, recognise that families come in a variety of forms. How those forms are understood can be important. For example, Shaw et al (2013) introduce the idea of 'satellite' and 'multi-local' families which come about when one adult family member works a long distance from the family home. This entails setting up a second home. We should keep this in mind when we think about people who move to different countries for work and not only in terms of people who may work a long way from their UK home and family.

---

**Pause for reflection**

Think of your own family and other families you know, and consider the differences. It may be that you do not have experience of different types of families, in which case you need to keep your mind open to the idea that families do operate in many different ways.

---

It could be more useful then to move beyond trying to pin down an unambiguous definition of family by recognising that family can be seen as both singular and plural (Morgan et al, 2019). So, each family may differ in terms of form, but it still corresponds to what we refer to as family. Of course, we might then think just what is it that makes it a family. Morgan et al (2019) point to three important characteristics: dependency, obligations and mutuality.

Think about how, within a family, we can often pick out the ways in which relationships exist that reflect dependency and responsibilities, mutual interests or concerns and a sense of obligation to others because of who they are. By looking at families like this we move away from the sort of approach whereby we have an idea or model that we then measure or compare others against to see if they fit the model or not. This gives us a much more fluid approach.

In recent years much academic research has come to be framed by this more fluid approach. This underpins the notion of 'family practices', a model identified and outlined by Morgan (2011). In this model the family is what the family does. This means that in identifying a family it is not necessary to have it correspond to some fixed or rigid definition. As a theoretical approach this places a greater emphasis upon agency, our capacity to act. It is less concerned with structures or structural forces. As a concept, agency is central to sociology.

---

**Note**

Sociology tends to offer explanations based on one of two positions, either structure or action. Action is often referred to as agency and you will come across these positions a lot.

In its simplest form structure refers to large-scale social structures such as how society is shaped by economic forces, religion or political values. From this perspective we, as individuals, are shaped by society.

The opposite position is that of action or agency. In this perspective society is shaped by the actions of people. It is what people do that is important.

---

The action perspective is an approach which works very well in explaining social change and that is where we started this discussion, by referring to changes in respect of the family. With this in mind it is useful to emphasise a point made by Morgan (2011: 3): 'there is no such thing as "the family"'. In saying this, Morgan is bringing diversity to the fore.

### Study tip

When reading the quote from Morgan, focus on the use of 'the' within the statement. Using 'the' always puts a particular slant on things and it is something that students often do, but very often shouldn't do.

We call using 'the' in this way 'the definite article'. What we mean by this is that by adding 'the' we present the idea that there is only one, clear definition or version of whatever it is we are referring to. So, Morgan says, 'there is no such thing as "the family"', and he is correct. What we can't say is that there is no such thing as 'family'.

Saying 'family' rather than 'the family' opens up the possibility of diversity. Think about this as you write your assignments and always be very careful how you use the word 'the'.

As a student, when you have an assignment that requires you to engage with the notion of family, you might find Morgan's approach very good for talking about families within contemporary society. There are families, but to refer to 'the' family is problematic. You can outline earlier approaches and refer to how they may be seen as rigid and then move on to say how the family practices approach put forward by Morgan (2011) is able to accommodate diversity and social change.

Importantly, though, you need to be careful not to assume that this more fluid approach that we have referred to is universally welcomed. From an academic perspective it is more accurate, and it is more useful, but that does not mean that it does not have its critics.

### Study tip

One thing that stands out in terms of academic issues is that very often ideas are contested. This can pose problems for some students as they have had years of being told that there is a right answer to the things we are discussing or learning about.

Once you start a higher education course you start to see that very often, especially in social sciences, this is not true.

There may be right and wrong ways of doing things, such as how to cite and reference, but most of the time it is up to you to demonstrate why you are right, or why your ideas are valid, and to do that you have to read a lot.

Frost (2011) is useful for illustrating this. Frost uses a quote from Smart (2007) relating to the decline of the nuclear family and the rise of the fluid family. This is characterised by two opposing views: one from Morgan and one from

CAVA. (Confusingly, maybe, the Morgan referred to here is Patricia Morgan rather than David Morgan as discussed previously. Patricia Morgan adopts a conservative approach towards families while David Morgan adopts a progressive approach. Do not get them mixed up!) Frost presents these two opposing views as being fear and concern versus appreciation and celebration. Almond (2008) provides a similar argument to Morgan regarding the ways in which legislation and social policies intersect with social change in being a threat to the institution of marriage. What both do is to reinforce the argument that is being put forward in this book that legislation and social policies, things which are put in place by the state, act to shape the lives of children and families.

## 2.2 Seeing the things we do for love as a script to be followed

So far we have been talking about families but we could also step back and ask about how families came to be. There are social, cultural and political aspects to this. Many of us will marry or live with a long-term partner in a monogamous relationship. Why? There is a strong emphasis in UK culture that this is for love but it is not as straightforward or as accurate as we tend to believe. Pinto (2017) provides a good overview of ways in which romantic love has changed over time illustrating how social and cultural behaviours may intersect with biological factors. There may be a biological basis to the feelings associated with love and attraction but how this plays out is social. Beck and Beck-Gernsheim (1995), in their book *The Normal Chaos of Love*, also point to how romantic love has changed over time as, they argue, we have become more individualised. This idea suggests that when we choose a partner we are making our own choice based on our own desires and needs, rather than for any social or family obligation.

The idea that we have become more individualised in our outlook can be linked to the influence of the political ideology that is called neoliberalism. A fuller discussion of neoliberalism is provided in Chapter 5.

It is not sufficient to say that neoliberalism explains these changes on its own because there have been other social changes which impact upon love and relationships also. The changing social position of women has also influenced attitudes towards love and marriage. So, be careful with theory; neoliberalism provides a framework within which we become more individualistic, but it may not be sufficient on its own to explain social change. It might be more reasonable to consider social change as a bit more complex and to recognise that often two or more things overlap and influence society and social behaviour.

Let us start by considering marriage, as this is central to how we understand families. Marriage plays a central role within our understanding of families but marriage on the basis of love is neither historically nor culturally universal. If we consider ideas about romantic love, we can see that a discourse exists regarding what love is and which may be read as a script. You may be wondering what is meant by the term discourse; if so, don't worry. We will explain discourse more fully in Section 2.5. For now, just consider the idea that discourse is like a script in terms of how it directs what we do. Discourse acts to shape how we understand the world and this includes a way of organising our feelings and making sense of them within a particular social condition. For example, there is a discourse that supports the idea that as adults we will meet someone special to us and settle down with them as a family. However, this way of living is not natural; it is socially constructed.

## Pause for reflection

To understand this better, apply it to a situation you may be more familiar with. Let's say that you have just started seeing a new partner.

Think about what you might expect within this relationship with respect to your new partner's behaviour towards you, or with respect to what you might do together, in terms of outings or gifts, for example.

Talk to friends and see what they think. You will soon start to see a pattern emerging which may suggest that there is nothing very spontaneous about how love plays out and the way in which relationships progress.

With an eye on gifts or outings, Mende et al (2019) point to the ways in which romantic love is bound up with consuming things and services and that this consumption acts to define and reinforce the romance part of romantic love. Think of the common sayings 'If you loved me you would …' (*reader to insert appropriate act here*) or 'Isn't it romantic?' as a term which signifies an act or thing as representing what is recognised or accepted as being romantic.

Wilding (2017) draws on the work of Bauman to explain this, and considers the point that, in a society dominated by consumerism, love also becomes a sort of commodity. A commodity is something that can be bought or sold. It may be difficult to say that we can buy or sell love but think about how we buy things to demonstrate our love, and that we might see a lack of gift giving as a lack of love. Now consider the idea that we regularly engage in practices which could be said to represent an act or acts which commodify ourselves.

## Pause for reflection

Do we commodify ourselves? Do you commodify yourself? Maybe not in terms of seeking an actual sale, but think about how we use clothes and make-up to enhance how we look and jot down some ideas about how you or people that you know might do this. This can sometimes extend to doing things that we don't like or which take a lot of effort in order to attract or please others.

Watch the currently popular television programme *Love Island*. Afterwards, think about what we have just said about how we may package and present ourselves for a purpose and reflect upon the events in the show as following a script that many of us find recognisable, even though we might not behave like that.

The aim of *Love Island* is, on the face of it, to develop a relationship, and this returns us to something that was said much earlier in this chapter about how relationships are central to families. As such it may be useful to say a bit more about relationships.

## 2.3 How have relationships changed?

Relationships can be seen and experienced in different ways. With respect to the family, relationships used to rest upon marriage and were deemed to be long term irrespective of what happened within them. As such, we can see how formal relationships act to constitute the nuclear family. We should be able to recognise though that in contemporary UK society there are different forms of family. Remember what Beck and Beck-Gernsheim (1995) said about love changing as we become more individualistic. This involves a greater sense of reflecting upon what we want for ourselves. What we can say about this is that as we have become more individualistic, so we have developed a greater concern with our own happiness and satisfaction.

As part of this change, we start to see relationships as sources of satisfaction. If you are in your teens or twenties, you might find it useful to stop here and read this again but in doing so try to suspend what seems to be natural or normal to you. If you are a female student, think about how at one time you would have been under pressure to find a man (ignore the assumption of a heterosexual relationship, we are thinking about social expectations in the past) who would provide for you. Now think about what you might expect a man to provide in such a situation. This will prove to be very important when we look at how the state also held views about men providing for women and organised the welfare state accordingly. See Chapter 6 for a further discussion of this.

### Study tip

To be a successful student you will very often have to try to understand a problem or an issue from a different perspective. The sociologist Max Weber considered this in the early 20th century. Weber said that it was important for sociologists to employ *verstehen*.

*Verstehen* is a German word which roughly means empathetic understanding. For us, the value is in terms of looking at something from somebody else's position: to look at something as though you were in somebody else's shoes.

So, if you are 18–25 and you read that society has become more individualistic, that can be hard to understand for some because this is all you have ever known. In other words, how society is now can seem to be perfectly normal and it is difficult to understand how it was very different just one generation ago.

To make sense of *verstehen* you have to try to step outside of what you know and look at things afresh. Sociologists sometimes say that it is necessary to defamiliarise; by this they mean that you should try to ignore what you know already, difficult as that may be. So, by the 2020s, UK society has become very individualistic. It wasn't always like this, or at least not to this extent. Something changed and as it changed so our understanding and expectations relating to relationships and families changed with it. At the same time what we might also see is that it could change again.

The way we live our lives, including social formations and/or structures such as the family, is shaped by the effect of external trends and forces. Social change, however, has been associated with the loss of traditional certainties, and not everyone will welcome that. For example, if we think back to the 1950s–1960s the social world was much more stable. Individuals tended to know where they stood in society and it was very possible to secure a job for life, or so it was thought. This was associated with gender, and it fed into how marriages and families existed. Our relationships within families were also seen as much more straightforward, certainly more straightforward than they seem to be now for many people. Be careful though; this could be a simplified version of the past that ignores that society was never really simple or straightforward but is used to suggest change in society is problematic.

### Pause for reflection

Think about how language normalises family practices.

Familiar language and terms that evolve in society make practices seem normal and acceptable even in the most complex of relationships.

Saltiel (2013) provides a good overview of the complexity of some family lives introducing the term 'not-grandma'. Not-grandma is of particular interest. The not-grandma referred to is a woman who provides care to a child and presents herself as grandma, but she is not a blood relative. Not-grandmas may be common in some cultures or families but not in others. Consider terms in your culture or family that shape family relationships, such as how female adults may be referred to as aunty.

Reflect on families you know and how different family practices exist and are normal for those families.

You might also consider what Zygmunt Bauman has to say about what he calls liquid modernity (2000) and liquid love (2003). For the idea of liquidity to make sense you have to take a historical view. For most of the 20th century UK society and ways of behaving were much more fixed or rigid than they are now. Social class, gender and ethnicity had much more of an impact upon how your life would unfold when it came to work and family life. Although tricky at times, the key idea that underpins Bauman's ideas here is that the demise of rigid social structures and the rise of a focus on individualism have led to more fluid social practices, hence the term liquid.

In many ways this is part of the normal development of society, but it may be worth considering that changes do not impact throughout society in a uniform or an equal manner. Issues to do with class, gender and ethnicity can be seen to result in different experiences for different individuals and groups in society, and it is argued that generally there is more flexibility than there once was alongside more diversity.

## 2.4 Does reflexivity mean that we project manage our own lives?

Think about how changes in a social context may create the conditions for different ways of understanding and for different ways of being, or doing, a family. In turn, this will feed through into how children understand and experience the world, presenting them with different ideas and options for their own lives. In relation to this, it is worth considering how situations are created where we are drawn into an increased concern with reflecting upon and working to establish our identity. In recent social theory this has come to be referred to as reflexivity.

### Note

The terms reflexivity and reflection are often used interchangeably but they mean different things.

Reflexivity is concerned with the ways in which we increasingly monitor ourselves and reflect upon what we do and who we are. If you work in children's services, you will come across the idea of reflective practice as it is quite commonplace in practice, and an expected skill of professionals.

There's a subtle difference in that reflective practice is concerned with reflecting on specific issues concerning the work role with a view to making changes compared to reflexivity, which is a much broader and more general social approach that has come to apply in everyday life for many in terms of personal development and identity.

It can be useful to think of reflexivity as a form of project management of our own lives. Think about how many people adopt a project management approach to life or how some parents adopt a project management approach towards their children. By this we mean that we spend time considering how we are living our lives, how we can do things better, what we should be doing to create a 'good life' for ourselves and for our children.

Consider how we may reflect upon being a good parent or a good friend. Think about how many people take a significant interest in 'likes' on social media as though this is some sort of true indicator of who we are. So, reflexivity is bound up with our understanding of who we are, especially in terms of relationships and aspirations or personal goals. Wilding (2017) provides a good summary of the reflexive self. Ferguson (2003) also shows how individuals who are the subject of welfare services, such as social work intervention, draw upon their knowledge and understanding of this discourse of reflexivity and personal development to influence how they are dealt with and to secure outcomes that are favourable to them.

What we have seen from this section is that, as the social world changes, so this has an impact upon families and family structures. The notion of nuclear families has become less common, and while the fluid family accommodates different forms it is much less certain in terms of roles and structures. However, although we may recognise diversity, there may be resistance to this, and to the way in which society can be seen as changing, usually by seeing past ways of behaving as preferable.

In recognising that there are tensions with respect to the family it is important to accept that this is because the family is not simply a term that is used to represent social relationships; the family comes to represent a particular set of values. However, in representing a particular set of values it can be seen as exclusive in terms of how other values, and alternative ways of behaving, are not recognised or are actively resisted as being lesser, inferior or problematic. In turn, this enables us to see the family as a site of cultural struggle (Chambers, 2001). By this Chambers refers to the way that groups struggle to have their ideas accepted as legitimate or right or feel threatened by ideas that they are unfamiliar with or do not understand. This is very often associated with discourse. Discourse also cropped up earlier, so it is now time to make sense of what discourse is and what it means.

## 2.5 How discourse makes us believe the way families behave is natural

Discourse is a concept that is strongly associated with the theorist Michel Foucault, though it can be traced back to the work of Ferdinand de Saussure (Inglis and Thorpe, 2019) and Claude Lévi-Strauss (Jones and Bradbury, 2018). You will be able to find lots of books on Foucault and/or discourse, but both Inglis and Thorpe (2019) and Jones and Bradbury (2018) provide an accessible account of the way in which discourse works to create rules which regulate the ways in which we think about the world.

### Pause for reflection

If you are uncertain about the term discourse, start with the idea that we act as though we are following a script which acts as a set of rules and shapes how we understand our life. Think about how the script reinforces ways of understanding different scenarios or settings. The script is the discourse, the framework within which we understand behaviour, family and society.

> Now turn your attention to the language that is used in the script. Discourse is rooted within language, and it influences our understanding. Think about the way in which our choice of language can influence what we mean about aspects of the social world or the ways in which it is understood. So, it can shape our feelings in terms of something being positive or negative, acceptable or unacceptable.

It is important to accept, however, that it is not the case that there is only one discourse about a subject. We may talk about discourse in general, but in practice there are always competing discourses. Each discourse shapes the way in which we understand social life by providing a general framework of meanings that are embedded within the language that is used. This section will provide lots of examples relating to children and families which show how particular words, and how we use them, shape our understanding in the way that they give meaning to what we see.

Importantly, the meanings which are embedded within the language that is used within discourses have consequences in respect of how social life works. Smith (1998: 254) explains this as being because discourse operates as 'a system of representation which regulates the meanings and practices which can and cannot be produced'. This is why we started off by suggesting that you initially view it as a script. We have a script that sets out a way of understanding the world and a set of rules to follow to fit into society. In this way, discourse is not just a matter of the use of language to describe our social reality; discourse is the thing which creates that reality.

Nicolson (2014) provides a good example that is relevant to family life focusing on domestic violence that illustrates how meaning and understanding exist within rules that are created within discourse. Most of us would accept that domestic violence is wrong and that it can be seen as a social problem. What Nicolson does, though, is to show that it is only a problem in the context of a particular discourse of relationships being based on mutual respect and equality, and where physical violence is seen as being wrong. In another discourse, one in which the use of violence by one partner against another was seen as being a normal and even necessary aspect of relationships, we wouldn't see domestic violence as being a problem. It may be hard to imagine how we might accept domestic violence, but think about how smacking children is still legal and acceptable in England and that this practice is often defended as being necessary to help children learn or keep them safe. So, discourse shapes our understanding of the world and makes things appear natural.

The key thing to focus on here is the idea of what is natural, or what we might believe to be natural. Discourse creates the illusion of things being natural rather than being a representation of something that is natural. Read that carefully: even we had to read it twice when we were proofreading! We are distinguishing between something *appearing* natural and something *being* natural. Consider the following from Smith (1998: 273): 'Discourse constructs the topic. It defines and produces the objects of our knowledge.' If this is the case, then we can only know what the family or childhood means within discourse. So, if typical family units such as a heterosexual couple with two children are put forward as natural in common discourse, we grow up accepting that and seeing other forms of family as unnatural.

Similarly, Wells (2018) talks about how pedagogy (a focus on teaching children) and psychology have been combined in a way which constructs childhood as a process of becoming as the consequences of a particular way of understanding development. The discourse here creates ideas about normal childhood and, thus, normal children, who have developed or are behaving in this way. So, children who do not develop in this way are seen as in some way abnormal or problematic. The point that is being made is that the language that we use has the effect of constructing the reality of our world. It has real consequences for us that lead to ideas of things being normal because they are natural, instead of an understanding of how things are constructed in society.

As an example of what this means for children's lives think about how children are much more restricted in what they can do or where they can go now than 50 years ago and how this is understood within a discourse of the risks that children face (Creasy and Corby, 2019). We can see how a discourse of risk shapes an understanding of threat to children. However, this overlaps with a discourse of parenting which promotes ideas about what it means to be responsible or to be a good parent. The result is that parents restrict the freedom of children because they 'know' that there are risks to children and they 'know' that, as good, responsible parents, they should protect their children. This leads to restricting children as this is a relatively easy way to protect them. Importantly, though, any parents who do not restrict their children may then come to be viewed as poor or bad parents and may find that they are subject to investigation or intervention by various social services.

---

### Pause for reflection

Consider the issue of risk, and how we see children as being at risk.

To understand how discourse becomes powerful in shaping behaviour consider how we think about the risks children face and what we need to protect them from. This is likely to be issues of protecting them from people that wish them harm, or risks in the wider world such as road traffic accidents or bullying in school. However, protecting children from these risks has inadvertently created other problems for children, such as inactivity and obesity. This can be understood if we think about short-term or immediate risks and long-term risks.

---

Discourse is one of those concepts that is embedded within academic work and it is a concept that you will be able to use in all modules that you study, so spend some time getting familiar with discourse. It will be worth it. Chambers (2001) illustrates how discourse operates in showing how what we understand as the family is shaped and how it makes sense as a consequence of the ways in which the family is presented to us. Chambers shows how we are exposed to messages and images which define the family and shape how we understand it.

---

**Pause for reflection**

Think about the ways in which, as soon as you hear someone referring to family, a set of linked ideas regarding what the family is and does automatically comes to mind. Now consider that the term family acts to focus what you are thinking about and that it makes a particular model of the family appear to be the norm.

Chambers focuses on the media and how the media provides a particular, but limited, view of the family and how this type of family then comes to be the focus of social policy and legislation which, in turn, have the effect of reinforcing this particular model. How social policy shapes the family is covered in Chapter 6.

---

Another good example of how discourse operates relates to people, including children, who are poor, and we can see how there is a long history of using language to distinguish between some poor people who are deserving of support or assistance and others who are undeserving, usually due to judgements we make about their behaviour or lifestyle. When we start to use the language of deserving and undeserving, we impose a particular understanding on what we see, which shapes how we might organise support or help for the poor. What we also do, though, is to construct an understanding of those people that the terms are applied to.

Jupp (2017) offers a more recent version of deserving and undeserving in using the terms 'strivers and skivers', but he also refers to families being labelled in other ways which act to differentiate between families and in doing so construct types of family, such as socially excluded, anti-social, responsible or resourceful. In terms of discourse these labels act to organise how we understand different families and how they come to operate in a way which gives the illusion that these are real descriptions. The overall result is that we come to see some types of family as normal and natural. Consequently, families which appear different are understood as being not normal or not natural in some way.

You have probably come across the term 'norms'. Discourse establishes the norms which we encounter in studying society and which guide how others deal with us (Smith, 2014). As an example of this read Moss et al (2000). They demonstrate how children are understood differently in the UK compared to children in Italy as a consequence of different discourses relating to children and childhood. In turn, this shapes the ways in which we provide children's services. For Moss et al, the Italian approach, often presented as the Reggio Emilia approach, sees the child as being resourceful and creative. The UK, on the other hand, tends to adopt an approach which casts the child as lacking or incapable, hence the title of the paper, 'The rich child and the poor child'. Rich and poor are used to describe not financial resources but abilities and opportunities. Similarly, Lambert (2019) offers examples of discourse in terms of 'children at risk' and 'families in trouble'. These terms shape how we see children and our expectations of children and families.

Cain (2016) is also useful in showing how a discourse about morals comes to shape single mothers by viewing them in terms of being workless and offering an impoverished family life to their children. The term single mothers in some instances is used negatively, reflecting a failure of the mother but ignoring the role of fathers and their involvement or absence. You will be able to find many other studies and papers which draw on the idea of discourse to show how we understand aspects of social life within a set of rules constructed within discourse. Our understanding of the world is influenced by discourses and, therefore, alternative ideas are either difficult to accept or even unthinkable.

## 2.6 How does discourse have power?

One very important aspect of discourse is that it operates in a way which means that it has power, or that it serves to legitimise the actions of one group against another. What is relevant to this book is the way in which discourses relating to children and families provide justification for how both children and families come to be acted upon by others: for example, the ways in which the state may act on families.

As a specific example of this, consider how a discourse of family makes it possible to conceptualise families as occupying a place upon a scale from good to bad and where terms such as troubled or failing families make sense and are used to identify a particular type of family. We see power within this when we recognise that the term troubled family has been chosen to represent a policy approach. Other terms could have been used.

---

### Study tip

There is a key point to be made here in respect of how the relationship between what a word is and what it means is arbitrary: that is to say that the meaning of any word is not fixed. There is no intrinsic value or relationship which ties a word to its meaning.

Government policy may make reference to troubled or failing families but that is not to say that there is any essential truth to this. We can see the point being made here in the ways that words and their meanings may change over time.

---

However, if we recap on a point that was made earlier, we can see that discourse not only acts to make it possible to speak of something in a particular way, but it also shapes the extent of what *can* be said about it. Thus, we can see a discourse of the family in which it becomes possible to categorise some families as troubled or failing. Within this discourse, though, it now becomes not only legitimate for the state to act upon such a family; it becomes presented as being something that is necessary.

In the previous discussion it was said that discourse is not simply the way in which language describes social reality but that it is the thing which creates that reality. Let us say a bit more about this. Think about how, when we use the term troubled, or failing, to describe a family, we do more than simply give meaning to that family. In using the term to define the family in question the speaker also distinguishes themselves as different, ignoring how families are complex and how such simple terms do not fully describe how that family is behaving or living their lives. In this way the discourse of troubled families creates what it means to be a troubled family, but it also constructs what it means not to be a troubled family. In other words, discourse can be said to operate in a way that defines and positions the speaker as being different from what they are talking about (Storey, 2018).

The discourse of troubled families makes it possible to identify some families as different and to elaborate upon why. However, this is only within a particular range of characteristics which both support and reinforce the idea that they are troubled: for example, where parents may not be working. When we recognise that the term troubled families is embedded within a policy programme set up and run by a particular government we can start to see how that government is using power to change the behaviour of some families within the UK. So, it is not that these families are troubled per se: they might be perfectly happy. Rather, it is that the government has created a discourse which constructs the reality of some families as troubled.

What follows from this is that we must accept that when a meaning is produced within a discourse the meaning itself is quite likely to further strengthen the discourse from which it was produced. Thus, 'troubled families' as a term becomes powerful in terms of the shared meanings created with its repeated use. The knowledge that is produced within discourse then serves to reproduce and legitimise that discourse. The same example of 'troubled families' demonstrates how we use terms that contribute to the development of a shared meaning but that this is very often without any real scrutiny of the bias or presumptions that these terms are making. In this sense we are left with the realisation that what we know about anything is less secure than it may appear. So, discourse not only constructs the issue that is being focused on: in this case, families who may be having problems functioning in society. It also acts to define it and produce the extent of the knowledge that we have about it (Smith, 1998).

To reiterate, what this means is that when we think about the language that is used in relation to any social phenomenon it is not that the language that is used reflects the reality of that which it describes but, instead, that the language that is used creates the reality.

With this in mind, think about what Frost (2011: 5) means when he says that the word childhood 'acts as a shorthand form that disguises a complex series of profoundly different life experiences'. Childhood is a complex and diverse experience but language simplifies childhood, so we think we know what it means and we see the meaning as obvious, until we have to explain it in more detail. Similarly, consider how we often use the term 'vulnerable' in relation to children and how it is applied in a way that assumes all children are vulnerable. This then has real consequences for children's lives (Creasy and Corby, 2019).

## 2.7 How state governance draws upon discourse

Discourse also provides us with an insight into why it is that the state may be concerned with children and families. How the state understands children, and the role of families in children's lives, is associated with the ways in which it understands one of the key concerns of the state, namely, the governing of society. The state can be seen to exist in some ways as a mechanism or system for social organisation. Planning plays a part in this with respect to future needs. This is evident in how the state can be seen to have adopted a particular discourse of childhood that views children in terms of their future. So, the way in which childhood is understood shapes the way that children are treated and the provisions that we make for them. In turn, this shapes the experiences that children have. In Creasy and Corby (2019), we propose that society in general sees children as falling into one of two positions: we either see children in terms of what they are now or we see them in terms of what they will be in the future. This can be summarised as seeing children as beings, or as becomings (James and Prout, 1997; Wyness, 2012). To add to this, we are going to say that in general the dominant discourse relating to children is that they are seen as becomings.

Within this discourse the child's future dominates our understanding, especially in terms of what children should be doing in the present if they are to achieve a particular outcome. This can be seen in respect of the state or in terms of services provided by the state. For example, think about how often government ministers or schools talk about children in terms of achieving their potential. Such a concern is vague as it is just not possible to identify what any child's potential actually is. The term is seductive, though, in that to challenge the idea of potential and be unsupportive of this notion is to be accused of holding children back. Therefore, to employ the idea of the child's potential within arguments has power as critics or resisters may be positioned as not acting in the child's best interests.

### Pause for reflection

Reflect here on your own experiences in school with regard to the idea of potential. Were you told you could be anything you wanted to be? Were you challenged that if you did not work hard you would not realise your potential? Consider how this discourse about potential shaped your understanding of what you might or might not do in the future, or could or could not do in the future.

Consider also the way in which children's development is seen in terms of milestones and how not reaching particular stages comes to be a cause for concern (Fattore et al, 2007). Milestones is another term which reflects the way in which childhood has come to be dominated by the ideas put forward within theories of developmental psychology, and which has had significant influence in terms of constructing an understanding of children as becomings (Walkerdine, 2009). As a concept, milestones rest upon, and reinforce, an 'ages and stages' approach to development. Theories that support the 'ages and stages' approach have come to dominate our understanding of children and how we treat children across all services. However, there are theories of development which take a different approach which are no less valid, just not dominant in our services for children.

It is also possible to see how the influence of neoliberalism results in the education of children being presented in ways which promote the idea of educational success providing social and economic advantages for children in later life. In this way, when potential is being referred to in terms of discussions about children it is not just in relation to the potential to achieve certification through educational success; it is also the potential to be economically successful in adulthood. This places the child as responsible for their future circumstances in that they are expected to work hard and do well at school in order to be able to do well as an adult.

The alternative discourse of childhood is that children are seen as beings. This is rooted within a more recent sociological understanding of childhood. This position presents the child as being important in their own right. It is concerned with the child as they are rather than in terms of what they will become. This is a view that is much more common in academic discussions but we can also see how it has had some impact upon practice with children. For example, you may be familiar with the idea of the child's voice and with concerns that the child's voice should be heard. What we must note here, though, is that although this has come to be seen as quite normal it is not something that would have been recognised in practice before the 1990s.

The fact that we identify these two basic approaches demonstrates that discourses compete, and it points to the idea that discourse makes some things possible and other things not possible, especially in terms of how we provide for children and families and whether we accept certain ways of behaving as valid. Discourse, then, should be seen as a form of power. It is not physical power. It is not something that forces us to behave in a certain way. Instead, discourse shapes behaviour because of the way that it makes things seem natural, the way that things come to be viewed as unquestionable. Once we accept something as being natural, as being common-sense, we generally stop questioning it.

## 2.8 How might you use this chapter?

In reading Chapter 2 we hope that you will have found it useful in terms of understanding the ideas that are held with respect to families and relationships.

We also hope that you have a much better understanding of discourse. However, at the same time, you may also be thinking about how useful this is for you in terms of the assignments that you will inevitably be faced with. As a student you cannot avoid being drawn into assessment at some point. Assessment is a fact of life for students, and it doesn't matter what you know or understand; how you perform in assessments becomes the measure of your ability. This is not to say that we agree with this; we see this as a rather limited or restricted approach. But, with the importance of assessment in mind, this section will try to identify key points from the chapter and to provide ideas as to how you might use this in an assignment.

So, in terms of the family there are some key points which we would certainly expect you to be mentioning or considering within an assignment:

- The family is a key concept within social life, but it is not as unambiguous or as clear cut as we may often think.
- We can talk about the family as singular and families as plural, which can be more useful in your academic writing.
- Stable, long-term nuclear families have become less common, but the fluid family is much less certain in terms of roles and structures.
- The family practices approach provides a good way of understanding the fluid nature of families in contemporary society.
- We may assume that romantic love is normal, but we haven't always formed relationships or married for love.
- The changing social position of women in society influences attitudes towards love and marriage.
- Children tend to be seen as becomings, in terms of their future, rather than as beings.

So, let us imagine that you have been given an assignment whereby you are required to discuss the family in contemporary society. This wouldn't be unusual on any course related to childhood, children and families, or a course related to working with children and families. You might choose to follow the basic structure of this chapter, but we would expect you to use Section 2.5 on discourse much sooner than we did. We dropped it in at the end because most students reading this want to read about the family and not about a key concept within social theory.

So, it makes perfect sense to always establish the key concepts early in an assignment. If the assignment is about the family, you could open with a critical comment to state that 'the family' is an insufficient term. That is what we did. We started by commenting on how the family is embedded within our ideas about society but then made the point that not all families are the same. We also made use of theory by drawing upon Morgan (2011) and promoting family practices as a good way to make sense of what a family is. As Morgan states, from the family practices approach, the family is what the family does. We did say, though, that although this approach works well in explaining family diversity, there are some who resist the move towards the acceptance of diverse family forms. From a conservative position, change is not good.

We then used Section 2.2 to question where families come from and to think more carefully about some ideas that we take for granted: in particular, romantic love. This is because we wanted to provide a critical understanding. We wanted to show that families are socially constructed and that what we might take for granted now has not always been the case. To help us to do this we commented upon how the social conditions that we live in shape how we live our lives and what we expect. Section 2.3 is where we did this. Look at how we commented on the changing social position of women and what this means for relationships. We then dropped a bit more social theory in by referring to Bauman and his concept that society has become more liquid. Tutors will always like to see you using theory in your work as this will demonstrate that you are providing an academic discussion, so for all assignments think about theory and what it can do for you.

We developed theory further by writing quite a bit about discourse and showing that the understanding of families and the social experiences that we have are rooted in discourse. Discourse makes sense of what we experience. It makes things seem normal and natural. The example that was used here is children. That made sense because the book is about children and families. So, we made the point that the social position of children and how we understand them is shaped by a discourse which positions them in terms of their future. If the focus is on children's future, then that has meaning for how families operate. As such you could follow this structure and use this final point to say that, although families may be diverse, very often the way in which children are understood is very much shared and this means that there are some things about families which seem to be universal.

We hope that makes sense. The following chapter provides a discussion of one of the key aspects of families – parenting – but uses this as a springboard into the idea that some families are problematic, that some families may be seen as failing or troubled.

### Further thoughts

Read some more about structure and agency and make sure you understand this theory as it comes up a lot.

Make sure you understand the basics of discourse then look for examples of discourse in everyday life. If you do not already follow the news it may be useful to at least look out for relevant news stories relating to children and families and look at how the ways in which they are written or presented shape a particular way of understanding them.

## Further reading

We recommend that you read further by selecting some of the sources that we have used within this chapter. Inglis and Thorpe (2019) provide a good introduction to structure and agency. Jones and Bradbury (2018) explain discourse well, and if you read Chambers (2001) and/or Moss et al (2000) you will be able to see how this is used in academic studies. Morgan (2011) covers the family practices approach and provides a basis for accepting diversity.

# 3

# Parenting and failing families

This chapter will help you to understand:

- why it is useful to see the state as regulating families;
- how ideology influences the need for parenting classes;
- how we can claim that some families fail;
- if we can say that failing families are part of an underclass.

## 3.1 How does the state regulate families?

In Chapter 2 we introduced some ideas about what we mean when we talk about the family, including how it is better not to refer to 'the family' but, instead, to drop the 'the' and to talk about 'family' or 'families'. This is to reflect the diversity of families which we see in contemporary UK society. It also reflects the changing nature of society itself. In thinking about the changing nature of society it often makes sense to consider the role or influence of the state, and although we often see the government as being the state, it is important to recognise that they are not the same. The state is much broader than the government. Considering the state is important because it is the state which sets the context within which individuals and families live their lives. The state has power, and this power can be brought to bear upon families in ways which regulate how they live.

Understanding the actions of the state as regulating families is a good way of considering what the state does as this refers to a way of acting upon families which may not involve direct or immediate force. Instead, regulation can be seen as actions which have the effect of encouraging, coercing or guiding families. That is not to say that the state never acts forcefully but for most of us it is more a sense that we comply with the state or fall in line with what the state wants, often because we have no choice.

---

### Pause for reflection

To understand how the state regulates us, think that most children go to school and that schools have a legal responsibility to monitor children's welfare. Parents who choose to home educate their children are required to register this and are then subject to inspections by the local authority to ensure that a suitable education is being provided.

Parents who do not send their children to school may be fined or even jailed.

If a parent is registered with a school then they may be fined for taking their children on holiday during term time.

So, this raises a question: what does the state want? It could raise the question: how does the state come to want anything? This returns us to thinking about how the government can be seen as the driving force of the state. The government is made up of individuals who want to achieve certain things for society or want society to take a particular shape. What they want to achieve can be seen to reflect their collective agreements regarding the benefits of political ideologies that they believe in. Political ideologies will be discussed in Chapter 5 in much more detail. For now, it is sufficient to accept that the government shapes the context of the state and that governments are influenced by ideas about what society is or should be and that this in turn sees governments introducing social policies and legislation which have a real bearing on the lives of children and families.

An example of this is the Labour governments' 1997–2010 concerns about what they termed 'anti-social behaviour'. This is behaviour that may not be illegal, but which can be a nuisance for others who have to experience it. Alongside this they argued that very often a small number of families in a community could make the general life of that community poorer by engaging in behaviour that was anti-social (Garrett, 2007). One policy programme that they set up to tackle this was the Intensive Family Support Programme (IFSP). This is a good example of how the state may act in ways which regulate behaviour because, as Nixon (2007: 548) notes, 'IFSPs do not solely contain and control behaviour, they also seek to transform "anti-social" subjects into active, self-governing, responsibilized citizens'.

Nixon (2007) is actually a paper which sets out to respond to a critical discussion about the IFSP by Garrett (2007) so it's worth reading both. The term 'responsibilized' seems a bit of a mouthful and it might seem odd at first reading. What it means is that through being subject to, or experiencing, an IFSP these families will come to recognise that they have responsibilities to others. This fits very well with New Labour's concerns about rights being associated with responsibilities (Driver and Martell, 1998; *Guardian*, 2002) but it also echoes neoliberal ideas about being self-reliant (Cain, 2016).

Garrett (2007) is a very useful read in relation to how the state may act towards families. He shows how the state has set up policy programmes aimed at changing family behaviours in a number of countries, something that can be seen both geographically and historically. For example, as well as in the UK these types of family programmes can be seen in the Netherlands in the 1950s and in Nazi Germany in the 1930s. These examples reflect the actions of the state to stop families behaving in certain ways, but policies can also be used to encourage types of behaviour. Consider the New Labour policy of the Working Families Tax Credit. This was clearly an incentive to get parents into work. It was embedded within the idea that there was a need to tackle child poverty and that getting parents into work was the best way to do this. On the face of it this seems reasonable but we will demonstrate later in the book that low pay means that very many families who experience poverty are not families where no one works (Hirsch, 2018; CPAG, 2019; Lyndon, 2019).

A very different example of the state regulating family life is provided by Walker (2020), who illustrates how some countries are providing financial incentives for families to have more babies as a consequence of concerns about falls in population, in contrast to policies that used to exist in some countries that forbade families from having more than one or two children. Or how, in the UK currently, Child Benefit is paid to parents for just their first and second child in most circumstances.

When we think about how the state often responds to problematic behaviour, we may think of the ways in which the law is used and how offenders may be subject to forms of punishment. What the IFSP aimed to do was to support families so as to change ways of behaving rather than to punish particular events. A similar approach was evident in compulsory parenting orders. Compulsory parenting orders were introduced by Labour for parents whose children were demonstrating problematic behaviour to the extent that parents found themselves in court. The orders required attendance on parenting programmes with the view that changing parenting would change children's behaviour (Holt, 2010), something that will be considered further in Section 3.2.

What stands out in any consideration of the relationship between children, families and the state is that the state can be seen to have a particular understanding of what children and families should be, what they should do and/or what they need. The issue of responsibilities plays a big part in this and it was under the Labour governments of 1997–2010 that parenting started to take on a much more substantial role in terms of what the state expects to happen within families (Lewis, 2011). Importantly, the state is much clearer within these policies about what responsible parents should do (or should not do), rather than how they can do this, when it talks about families that are considered to be failing. Later in the chapter we will argue that this has overlaps with the idea of there being an underclass, a social class that tends to be associated with relying on welfare benefits. Section 3.2, however, says more about parenting.

## 3.2 Is it the case that what parents do is more important than who parents are?

Let us start by stating that there is a sense in which parenting can be seen as natural. We have children and we take care of those children; that is parenting. However, in recent years concerns about the ability, or even the inability, of parents to parent has become very common. Parenting as a term is so obvious it may go without any scrutiny but as students of childhood and/or families it is always useful to be precise in stating what we mean. As such, the definition given by Hoghughi and Long (2004: 5) is a useful starting point. They refer to parenting as 'purposive activities aimed at ensuring the survival and development of children'. If we adopt a critical approach, however, we might recognise that this definition is somewhat limited. The key thing to accept is that children will survive, and they will develop within a wide range of conditions.

In recent debates about childhood it is the question of how children develop, and the role of parents in ensuring that children develop in a socially acceptable way, which is often the main issue. For example, we can see evidence of the state being concerned about how parents parent with the introduction of parenting programmes and/or parenting orders.

As this section is concerned with parenting, and in particular the ways in which parents may be supported, it is useful to establish what we mean by parenting programmes. Whittaker and Cowley (2012: 138) state that 'parenting programmes (social interventions designed to increase parental knowledge, skills, and self-belief in their own capabilities in raising children) are key components of wealthier nations' strategies for the prevention of child maltreatment and improvement of life chances'. In the UK the Labour governments that were in power between 1997 and 2010 oversaw a number of parenting programmes being introduced and promoted. Sure Start Children's Centres played a key role in supporting parenting, with named programmes being used in some cases, such as Incredible Years, Triple P, Strengthening Families Strengthening Communities and Parent Gym (Lindsay et al, 2011, 2019). In a study of parents who were on, or had been on, parenting support classes, Corby (2015) points to the ways in which parents saw these as positive and beneficial.

---

### Pause for reflection

It may seem obvious that parents access some sort of parenting programme as these have been made available for a long time. However, in the past parenting was something that was seen to be learnt within families, or which was guided by health visitors. Health visitors have existed for over 100 years and were originally middle-class women who worked through charities to help poor women parent their children.

---

However, what parents do is always within a social and political context. One aspect of the social and political context that is very important and that has already been raised is the impact of neoliberalism. We mentioned how neoliberalism was said to promote the idea of individualism earlier. By this we mean that we, as individuals, are seen as being responsible for our own lives. If we are parents, it is not unreasonable to extend this idea to a sense of responsibility regarding our children's lives. This includes our successes and failures. Therefore, in a neoliberal context, the state expects us to take responsibility for our children regardless of what circumstances we face.

This is a good example of how different social issues overlap. For example, we live in a society that is unequal. UK society was steadily becoming more equal up to 1979 but policies introduced by the Thatcher governments of 1979–1997 led to inequality increasing. Very often this was the government's aim (Dorey, 2015). Importantly, neoliberalism presents inequality as being the outcome of individual choices and abilities. One explanation for being successful in life, and which rests upon an individualistic base, is the idea that some of us are more aspirational. This is the idea that some of us want success more than others and therefore we will work harder for it. Although this is a limited theory in respect of how it explains and accounts for inequalities, it is one which tends to be drawn on quite a lot so we need to consider how this might feed into issues concerning parenting.

To start, though, it may be useful to consider that we can distinguish between the concept of parenting and a concern with parenting as reflecting the ability of parents to control their children and to ensure that their children display appropriate social behaviour. This concern with control is not particularly new. Gorer argued that in the early 1950s, the development of a 'tough love style of parenting had been the agent that changed England from a century's long tradition of brutality' (Field, 2010: 18). Tough love was a much more involved parenting that encouraged parents to guide their children but to punish them if they did not behave in ways that were seen as socially acceptable. This led to ideas that authoritative or even authoritarian parenting was the best way to raise children. These ideas can still be found today but Field has raised concerns that parents are no longer practising 'tough love' and considers that this has contributed to social problems.

Field (2010) comments upon the actions of parents and considers how what parents do has an impact upon children. This is echoed by Allen (2011: xiv) in a report promoting early intervention. Crucially, Allen states that: 'What parents do is more important than who parents are.' This idea mirrors the idea that was raised in Chapter 2 regarding what a family is and the development of the family practices approach. You will remember that, for the family practices approach, the family is what the family does. Allen's point is that regardless of who the family is, the success or otherwise of their children is dependent on what they do, not on whether they are rich or poor. In turn, this accommodates the diversity that we see in contemporary society.

---

**Pause for reflection**

It might be worth considering how in our society we tend to see family as our biological relatives. Law and policy support the right to family life for those who are biologically related. This reinforces the idea that the best parents for a child are their biological parents. However, many cultures and societies recognise social parenting, or adults parenting children who are not biologically theirs.

Mullin (2012) provides a useful discussion about the relationship between children and adults in contemporary society and introduces the idea of being a social parent as distinguished from being a biological parent. It is quite easy to become a parent biologically but considering Mullin's point we can see a distinction between being a parent and parenting. A parent may not be good at parenting, just as a child can be parented well by someone who is not their biological parent; remember the 'not-grandma'?

## 3.3 Does social class influence parenting?

A concern with what the family does, and how it does it, can be seen as being central to the work of Lareau (2011). Lareau is an influential figure in how we understand parenting, arguing that, in America at least, there are clear differences between how parents parent. She argues that these differences reflect differences in the social class of the families. As such Lareau argues that middle-class parents engage in what she calls concerted cultivation. This is compared to working-class families who, she claims, adopt a parenting strategy which she calls the accomplishment of natural growth.

Concerted cultivation is a style of parenting that is actively engaged with the children's education and development and as such is a very involved style of parenting. If concerted cultivation represents 'hands-on' parenting, natural growth reflects parenting that is 'hands off'. This does not mean that parents don't care or are not involved but just that they are not so concerned with children's educational outcomes or personal development.

In the UK, Lareau's identification of two types of parenting can be seen as underpinning the Effective Provision of Pre-school, Primary and Secondary Education Project (EPPE) project. The researchers behind EPPE do not focus on differences in parenting due to class. They promote active cultivation and place more emphasis on types of parenting than on social class, arguing that it is what parents do that is important rather than their socio-economic position (Siraj-Blatchford et al, 2013). This suggests that there is a belief that regardless of circumstances parents can practise active cultivation and parent their children in a way that will enable their children's successful negotiation of school and society.

From this position social structures, such as class, and the social conditions in which families live take second place to the actions of parents. This reflects neoliberal ideas about the importance of being active in terms of taking responsibility for our lives (Simpson et al, 2015). This is a good example of an issue which illustrates the way that neoliberals view social life as something we shape ourselves by our own choices and actions. As such, we are left with the idea that good parenting is parenting that reflects the idea of active cultivation but where any consideration of the conditions under which families live, such as experiencing poverty, is not seen as valid.

It can also be seen that a range of commercial enterprises – for example, children's activities, toys and additional tutoring – can be seen to have developed to support the active cultivation approach providing activities which emphasise long-term benefits for children. Such activities not only reinforce active cultivation as good parenting; they also reinforce an understanding of children as becomings and as being a project that good parents actively manage (Vincent and Maxwell, 2016).

However, this also demonstrates how being poor may limit opportunities for parents to provide activities that are seen as part of good parenting.

---

### Pause for reflection

Try to find examples of how goods and services for children may be marketed in ways which emphasise that good parents would choose them because of the advantages they provide for their children.

For example, look at the way that goods and services might promote children's learning.

So, what message is being sent to parents who choose not to use such goods or services, or who cannot afford them?

---

Wheeler (2018) provides a good account of how Lareau has influenced thinking about parenting and has also demonstrated some weaknesses with Lareau's work. This is not to say that Lareau has no merits, but Wheeler draws attention to some of the problems in using social class as a descriptor in 21st-century Britain. Social class is no longer as obvious, or identifiable, as it once was and because of this it is not so easy to suggest that what working-class parents do is different to what middle-class parents do. What Wheeler adds is a way of seeing social class as a continuum, where parenting may change along that continuum.

Furthermore, Wheeler refers to 'essential assistance' rather than natural growth. Wheeler's rejection of the term natural growth is due to the fact that it suggests that parents don't involve themselves at all in their children's development and leave them to develop 'naturally'. This is not what Lareau meant, though, as parents in this group do carry out the essentials of parenting. They just do not attempt to cultivate their children's success.

This concern with how parents parent is both important and relevant when it is considered alongside the idea that parents should be involved in raising the aspirations of their children. Aspiration is another concept that fits comfortably with neoliberal thinking and is linked to expectations that parents will play an increasing role in the lives of their children. However, this can go too far, as in the case of helicopter parenting (Creasy and Corby, 2019). Helicopter parents can be said to intervene excessively, and thus detrimentally, in their children's lives. Helicopter parenting can be understood in terms of the increased pressures that are brought to bear on parents with respect to their responsibilities towards their children and how parents feel that they are judged on their involvement in their children's lives.

## 3.4 Should the state help parents?

There is some recognition in our society that parents need support in raising their children. The debate tends to be about how much help, what help and which parents deserve help. It has become expected that parents should get some support in terms of their parenting, though sometimes for different reasons. For the Labour governments between 1997 and 2010, an extensive system of parenting support was established through the Sure Start Children's Centre system.

---

### Note

'New' Labour as it was referred to during this period drew on the political ideas of communitarianism, an approach which emphasised a need for a relationship between rights and responsibilities (emphasising that there should be no rights without responsibilities) alongside the benefits of strong communities (Parton, 2006). From this position state support for families will benefit society as a whole.

This message was presented as a response to the individualism of the Conservative governments from 1979 to 1997, a time when Margaret Thatcher famously said, 'There is no such thing as society, there are only individuals and families' (Thatcher, 1987). From both a neoliberal and a neoconservative position families are private matters and this justifies the state not providing support.

---

What Thatcher's neoliberal message did was to reinforce the idea that we have no responsibilities towards anyone else other than ourselves and our families. As such you might recognise that it undermines concerns about communities. So, from a neoliberal perspective, children are the responsibility of their parents and families are seen as self-sufficient. It is important to recognise that it reinforces the idea that we should support ourselves. Labour responded to this by pointing to the idea that there are times when we all need support, that we will all do much better when there is support and that parenting is not always easy, so a successful society will come together to help raise children.

In some ways the COVID-19 pandemic of the early 2020s demonstrated the failings of neoliberalism and illustrated why a political theory which promotes self-centred behaviour, as neoliberalism does, only benefits some in society rather than society as a whole. Lots of people in society were isolated and struggled in the pandemic due to a lack of support but many communities attempted to come together and help each other.

It could be fair to say that between 1997 and 2010 Labour changed the landscape of parenting within the UK. The aim to benefit society as a whole saw Labour doing much to support children and families, and although the state had taken an interest in families previously, this had never been structured in such a positive way before.

One reason for Labour's concern to provide support for parents can be seen as a response to poverty in the UK. More will be said about poverty in Chapter 12 but for now it is generally accepted that poverty often disadvantages children. If so, then we can argue that if parents are offered support they will be better equipped to address the needs of their children and in doing so they will be in a better position to overcome the disadvantages of poverty (Hoghughi and Long, 2004; Field, 2010).

Although this argument has previously been put forward to make the case for ensuring that all poor parents have access to parenting programmes, other reasons can also be seen. For example, parenting programmes can be seen as part of a raft of measures which fall under the umbrella term 'early intervention'. One important argument in support of early intervention is that it addresses a range of issues that, if unaddressed, can become complex and expensive (Allen, 2011; Gillies et al, 2017). Early intervention is argued to save the state money as well as providing better outcomes for children, especially those children who live with some disadvantage such as poverty.

We do need to be careful; although the growth in parental support is often seen as being attributed to Tony Blair's Labour governments, it does have a long history. Tisdall (2017) considers guides for parents such as Dr Spock's but also indicates how parenting has often been dominated by psychological theories. Health visitors have also offered support in the form of early parenting advice and 'parent craft' as a universal programme for decades. Other organisations such as the National Childbirth Trust and other voluntary agencies have provided programmes for pregnant women with respect to the early care of infants.

In general, though, the provision of parenting programmes beyond the early years has typically been aimed at families deemed to be having problems with respect to managing their children's care and behaviour. This supports the idea that some people know how to parent and only those having problems will need support. The idea that some families don't just have problems but are problematic, however, is a recent concern that has been presented as the idea that some families fail.

## 3.5 What do we mean by failing or troubled families?

The idea that some families fail seems to have engaged a number of governments. Consider the following quote from Tony Blair, the Labour prime minister, referring to the unborn children of lone mothers in 2006: 'there is no point pussyfooting ... if we are not prepared to predict and intervene more early ... pre-birth even ... these kids a few years down the line are going to be a menace to society' (Gregg, 2010; Garrett, 2018). Without disputing that some families are faced with significant problems and may sometimes appear to be struggling, when you read about failing, or troubled, families what tends to be seen is that families that are referred to as failing are nearly always poor families. A word of caution is required here. We are not suggesting that being poor means that a family will be problematic, not at all. What we are suggesting is that when we start to look at families who come to be referred to as failing it is not at all unusual to see that they are families who experience financial hardship (Jupp, 2017; Rose and McAuley, 2019).

---

**Pause for reflection**

The idea that some types of parents are a menace to society prevails.

Consider which types of parents are seen as problematic.

Very often it is parents who are poor, but we might suggest that teen parents, even parents under the age of 22, are also very often seen as the ones who are likely to need support. This tends to be a judgement based purely on age.

---

Discourse, as was discussed in Chapter 2, is rearing its head again here because the terms failing and troubled families set the scene for how we understand the living conditions and behaviours of some families (Garrett, 2018). They carry with them the idea that families can be measured against particular standards and that not all families come up to the mark. However, we can draw a distinction between families who seem to have specific problems that are restricted to their own circumstances and families who are deemed to be problematic on a wider scale in that they impact upon the wider community.

You may be aware of the television programme *Supernanny*, in which Jo Frost intervenes in the lives of parents who are portrayed as struggling with their children's behaviour. This represents families with problems that we can categorise as private; that is to say, the problems are within the home rather than having an impact on the wider community. *Supernanny* presents a particular view of families, one where Jo Frost's parenting techniques will provide a solution for that family (Jensen, 2018). In terms of parenting, though, *Supernanny* could be seen as promoting the idea that all problems are rooted in individual families rather than in social conditions; these are problems that individuals can solve by behaving or parenting differently. This is not to dismiss Jo Frost out of hand; rather, it is to encourage you to consider that families which come to feature in each show are families where specific parenting behaviours can be focused on. For many families, though, their problems are rooted in the social conditions of their lives, and these are less easy, or even impossible, to solve by changing our behaviour and/or our parenting.

Underpinning arguments about parental support is the idea that when parents fail this leads to social problems that will affect children's outcomes. What is deemed to be problematic will, of course, change and what is expected, or what is deemed to be normal for families and for parenting, changes: for example, how we no longer consider it acceptable to smack children. There are times, though, when moral panics follow high-profile incidents as well as more general concerns about dysfunctional families or social breakdown, which leads to state intervention into family life (Frost, 2011). One such moral panic is exemplified by the claims made by the Conservative politician David Cameron when he was prime minister, in response to a series of riots which took place across the UK in 2011. The riots were presented as the result of social and economic unrest in deprived areas but were in fact triggered by the death of a young man who was shot by the police.

Cameron did much to locate the causes of the rioting within families which he deemed to be failing, referring to 'troubled families' (Welshman, 2013; Parr, 2017; Crossley, 2018a; Garrett, 2018; Hoggett and Frost, 2018). In referring to troubled families, Cameron echoed Blair in talking about parents who are seen to be a problem for those around them. In this way, the private troubles experienced within families come to be public troubles that are the focus of state intervention (Ball et al, 2016). However, this ignores the issues of social and economic inequality that may contribute to social tensions.

This is nothing new. Historical concerns with problem families have a long history (Welshman, 1999; Garrett, 2007, 2018; Lambert, 2019). The Troubled Families Programme can be seen as following on from the previous Labour government's concerns with families who experienced social exclusion and this in turn reflected the Family Intervention projects set up in Dundee by the Conservative government under John Major in the mid-1990s.

Lambert (2019) offers a good account of how a discourse may persist, but where the focus has changed over time, from 'problem families', to 'children at risk', and then to 'troubled families'. Lambert opens with a quote from Cameron in 2011 that is seen to mark the beginning of the Coalition and Conservative focus on troubled families, one that is often used: 'we've known for years that a relatively small number of families are the source of a large proportion of the problems in society' (2019: 82). Take note that the focus of this speech was not poverty, not a lack of jobs and not social exclusion; it was families. The response was to set up the Troubled Families Programme (in England only) to work with families, rather than individuals in families, with the aim being to change their lives.

The definitive guide to the Troubled Families Programme is provided by Casey (2014: 82), who was appointed by the government to lead the programme, and who writes that the programme is:

> working to 'turn around' 120,000 families over the lifetime of the programme. To be eligible for help under the Troubled Families Programme, families have to meet three of the following four criteria:
>
> - Are involved in youth crime or anti-social behaviour
> - Have children who are regularly truanting or not in school
> - Have an adult on out of work benefits
> - Cause high costs to the taxpayer.
>
> However, for most of these families, such problems are often part of a much more complex picture where many other issues are at play. We published a report – 'Understanding troubled families' – which is based on data collected by local authorities of a sample of families

who have been helped by the Troubled Families Programme. This showed in addition to the expected problems related to crime and anti-social behaviour, absence from school and unemployment, that on entry to the programme, troubled families had the following characteristics:

- 71 per cent of families had a health problem;
- 42 per cent of families had had police called out to their address in the previous six months;
- 29 per cent of troubled families were experiencing domestic violence or abuse on entry to the programme;
- over a third of families (35 per cent) had a child who was either a child in need, subject to child protection arrangements or where a child had been taken into care; and
- one in five (21 per cent) had been at risk of eviction in the previous six months.

Families had on average nine problems related to employment, education, crime, housing, child protection, parenting or health on entry to the programme. This is based on those families for which full data were available across every problem (1048 families).

Casey is understandably positive about the programme but more critical accounts are available and you are advised to read some of these. Fletcher et al (2012) provide some explanations as to why they considered that the Troubled Families Programme was unlikely to work, while Jupp (2017), Crossley (2015) and Levitas (2012) point to some major weaknesses in terms of the claims that have been made in respect of the programme (Levitas and Crossley are easily accessible online). These accounts are often critical of the figures that the Troubled Families Programme is based on, such as how the number of so-called troubled families was arrived at, and in terms of the success of the programme, something which Crossley refers to as 'unbelievable'.

One problem with the Troubled Families Programme is that it assumes that families have persistent or stable problems – that is to say, problems which do not change – when this is not the case. So, a family where children regularly truant may find that they are recorded as having been successfully turned around on the basis that their children have left school, or where adults find work. These are changes that families make in their lives without intervention. It is not clear in this programme what support is provided that actually helps families. Instead, it appears to just monitor families who are identified as troubled. However, in spite of these weaknesses, in January 2020 HM Government (2020: np) announced up to £165 million for 2020–2021 for the programme on the grounds that:

compared to families with similar characteristics who have not been on the programme, 19–24 months after starting to receive support:

- the proportion of children on the programme going into care has reduced by a third
- the proportion of adults on the programme going to prison has reduced by a quarter and juvenile convictions reduced by 15%
- more people on the programme are back in work, with 10% fewer people claiming Jobseekers Allowance.

The programme was originally set to run for five years from 2015 to 2020 but was extended by a year in 2019. There was £165 million of funding confirmed for 2020–2021.

Since the current programme began in 2015, 297,733 families have made improvements with the problems that led to them joining the programme. In 26,848 of these families one or more adults has moved off benefits and into work.

Note that the programme was renamed Supporting Families in 2021 (HM Government, 2021).

One thing that stands out in a number of the books and papers that you will encounter regarding problem, or troubled, families is an association with the idea that within society it is possible to identify a class of people who form a group at the very bottom of society. This has been called a number of things over time but since the 1980s it has usually been referred to as the underclass. It is hard to explore the issue of failing families without considering how this overlaps or draws upon ideas about an underclass. As such, Section 3.6 introduces ideas about the underclass debate.

## 3.6 Can failing families be seen as part of an underclass?

The link between failing, or troubled, families and the underclass is evident in a number of books and articles. For example, in his book on a history of the underclass, Welshman (2013) also quotes Cameron, referring to a need to sort out the lives of 'troubled families'. Cameron is one of a number of prime ministers who have expressed a desire to tackle the problem of troubled families. This is relevant because although on the surface debates about the underclass can be seen as being rooted in concerns about poverty, discussions of the underclass often focus on a particular type of family, suggesting it is not just poverty but a particular response to poverty. Welshman makes the point that his book is a history not really 'of poverty *per se*, but of a particular interpretation of the causes of poverty that has reappeared periodically under slightly different labels' (2013: 1–2).

In many texts about the underclass, such as Murray et al (1996) or Neckerman (1993), the place of families is of major significance. They suggest that there are cultural issues related to poverty that are problematic, as opposed to poverty itself. In some ways the 21st-century concern with families who may be referred to as troubled, failing or problem families is simply the latest version of an enduring concern with poor people who are portrayed as being 'not like us' (Welshman,

1999). Setting up the discourse in this way allows others to distance themselves from these families.

The rise of a concern with problem families can be traced back to the 1940s and it can be seen to have emerged at a time when previous explanations which proposed that poverty was caused by biological weaknesses among some groups within society had become discredited (Garrett, 2007, 2018; Welshman, 2013; Macdonald et al, 2014). That is not to say that the idea that poverty is somehow the fault of the poor never resurfaces: for example, Margaret Thatcher claimed that poverty results from a character defect (Dowden, 1978). However, there has been a general rejection of the idea that poor people are poor due to their biology.

Since the 1970s the underclass has tended to be associated with the state provision of welfare. Although the welfare state has been very successful in raising the living standards of millions of people in the UK, there has been widespread criticism of it, particularly from right-wing commentators.

One of the main critiques of the welfare state, especially that put forward by right-wing commentators, is a concern with the creation of a 'dependency culture' (Garrett, 2018). This refers to the ways in which people are said to become dependent upon welfare benefits to the extent that they cease to look for work and start to expect that the state will look after them. This overlaps with ideas about the development of the underclass. Although hard to define, as will become obvious, the essence of the notion of the underclass is that of dependent 'scroungers' who have not only no desire to work but who also hold different values to the rest of society, and this is characterised by the spread of single-parent families and of crime. Bagguley and Mann (1992) sum this idea up quite succinctly in the title of their excellent review of underclass theories, 'Idle thieving bastards'.

To make sense of the idea of an underclass, though, we have to accept the idea that society is stratified or layered in ways which we typically refer to as social classes. Typically, in the UK, social class has been considered in terms of upper class, middle class and working class; the underclass is not an official part of any class model. Official statistics within the UK adopt the National Statistics Socio-Economic Classification (NS-SEC) (Goldthorpe, 2016a). The seven-class version of this class scale is as follows:

Class description
1. Higher managerial and professional occupations, Salariat
2. Lower managerial and professional occupations
3. Ancillary professional and administrative occupations* Intermediate
4. Small employers (fewer than 25 employers) and own account workers classes
5. Lower supervisory and technical occupations
6. Semi-routine occupations Working class
7. Routine occupations

---

* NS-SEC names Class 3 simply as 'Intermediate occupations'. We elaborate on this to give a better idea of the occupations included. (Goldthorpe, 2016a: 90)

Looking at the categories, it can be seen how this scale may be better understood as a model of occupational class because it does not include those who do not work, whether that is because they have no work and therefore may be seen as falling into an underclass or because they are those who are wealthy enough not to need to work.

Social class itself is something that is often debated, but for now don't worry about what determines membership of social classes, just accept that there are arguments which propose that there is an identifiable underclass. For example, Runciman (1990) argued that there is definitely a class below the working class in the same way that there is a class above the middle class. This underclass constitutes those members of society who are more or less permanently at the economic level at which benefits are paid. Jordan (1973) also pointed to benefits as a decisive factor in defining the underclass calling welfare dependants a claiming class. This ignores that some of these people may not claim benefit or may not be eligible for benefits but have little or no regular income and may depend on others (friends, families or charities) for their survival.

In contemporary society, however, it is a term that is often used when referring to the poorest sections of society but in a very specific way, in that it is used in relation to cultural issues. In raising the issue of culture, we are considering how the underclass are often portrayed as living a particular lifestyle or holding particular values which shape their behaviour. It is not simply a label that is applied to individuals who claim benefits. For an example of this read Bom et al (2018) or Paterson et al (2016). Bom et al (2018) analyse public tweets that were posted in response to the UK television programme *Benefits Street*, Series 2, and the way in which tweeters make reference to lifestyle choices, usually in negative ways. This shows how we continue to see these families as responsible for their own circumstances due to the lifestyle choices they make.

In respect of the underclass there are two specific perspectives that can be taken to explain how it has come to be formed:

1. Cultural: they create themselves. This is a right-wing view which sees the problem as the poor themselves. Thompson (2017) explains this as a pathologising explanation. By this he means that the poor are claimed to have some personal failing which sees them as unable to escape poverty.
2. Structural: they are created by social structures. This is a left-wing view where the problem is explained as the structural conditions which create poverty. In this perspective, inequalities result from how society and the economy are organised.

The modern usage of the term the underclass can be seen in Sir Keith Joseph's concept of a cycle of deprivation (Welshman, 2013; Macdonald et al, 2014; Page, 2015). Joseph is important because he played a central part in the Thatcher governments after 1979 and, as a consequence, was able to influence social policies relating to poverty. During the early 1970s Joseph argued that even in a period of economic prosperity it was possible to identify groups who were living in poverty and claimed that this was being transmitted through generations. Joseph described this as a cycle which continually acted to reproduce poverty.

This idea has become a common-sense explanation in relation to children and families living in poverty, as is illustrated by Simpson et al (2015), who interviewed early years' practitioners in a deprived town in the northeast of England and found that it was not uncommon for them to describe their role as intervening to break the cycle of poverty. Respondents – that is to say, early years practitioners – tended to hold a view of poor families as not being aspirational. This reinforces the cultural explanation of poverty that is seen in the arguments put forward by Joseph. There is a sense that Joseph is suggesting that children in some poor families were being socialised into accepting poverty, and a reliance on state benefits, as normal. This is an idea that is very strong within popular depictions of poverty as being cultural within the UK (Macdonald et al, 2014; Simpson et al, 2015; Calder, 2016).

The problem with this explanation, however, is that this is very generalised and there is little evidence to support it. Many people move in and out of poverty and the theory of a cycle of poverty is unable to account for any significant continuation of intergenerational poverty. In spite of influential commentators talking about families where three generations have never worked as being a fact (Calder 2016), the evidence is very hard to find. Macdonald et al (2014) detail how they tried to find families where three generations had never worked by carrying out research in deprived communities in both Glasgow and Middlesbrough but failed. Glasgow and Middlesbrough are both areas where widespread poverty has been located for quite some time, so it was reasonable to investigate intergenerational poverty in these areas. Although welfare practitioners in these areas would often talk about such families and the idea of such intergenerational poverty as being firmly in place, the reality was somewhat different. What stands out from all of the interviews carried out by Macdonald et al is a strong commitment to working rather than relying on benefits.

This focus on the family as a transmitter of poverty leading to generational poverty shifts concerns away from the structural roots of poverty, such as the availability of jobs or the level of pay, by blaming the poor for their own poverty. This is why it is termed a cultural explanation. It is an explanation which can be seen as underpinning the very influential work of Murray (1984; see also Murray et al, 1996).

## 3.7 Murray and the start of concerns

Murray makes an important distinction in his work in saying that he is referring not to the degree of poverty (the extent of how poor someone is) but to a type of poverty (though it may be more accurate to substitute a type of response to poverty rather than simply a type of poverty). This clearly defines Murray's argument as a cultural argument. Arguments such as this can be seen to be adopting a victim-blaming approach in that they locate the reason for poverty in the person, or family, that is poor.

It is worth pointing out that Murray's type of poverty is not really new; nor does he claim it to be, and he cites poverty in Britain in the 19th century to show this. Murray's type of poverty, the type that he sees as belonging to the underclass, is what has been called a number of names such as the undeserving poor, the feckless and the residuum (Mann, 1992; Welshman, 2013). Murray considers that the people who constitute these groups are dishonest and distinguishes between the 'honest poor' (as he claims his parents had been) and the 'dishonest poor' who he is focused on. You might recognise a process of othering going on here. Othering refers to a group being cast as different in some way.

Murray is quite provocative in how he writes about the underclass, referring to the underclass as being of a similar nature to a disease. In talking about his work in Britain he claims that he set out to consider whether or not the plague (a term which he uses), which he has identified in the US, is spreading to the UK, asking if we in the UK are being contaminated (Levitas, 1998). Importantly, though, Murray argues that this plague cannot be cured by providing more jobs or by providing higher benefits. This is because the people who constitute the underclass are healthy people of working age but who have a very different understanding of life from the rest of us. For Murray et al (1996: 26), they 'live in a different world'. Now, as a student you will no doubt have been told on numerous occasions that if we are to make claims, as Murray does, then we need some evidence.

The question then is: what evidence does Murray have? Murray's original work relating to Britain is freely available online – do an internet search for *Charles Murray and the Underclass: The Developing Debate*. Reading it, you will see that Murray concentrates on three factors which he terms the early warning signs (1996: 26):

- illegitimacy (which Murray says is the best indicator);
- violent crime; and
- dropping out from the labour force.

Taken together, he argues that the statistical evidence of growth in each of these factors provides proof of the existence of an underclass in Britain: 'If illegitimate births are the leading indicator of an underclass and violent crime a proxy measure of its development, the definitive proof that an underclass has arrived is that large numbers of young, healthy, low income males choose not to take jobs' (1996: 38). Murray also goes on to state that 'the young idle rich are a separate problem'.

**Study tip**

Remember that as a student you are usually asked to be critical. So, consider the claims Murray makes.

He presents illegitimacy as a way of having children outside of marriage that is particular to this group. It might be worth considering how he is using this term and whether it is outdated, given that many women have babies outside of or before marriage.

Also, consider the idea that he suggests that this group is dropping out of the labour force. He is suggesting that this is a choice but think back to what we said about deindustrialisation and the way that many traditional industries closed down during the 1980s. What opportunities to work are such people likely to have?

What is evident in Murray's work is that he sees the underclass as being of their own making and as such his argument is clearly a cultural argument. The message is quite clear; members of the underclass don't want family responsibilities or jobs, just benefits and easy money. He claims that the underclass has developed in response to high benefit levels, easy access to subsidised housing and a reluctance to punish criminals. This is presented as being understandable: such a lifestyle is obviously very attractive to some. Who wouldn't want free money, cheap housing and not to be punished if you do anything wrong? So, the underclass is a cultural phenomenon explained by cultural theories. Or is it?

Dean (1991) suggests that poverty can be seen to be something that is rediscovered as a social problem in certain periods, such as in the late 19th century and the latter half of the 20th century. When this happens notions of an underclass based on cultural caricatures are also reinvented. By caricatures, Dean means that exaggerated stereotypes are referred to in ways which are said to represent a group overall. What Dean is saying then is that the argument that the poor created themselves is actually a defence that the non-poor use as a way of defending a social system which creates inequality and poverty. As such, what happens is that an argument is presented which states that the problem is not the system, it is certain types of people: the poor are the problem. They are different.

This idea can be seen in the words of Margaret Thatcher, prior to becoming prime minister, when she asserted that 'there may be poverty because people don't know how to budget, don't know how to spend their earnings, but now you are left with the really hard fundamental character – personality defect' (Dowden, 1978). Thatcher was arguing that absolute poverty was not a problem within the UK, therefore what we might see as poverty was in some way self-inflicted. In doing so, however, she negates any concern about inequalities and rehashes the old idea that the poor are feckless. This is relevant now because there is lots of evidence to show that after Thatcher became prime minister inequalities widened in the UK and that they are continuing to get wider under current government policies (Alston, 2019). What is more, whereas at one time poverty was seen as being a consequence of worklessness, what is now evident is that the poor are increasingly comprised of people who are in work (MacInnes et al, 2013; Hick and Lanau, 2018; McBride et al, 2018). Consider this in regards to Murray's comments about people 'dropping out' of work.

## 3.8 Being critical and using this chapter

Before we consider how you might use this chapter in an assignment, it is useful to think about how a focus on the Troubled Families Programme offers some good opportunities to develop your skills of being critical. We have said elsewhere that it is important to be critical. Most students study for a degree with the intention of getting a job, and a critical approach is a useful skill to have in graduate-level jobs. Employers will value staff who can identify weaknesses in arguments and processes. It is by identifying weaknesses that we can progress. However, you do have to be clear about what being critical is. Being critical in higher education assignments is not just a matter of finding authors who provide opposing views. As we have already said, that just leads you to the type of essay where you write Smith (ref) says this but Jones (ref) says the opposite.

As an example of a critical approach, locate and read the papers that were referred to in the previous section by Crossley (2015), Fletcher et al (2012) and Levitas (2012), and think about how these enable you to demonstrate weaknesses with the Troubled Families Programme.

### Study tip

At this point, consider how the Troubled Families Programme is a good example of rhetoric. Rhetoric can be explained as persuasive language.

See rhetoric as the use of language which seeks to present a particular image of something, but which doesn't really stand up to scrutiny.

As a student, one good approach to developing criticality is to try to test what you read or hear as being either rhetoric or reality. So, think about the COVID-19 pandemic of the early 2020s and then look at the ways in which the government and the media constantly referred to dealing with the virus by using the analogy of a war. Think about how the virus was often presented as clever, as having the ability to plan and attack when, of course, that is wholly unrealistic: a virus doesn't think. However, in terms of a message this type of analogy is very persuasive.

So, are troubled families real or are they a rhetorical device which justifies a government adopting certain policies?

In the discussion above we demonstrate how you can use academic papers or books to build up an argument which identifies weaknesses in the Troubled Families Programme. You could use Levitas to question the methodology used in arriving at a figure of 120,000 families. A further approach is to consider the claims being made. For example, the Troubled Families Programme was introduced as being concerned with achieving social justice (Crossley, 2018b). This seems admirable. However, it is an aim that we would call seductive; who wouldn't want to achieve social justice, when the alternative after all is social injustice? Yet, as Crossley notes, there is nothing in the government's proposal which actually states what is meant by social justice. Now, in terms of being critical, if we were to read something in a student assignment which establishes what is meant by a key concept such as social justice, we would be much more confident that the student understands what they are doing and that in turn is likely to be reflected in the grade. As a student, your task is to convince the marker of your work that you have read widely and that you understand what you have read.

One thing that we have said previously is that as students you have to be precise when you use terms. You must make it clear what you mean when you use a term such as social justice. In proposing the Troubled Families Programme, the UK government did not do this. That means that we ought to explain what social justice is. It is maybe easier to do this by starting with social injustice.

Social injustice can be defined as unfair treatment or discrimination within society. So, social injustice can be said to be present when the rights and responsibilities of individuals, groups or categories of people are not respected. The Black Lives Matter movement is concerned with social justice in that it is focused on the experience of differential treatment for people of colour and seeks to change this so that all groups, irrespective of ethnicity, are treated fairly. This doesn't mean that everyone has to be equal or the same. Equality is not the same as treating everybody the same, just as diversity is not synonymous with inequality. Some groups may be treated differently because of historic injustices and as such we may recognise the idea of positive action.

Different treatment only becomes a problem when it rests upon ideas about some groups deserving better and some groups deserving poorer. We have social justice when we are all treated fairly rather than when some groups experience discrimination, when everyone's rights are respected and where we all feel that our efforts are fairly rewarded. This has not always been the case, and some may say that it is not the case now. An excellent book for exploring social justice is Thompson (2017). Being critical can enable you to investigate such claims.

There was a lot in this chapter, so let's try to pick out some of the key points if you were required to write an assignment about parenting or about failing or troubled families. Let's just add the warning, though, that the term troubled families is politicised in that it is rooted within a particular policy response to something that a particular government sees as problematic. So, the key points are:

- The state often intervenes to regulate family behaviours.
- We can distinguish between being a social parent and a biological parent.
- It has been argued that what parents do is more important than who parents are.

- Parents are often seen as responsible for ensuring that children develop in a socially acceptable way.
- How parents 'parent' can be seen to have changed.
- Different social classes are said to parent in different ways.
- Support for parents has sometimes taken the form of parenting programmes.
- Some families are characterised as anti-social, often being referred to as troubled or failing.
- The state has focused attention on those families who are said to be failing families.
- Failing families are nearly always families that are in poverty.
- Failing families can be understood in relation to ideas about an underclass.
- Children within failing families experience obstacles to achieving.
- The actions of the state provide the context for family life; this may help or hinder families.

This has been an extensive chapter and we have covered a lot of ground, but we can still pick out ways in which you might use this chapter to build up a focused and structured essay. So, if you have an assignment on failing, or troubled, families, how might you go about it? If it were us, we might start by establishing the central role that families are seen as having in society, and then state something like 'however, some families can be seen as failing'. By starting with this claim, we can then go on to say that there is evidence from historical and cross-cultural sources which indicates that the state can act to regulate family life. Note, regulate rather than control.

In terms of how the state might regulate or what they might seek to regulate we could use the example of parenting as covered in Section 3.2. This lets us talk about parenting as a social role and comment upon how it has changed. We could use Lareau (2011) to do two things: firstly, to introduce the idea of parenting reflecting social class, and secondly, to make use of theory. If we are going to say that parenting differs based on social class, then we need to support this claim and Lareau works well. We might also comment upon helicopter parents as being one extreme and neglectful parents as the other. That could work.

The structure in this chapter sees us providing a more focused consideration of failing families by focusing on the Troubled Families Programme. This provides an opportunity to support the claim made earlier that the state will intervene in family life. We can also show how this is shared by governments of different political persuasions. In this chapter we introduced the idea of the underclass and illustrated how influential this was, but you might not have the space to write too much about this. If that is the case, just provide a brief discussion but add a few references. If you don't have space to discuss something fully, dropping a few references in can help to give the marker confidence that you know what you are talking about, and it shows that you have read around the issues. If anything, an assignment on failing, or troubled, families is likely to be quite focused, so take note of your assignment guidance and don't go off at a tangent.

## Further thoughts

As a student it is useful to recognise your own position in terms of values.

Think about whether you agree with the idea that the state should provide support for parents. If you think support should be offered, what support and for which families?

Now consider your view on poverty. Give some further thought to the distinction that we made regarding cultural explanations of poverty compared to structural explanations. How does this fit with the sociological approaches referred to in Chapter 2 regarding structure and agency? Consider you own view on this and what that is based on.

Make sure that you are clear what we mean when we say that the state regulates families rather than controls them. How does regulate differ from control, and are there any instances where you feel it is control rather than regulation?

## Further reading

Read books on poverty and inequality to help you form your own opinion based on research. Crossley (2015, 2018b) illustrates the approach taken within the Troubled Families Programme. See also Lambert (2019).

# 4

# The state

This chapter will help you to understand:

- what the state is and why the state is not the government;

- why we might benefit by giving up some personal freedoms;

- what we mean by rights and how the state shapes the rights that we have;

- the basic approach to democracy within the UK and what we mean by populism.

## 4.1 Why is the state relevant to studying children and families?

In starting to consider the relationship between the family and the state it is important to be able to define what each of these is. As a basic definition we can say that a state exists when there is a political system in place governing over a definable area and reinforced by the law. A state is not the same as a country. So, for example, England is a country but is part of a bigger state, the United Kingdom of Great Britain and Northern Ireland. Note also that the state is not the government; the government is a part of the state. The government can be seen as directing what the state does in terms of policies and legislation, but it is only a part of the state. Defining the state makes it appear quite straightforward but the state, like the family, is quite a slippery concept.

As this book is aimed at higher education students on courses which are focused on childhood and families, it might be fair to ask why it is that such a student would want to read a chapter about the state or what the state does. The response to such a question is that the state regulates and shapes the context of the lives of children and families. By now this should have been made obvious as we have looked at a range of ways in which the state does things which make the lives of children and families either easier or harder, and in doing so actually shapes how childhood and family are experienced.

You might also want to think about how important Bronfenbrenner (1979) has been in shaping our understanding of children and how the state is firmly located within Bronfenbrenner's socio-ecological model.

**Study tip**

In your assignments you should always be trying to make links between ideas. You will look stronger if you can make good links between ideas. This might be from other modules. In Chapter 1 we referred to Bronfenbrenner's socio-ecological model and you can see how we are linking back to it here.

If you are not familiar with it or feel you do not fully understand it, then go back to Chapter 1 now and think about how it links.

In terms of how the state operates it might be useful to draw a distinction between legislation (laws) and policy (guidance for practice). Legislation creates a legal requirement to do something. As such, legislation is very likely to be put in place when a government wants society to operate in a very specific way, and therefore to achieve a policy outcome. However, policy is not the same as legislation. A government will develop and use policies to achieve its aims. To ensure this happens, or to enforce these aims, it will often introduce legislation, but policy can be put in place without a legal requirement.

To understand this point better, think about how organisations or companies that you may have worked for have policies which dictate what you do but which there is no legal requirement to actually do – safeguarding, for example. At the same time, a government may introduce legislation which aims to provide some service provision but without specifying how this service should be delivered. So, schools may be required to teach the National Curriculum but not in any particular way. Policy specifies how the legislation is put in place, but this may vary across the country.

As an example of this, within the UK local authorities must provide Children's Centre services. This is a statutory service, which means they must provide the service. However, a local authority is not compelled to provide such services in any particular way. With regards to Children's Centre services, local authorities do not even have to provide a physical building, just some means for parents to access support and advice. As such we can see that the law says that an authority has to provide the service, but it is up to each local authority to determine its own policy of how that service is provided. What you might consider then is that we tend to encounter the effects of policy in our everyday lives to a much greater extent than we encounter legislation. However, we may not be aware that what we encounter is the result of policy or legislation.

We should also be aware that legislation and policy might not change as much as we think and although they can be seen as a means to create social change, they actually often lag behind social changes in society that can be seen as issues or problems for members of that society. Consider childhood obesity. It is commonly accepted that childhood obesity is a problem. This problem can be seen when we encounter children who are overweight but there is little policy that is addressing this issue. So, we may be right in thinking that the landscape of social policy is subject to change, but always bear in mind that changes might not be substantial, and they may be slow or even ineffective.

---

### Pause for reflection

It may be worthwhile to take a moment and think about obesity in childhood. Many children are obese yet there is little evidence that we are finding solutions to address this issue.

Think about what might be the cause – lack of exercise, or the growth in fast food, for example – and what might be the solution. Then think who should be involved and who could bring about change. Difficult, isn't it?

---

## 4.2 Can the state do things that individuals cannot?

In terms of problems that societies might face, we are writing this soon after events in the UK that devastated the lives of very many families across the country and during the ongoing consequences of another threat. The first event is the devastating floods that caused misery for many families early in 2020 and which are associated with global warming and the climate crisis. The second event is the spread of a coronavirus, COVID-19, a flu-like virus that has had an impact around the world and which has seen extensive restrictions on social life that were unprecedented in our lifetime. We are commenting upon these events because each is something that individuals are relatively powerless to deal with; individuals have neither caused these events on their own nor can they prevent these events when they act as individuals.

In both cases, we can see that something needed to be done to address these issues and the problems that they caused. The question is, who should do this? When we see that something needs doing about such important and complex issues, we tend to see this as something that someone else should do: someone who is in charge, who has power and influence. This tends to be seen as being the state, though this may also be referred to as the government. We will distinguish between each of these. However, there is a difficulty here in that we often feel that the state either does too much and is too intrusive in our lives or that the state does not necessarily do the right thing, or does too little. It is the case, though, that problems such as the floods experienced as part of the climate crisis or the COVID-19 pandemic can only really be dealt with at the governmental level.

When we consider events such as flooding and the spread of disease it seems evident that responses have to be above the level of individuals or even above the level of communities. This is because the costs are often too high and the planning is just too much or because the problems just seem to be too complex. When we think about life in a complex modern society such as the UK, events such as these remind us that very often we need a level of government which can act in a manner in which individuals and communities are unable to. So, we need someone to represent and act in our interests who does have power and influence.

As such, we could say that there is definitely a role for a body that has the power to operate at the national level, and even to represent and act on our behalf at the international level. However, how that body operates is open to debate and, as we shall see, it relies on the possession of power so as to be able to achieve things. At the same time, it is also fair to say that it inevitably becomes difficult to satisfy the vast range of demands that are placed upon it. The state or government cannot do all things for all people, given that we all might have different needs and differing ideas of how things should be done. What we will consider then is a number of issues that relate to how the state operates and how the role of the state impacts upon the lived experiences of children and families.

---

**Pause for reflection**

Make a quick list of services or provisions that are provided by the state for children and/ or families.

Now consider why the state might provide services for children and families. What might the state want to achieve in providing services?

Think about how these services may be compulsory, such as education, or how parents may be able to opt out of accessing service provision. Consider why we expect some services to be used and others to be optional. Why might this be?

---

## 4.3 How values shape what the state does

It is not contentious to say that the state has a concern with children and families. Examples drawn from previous chapters illustrate that the state has concerns about what the family is and even who might be entitled to form a family. We can see this in the recent development of same-sex marriages. The development of same-sex marriages rests upon actions by the state which permit a new type of family to exist as a legal entity. This example also shows how ideas may fall on a continuum of ideas from liberal (open to new ideas) to conservative (averse to change). Also consider how ideas in society change, and why they may change.

So, to explain this, if you are socially liberal you will generally be open-minded and tolerant. Being socially liberal means not being prejudiced such as being homophobic or racist. Being socially conservative means the opposite, being resistant to inclusive practices and generally prejudiced against groups which you somehow deem to be inferior, wrong or unnatural in some way. We might see this being played out during the 2020s in terms of culture wars and debates about being woke or being critical of wokeness. Woke is a term adopted to describe people who are open to new ideas or who recognise critical views of social matters such as why statues of historical figures who were involved in slavery can be seen as offensive.

In the early 2020s in the US we have seen how the president is able to appoint judges whose values resonate with their own to the Supreme Court, which can then have significant consequences for children and families in that the Supreme Court makes laws and judgements that shape how children and families can live their lives. The most obvious example of this is how the balance of values within the Supreme Court was changed to make it more conservative and how this led to sweeping changes to legislation and policy relating to contraception and abortion. Of course, this can be a complex issue and contradictions are commonplace. The key thing is that liberal values tend to be accepting of difference and change whereas conservative values tend to resist difference or change.

Be careful not to make the mistake in assuming that the Conservative Party will inevitably be socially conservative. They often are but not always. For example, it was a Conservative government in 1988 which introduced a clause in the Local Government Act prohibiting 'the teaching in any maintained school of the acceptability of homosexuality as a pretended family relationship' (Wilson, 2001: 124). This is clearly socially conservative. Look at the language that is used to denigrate same-sex relationships by calling them 'pretended'. The clause was generally referred to as Clause 28. Clause 28 was scrapped by Blair's Labour government. However, it was a Conservative prime minister, David Cameron, who granted same-sex couples equal rights to marry through the Marriage (Same Sex Couples) Act 2013 (Gilbert, 2018). This is socially liberal. This example also demonstrates how important it is to consider the ways in which different leaders of political parties influence the types of legislation and policies that governments may introduce.

There is a further aspect to this, though, in that we can see how social and public policies can have what we call a normative effect: that is to say that they shape our understanding of what is normal. So, with respect to Clause 28, homosexuality was presented as being socially unacceptable with the consequence that individuals who are homosexual may have experienced being discriminated against as their behaviour was presented as not normal. To add to this, we can also say that social and public policies can be prescriptive in that they act to assert what can and cannot be done, as in the case of Clause 28, so regardless of an individual school or teacher's beliefs, they could not talk about homosexuality to pupils in a way which suggested that it was normal.

However, we also need to consider what influences or drives the development of social policies. This might not always be as simple as it seems. There may be multiple things which drive a government to introduce a policy. For example, many policies that are referred to in this book can be seen as being influenced by two particular ideologies, neoconservatism and neoliberalism, both of which have been very influential within UK society for over 40 years. Both will be explained in some detail later in Chapter 5.

For now, it is enough to recognise that neoconservatism operates in a way which sees particular types of behaviour as being unwelcome. Neoconservatives would usually tend to resist or try to prevent social practices which they would say are not normal or not socially acceptable. Homosexuality is a good example of this. That is not to say that it is not normal – we are definitely not saying that – just to say that neoconservatives are likely to say that it isn't normal. During the 1980s a lot of concern was focused upon homosexuality, particularly after the identification of Acquired Immunity Deficiency Syndrome (AIDS) (Wilson, 2001). AIDS is a health problem experienced by individuals who have contracted the human immunodeficiency virus (HIV) and contracting HIV is linked to certain types of sexual practices.

So, the combination of neoconservative influences in the government alongside more general concerns about a particular health concern, AIDS, can be seen as influencing a change in policy. Alongside this, the 1986 Education Act had already indicated that the Conservative government at the time was concerned about sexual behaviours and this legislation had transferred responsibility for providing sex education within schools from Local Education Authorities (LEAs) to school governors. For Wilson (2001), this policy aimed to shift responsibility away from what the government saw as socially liberal bodies (LEAs) and towards what they thought would be socially conservative bodies (school governors).

This came after a great deal of attention had been given to the idea that sex education led to promiscuity. This is based upon the idea that if you know about something then you will want to do it, though this is a very weak argument; we both know about skydiving, but neither of us wants to do it. Sexuality and sexual practices are aspects of human life that the state often seems to be concerned with.

### Pause for reflection

Why might the state be concerned with sexual practices, which may be argued to be a private matter?

One reason we tend to accept is that children need to be protected so an age of consent seems reasonable. Thus, sex is established as non-consensual before the age of 16 in the UK. Is 16 the right age? What about when the age is 18?

Different countries or states have different legislation about this. Why might that be?

Both Dauda (2010a, 2010b) and Waites (2001) consider how the state regulates sexuality by imposing an age of consent for sexual activity in ways which draw on ideas about what is appropriate and when. More will be said about matters relating to types of sexual or sexualised behaviour in Chapter 11. However, it is worth considering here a point made by Waites. In the UK the age of consent for sexual activity can be 18 rather than 16 as is commonly understood. This is when sex involves an adult who is deemed to be in a position of responsibility, such as a teacher, and the other person is, say, a 17-year-old student. In establishing an age of consent, you might consider the argument that it is necessary to protect young people from entering into activities which they may not be ready for, or which could have serious long-term consequences, such as pregnancy or exploitation. In this way the actions of the state can be seen as protective. Bear in mind, though, that the age of consent varies quite a bit across the world so there is nothing inevitable or obvious in the setting of such an age restriction.

As such, we should be able to see that a concern that something needs to be done often translates into something being done in the way that a change of policy comes about as a consequence of government actions which could include new legislation. This shows that the actions of the state can have real consequences for how we live and experience our lives. Mind you, at this point we still haven't really explained what the state is. That comes next, but if you feel that for your assignments you need to know more about policy and less about the state feel free to jump to another section or even another chapter. You rarely have to read academic books in a linear fashion. Use them in ways which work for you.

## 4.4 What do we mean by the state?

Trying to pin down just what is meant by the term the state is not easy, and just what it is is contested (Hay, 2014). Hay provides a good position to take regarding the state in arguing that although the complexity of the state means that it is difficult to define in a conventional sense, the state does exist. There is a state, but we have to see it as something that is abstract. So, in respect of how you understand the state, and in terms of how you talk about, and write about, the state it is useful to think of it as a political force which has power, but which can never be defined in a way that is wholly without question. The state is a slippery concept. It is contested and is perceived differently by different groups and individuals. Accept that and a lot of other things become easier to understand.

Skinner (1997: 8) offers a useful description when he says that the state can be understood as 'an apparatus of power whose existence remains independent of those who may happen to have control of it at any given time'. So, see the state as an indistinct apparatus that has power but that it is not fixed. It has power, but that power operates in a range of ways, some of which are obvious and some of which are subtle, or even hidden. Importantly, note that the state is not independent of society; it is a part of society itself (Coates, 1984). The way in which some people talk about the state may suggest otherwise, but that is not the case.

---

### Pause for reflection

You may want to take some time here to think about this concept.

We can confidently say that a state exists when there is a political system in place governing over a definable area and reinforced by the law.

A state is not the same as a country: for example, England is a country but it is part of a bigger state, the United Kingdom of Great Britain and Northern Ireland.

---

A state tends to be self-governing but in some circumstances a state can be subject to a higher authority, something that we might see being referred to as a supra-national power. Supra-national simply means above the nation. So those with power and influence over our society may even be those in other countries, or not obviously part of our society.

For example, the European Court of Human Rights is a supra-national body that has the power to restrict what the British government does. It is important to note that the European Court of Human Rights is not a part of the European Union (EU). The European Court of Human Rights pre-dates the EU. It was set up in 1959 by a number of European countries including the UK to enforce the European Convention on Human Rights, which in turn was established in response to the actions of Nazi Germany before and during the Second World War. Its aim was to prevent the sort of atrocities experienced in the Second World War by identifying and protecting individual human rights.

Similarly, when the UK was part of the EU it was obliged to comply with EU legislation, and this can also be seen as an example of supra-national power. It is important to point out, however, that as a member of the EU the UK was involved in drawing up EU legislation. It was not the case that the EU drew up legislation which was imposed on the UK. Instead, the UK, as a country which had joined the EU voluntarily so as to benefit from membership, was therefore obliged to follow the rules that it contributed to making, even though there was still considerable scope for different approaches to be taken.

That can be contrasted with the way that Great Britain took control of other countries as part of the British Empire. The British Empire is an example of how one country may take control over another country, often through force and as a part of the act of colonisation. In these circumstances the colonising state imposes laws and regulations on the country that has been taken over. Many European states did this during the 18th and 19th centuries with significant consequences for the rights of millions of indigenous people across the globe. In turn, many colonised countries gained independence during the mid- to late 20th century, often having to resort to violence to achieve independence.

You may also come across the idea of states within a federal system. The United States of America is the most common example of this system, but Australia and Germany are also federal states as are many other countries. A federal state represents a group of states working together to benefit all. A state in the US sense has limited powers within a federal system. So, in the US individual states set taxes such as sales tax within that state. States may also tax income in addition to federal income tax. The federal government has authority over all states, with individual states having more limited authority over themselves. The EU is not a federal system and this is why countries within the EU have much more freedom than individual states have within the US.

It is very important then to note that the state is not the government. The government is part of the state, albeit a very important part. The government can be seen as directing what the state does in terms of policies and legislation, but it is only a part. The state represents the broader systems involved in running the country. One way of making it clear why the government is not the state is that governments can, and do, change; however, the state remains.

Governments influence the state but should not be seen as being the state, as per the quote from Skinner (1997) at the beginning of this section.

---

**Study tip**

You should always take note of which political party, or which prime minister, was in power when a particular policy or piece of legislation was introduced or removed. This is because prime ministers and political parties will change the approach that is being taken to a particular issue, but this can be seen as temporary or for only as long as that party or prime minister remains in power.

Think about working for a company or an organisation and the manager or chief executive changes. The organisation remains but it may be that you start to see the new person in charge introducing changes to what you do or how you work.

---

## 4.5 How the state can regulate the context of your life

In beginning to think more about what this means for us in terms of our everyday lives, you can usefully consider that the state is the context within which we have, or do not have, rights (rights are discussed more fully in Section 4.8). As such, the state exists as a framework within which our rights as individuals or groups are established, maintained or removed. It is the power of the state that acts to provide or remove rights. As an example, think about the issue that emerged during early 2018, usually referred to as the Windrush scandal. In this example, we can see how the government can change the context of our lives.

---

**Pause for reflection**

If you are not familiar with the Windrush scandal, look it up now. See Gentleman (2022) and Rawlinson et al (2022).

---

Because of growing criticism about the scale of immigration, the Conservative government under Theresa May had determined that it would target illegal immigration and set about establishing what it referred to as a hostile environment. This had consequences for many individuals who had legally moved to the UK as children but were unable to provide documentation to prove this (Dorling and Tomlinson, 2019). This meant that many individuals suddenly found that they had lost their right to live and work in the UK. Despite having worked and paid taxes for around 50 years many found that they were now being denied benefits and healthcare and that they either lost their jobs or were unable to get new jobs because employers were being required to check that individuals had the right to work in the UK. They suddenly had no rights. This is quite an extreme example of how the state impacts upon our lives; however, for most of us the state acts upon us in a more subtle way; a way that is maybe best understood as regulating.

In thinking about how the state shapes our lives we have already said that it is very useful to see it in terms of regulating. In using the term regulating we are able to accommodate the fact that the state rarely uses force to compel us in what we do. Instead, we can see that the framework of legislation and policies which the state sets up means that the context of our lives is subject to regulation as we are drawn into complying with them. Of course, we may find that not complying does not necessarily result in a penalty. For example, if you break a law, you may be subject to a penalty such as a fine or even imprisonment, but that is not always the case. However, if you do not comply with policy, you might simply find that you do not get support. For example, applying for the 'Care to Learn' benefit but then refusing to provide certain information will mean that the benefit is not given to you. In this way we can see how legislation and policy encourage, coerce and guide our behaviour but in a way that is often not through direct force. As such we often find that we comply with what the state wants, simply because we have no real choice.

---

**Note**

Education is compulsory until the age of 16 in Great Britain. However, policy introduced in England in 2013 meant that young people had to go to college, take up training or work until they are 18. While this is not enforceable by law, it means that under the age of 18 you are not entitled to benefits if you are unemployed.

This has the effect of restricting the independence of young people in England, by regulation.

---

So, in considering the relationship between children, families and the state it is important to say what we mean when we refer to the state and why it is relevant. In terms of children and families it is reasonable to say that childhood and the family are both regulated by the state. As indicated, though, we say regulated because this is more accurate than saying that childhood or the family is controlled by the state. Control is difficult to achieve but if we say regulate, we can see how legislation and policies shape the context of both childhood and family life and how it is that this has a strong influence upon how we experience them. This can even extend to the size of families.

For example, some Eastern European countries have recently introduced financial incentives such as payments and loans so as to encourage larger families (Walker, 2020). Similarly, in the UK, changes to the welfare system that were introduced in 2017 have meant that families receiving benefits now only receive payments for the first two children born to a mother. This could be seen as an attempt by the government to restrict the size of those families who are reliant on benefits but applies to all families, so can be seen as suggesting that having more than two children is unacceptable. A somewhat similar example can be seen in respect of Child Benefit. Before 1975 Child Benefit was not payable for the first child, something that one of the authors, Creasy, was always aware of; as the eldest of four children his mum often told him that she didn't receive Child Benefit for him. As the second child in her family, Corby's parents did receive Child Benefit for her!

These examples can be seen as relating to how state support for families in respect of payments can be said to regulate family size, yet family matters are often presented as being a personal or private matter. One issue in relation to this can be seen to be the question of exactly what the state should be seeking to regulate or control.

---

### Pause for reflection

To help you decide whether or not the state should act to regulate or restrict some things consider the following examples.

1. During the 19th century it was common for children from poor families to work in industry, often in dangerous and hazardous jobs. Children worked in factories, mills and coal mines, for example. The state faced pressure from social reformers who campaigned to prevent children from working in industrial settings and eventually legislation was introduced which restricted child labour.
2. In the early 21st century many infants are fed with what we call milk formula. This is marketed as being good for children. However, many types of milk formula have high levels of sugar, and sugar is associated with health problems (Bridge, 2020). Regulations to control the amount of sugar in milk formula and to ensure that consumers know how much sugar is present are often absent.

Would you support campaigners seeking to remove children from industrial workplaces?

Would you support regulations to restrict the amount of sugar that is in baby milk formula?

In each case, can you say why?

---

In the first example regarding child labour, it seems quite clear that restricting child labour is good for children. In the second example the issue might appear less obvious so we have to think about whether or not the amount of sugar in milk formula should be restricted or regulated. In both cases, though, who should be responsible? You might draw the conclusion that the state is the obvious source of regulation and has a role to play in protecting children's health, but not everyone would draw the same conclusions. There are many people who would argue that it is parents who should be responsible for their children's health and it is up to them to choose healthy foodstuffs. Bear in mind, though, that during the 19th century there were similar arguments regarding the rights of parents to send their children out to work, which was often seen as necessary in order to have sufficient money to support the family.

Now consider what society might look like if the state did not regulate social life or behaviour. You might ask why parents would send their children to work or feed them milk that was potentially unhealthy. However, we should be able to accept that parents generally behave in a way that they see as normal and acceptable in society and, thus, they are not intending to harm their children. Sending young children to work at an early age can seem like a rational decision in respect that this can enable them to contribute to the household budget. We, the authors, have children – they are expensive! At the same time, unless parents are aware that milk formula contains sugar, and that sugar is unhealthy, they will not be in a position to make a rational decision. They may also feel that if baby milk is sold in shops then it must be OK to use for their baby.

---

### Note

Remember we asked you to consider obesity earlier? One of the issues with obesity is that sugar is in so much of our diet that we may not be aware of, in processed food. Baby milk is a processed food and it can contain a lot of unnecessary sugar. Sugar is believed to be addictive. Thus, babies are being introduced to sugar which will shape how they experience food from an early age, and what they like to eat.

---

## 4.6 Should we give up personal freedoms and let the state have more power?

We might see that the state is a social body that can do much that is good if it intervenes to challenge and shape what is normal. However, there is often a trade-off in that as individuals we have to give up some of our personal freedoms so that the state can exercise power. We accept fewer freedoms so that we may benefit from the power of the state. The pay-off for us is that we benefit from the things that the state can do which we as individuals may not be able to achieve on our own or are even unaware of. Of course, when children were prevented from working some parents would have been unhappy as it meant that their household income declined

Think about ways in which the state may regulate the lives of citizens for good reasons, or to achieve positive outcomes.

---

**Pause for reflection**

Take a moment to think about a list of things which the state prevents you from doing or which it restricts so as to achieve positive outcomes.

As an example, you could start with restricting children working, but what else does the state do? If you struggle with this, then consider age restrictions.

---

Having given some thought to how the state may restrict what we can do, consider how government policies about smoking, alcohol use and road safety are all examples of regulations which aim to improve our lives (Jochelson, 2005). For example, in the UK since October 2015 it has been illegal to smoke in a car when an under-18 is present. Given that there is no doubt that smoking is harmful, the legislation which prevents smoking in cars acts to benefit children, but you can see how acting to establish the rights of children to be protected from second-hand smoke simultaneously restricts the rights of adults to smoke when and where they want to.

If you think that the state should have some responsibility and that the law about smoking in cars is something that is positive, it may be seen how this leads to the idea of seeing the state as being paternalistic, or what Jochelson (2005) calls the steward state. The paternalistic state is the state that is seen to be acting towards citizens as though it were a parent. There is a sense in which the paternalistic state is a state which seeks to protect us. It may stop us from doing things but that is for our own good. In suggesting that the state may stop us doing something, though, we have to recognise that the state has the power to stop us.

---

**Pause for reflection**

This intervention by the state was evident during the COVID-19 pandemic in 2020 when the government aimed to limit the spread and effect of the virus by introducing a range of what could be seen as extreme measures, such as preventing people from leaving home.

While most of the country went along with these measures some people challenged and resisted them. On reflection, we may consider some of the measures unnecessary or ineffective. However, it might be argued that the government felt they were doing the right thing at the time. What are your thoughts and experiences of this? Consider how others might have experienced the pandemic.

---

This idea suggests that the state has a duty of care over its citizens and therefore should act in their best interests. Regulation by the state can be compared to the way parents make decisions for children that are intended to be in their best interest. There is often resistance to such policies, though, and those who oppose policies of this nature often refer to the state as being a nanny state.

The term nanny state refers to the claim that the state is not allowing us to act as we would want to, it is telling us what we can or cannot do or it is making decisions on our behalf based on the idea that we are not capable of making decisions for ourselves (just as nanny is said to do for infants). This is often used as a derogatory term in that 'nanny' is not respected as knowing best but, instead, is seen as controlling small children. The implication is that we, adults, are being treated like children.

You may also read or hear of states being referred to as authoritarian. The authoritarian state refers to a state where those that hold power restrict the freedoms of individuals based on their own beliefs and ideals but also retain that power in the long term. Those in power do not see a role for others in society to have a say, offer ideas or challenge that power in any way. Chapter 8 of Sayer (2008) provides a very good introduction to issues surrounding the ways in which the state can be seen as authoritarian.

## 4.7 Considering the power of the state

One thing that should be obvious is that, if the state is to carry out the roles that are related to administering the country, it must have power. That the state has power is something that cannot really be contested; however, the thing that always concerns writers and commentators is not that the state has power, but rather, the ways in which it exercises its power. When we think about power and how the state acts, this often leads to the state being seen as something separate from us and acting in a negative or controlling way.

Power is important because it can be seen to underpin everything that we consider when we analyse and evaluate children, families and the state. Frost (2011) reproduces a useful model of power that was first put forward by Dencik. In this model the relationship between children, families and the state is represented as a triangle where the state is at the top and children and families are on either point at the base. What is then identified is the direction of influence between each party, showing how there is strong influence from the state to both families and children and there is also strong influence from the family to children. There is weak influence from children to the family and there is weak influence from the family to the state. So, where Dencik refers to influence we might find it more useful to see influence as power. If we can influence something, then we have power. Consider how our right to vote is seen as our power to influence government. If we believe our vote counts or has influence, we may vote during an election; however, if we think our vote is not of influence then we may be less likely to bother.

One thing that is apparent is that power is always relational (Burkitt, 1993). It exists as a characteristic of the relationships that we find ourselves in. So, sometimes we have power and sometimes others have power over us. But think about what it is that gives power in each situation; how do we hold power in some situations and why is it that in other situations we do not? Also, we may not always be aware that we have power.

You can make sense of this by thinking about yourself as an individual. There are some situations in which you have more power and some situations where you have less power. So, it is not that you have power as such but that at certain times or in certain circumstances or situations you have more or less power. This applies to our private relationships and our public ones. Often this is because of our role at the time and how that role is understood within a social context. So, as an example, at home you may be able to say you hold power within your family and can set the rules for how your family will behave; however, in work, you may hold little or no power and have very little control over how you carry out your work.

Considering Foucault is useful here. Foucault is important because of his ideas about power and his approach to the way that it is manifested or exercised. For Foucault power is hard to define; it is indistinct. It operates in many ways and is held by different individuals at different times. Importantly, though, for Foucault power should always be understood as existing within a relationship where resistance is possible. This is fairly easy to recognise when it comes to relationships between people, but you may recognise from our earlier discussion of discourse that Foucault does not restrict his argument to relationships between individuals regarding power. He also argues that power exists in many forms, some of which are much more taken for granted and are much more resistant of debate.

## 4.8 Rights, and some arguments for restricting or removing them

By this point you should have a better understanding of what we mean when we refer to the state and the ways in which it has power. In general, think about power in terms of being able to do things but also consider it as being exercised when we get others to do, or not to do, certain things. So, we could consider that our individual power is concerned with how we have the ability or freedom to do certain things, our freedoms to choose what we do within our society and our ability to influence others. However, we can also recognise that different societies have different levels of freedom and recognise also that those freedoms exist as part of the relationship between the state and citizens. We can also see that where a state has more power then this tends to mean that a citizen has less power. To explore this further in respect of children, families and the state it is useful to say more about the issue of rights.

One important aspect of the relationship between the state and individuals is with respect to the rights that we may hold. We commented earlier on how European countries established the European Convention on Human Rights followed by the European Court of Human Rights as a strategy to protect an agreed set of ideas about the rights that we should all benefit from. That is not say that such rights, or the legitimacy of the European Court of Human Rights, will always be accepted. The Conservative Party has a long history of criticism of the European Convention on Human Rights with the European

Court of Human Rights often being subject to a more general antipathy commonly directed towards organisations that are seen as European (Grieve, 2020; Jay, 2021).

The issue of rights also links back to the discussion of discourse in Section 2.4 when we consider that rights may be promoted or attacked within competing discourses, and which were raised in the example of the Windrush scandal that was considered in Section 4.5. As a further example of this we could consider the significant number of protests that were held in towns and cities around the UK in 2020 as a consequence of events that had happened in Minnesota in the US and which took place as part of the Black Lives Matter movement. On one hand we might take heart from the fact that many people across the UK, of all ethnic groups, were motivated to make a stand against racism; however, we also have to see this in context. Racism is still evident within the UK and significant numbers of protesters also took to the streets as a counter-protest. In terms of the counter-protests think about what this means; it means that significant numbers of British citizens were protesting in support of ethnic inequality.

---

### Pause for reflection

Black Lives Matter or All Lives Matter?

As an example of how language has power, consider the ways in which these two terms operate.

Black Lives Matter is a slogan that is used to draw attention to the inequalities and injustices that are faced by people of colour. As such it operates to motivate support for change so as to improve the lives of people who experience inequality and injustice.

All Lives Matter is a slogan that is used to promote the idea that we are all human and therefore all matter. It is very seductive in that it is hard to say that this is not the case.

But think about what All Lives Matter does in diverting attention away from the inequalities and injustices that are called out in the term Black Lives Matter. As such we can see All Lives Matter as operating in a way that is conservative in that it glosses over the particular inequalities experienced by some groups (Stollznow, 2021).

All lives do matter, but the term Black Lives Matter does not deny that; it simply points to the fact that some people experience discrimination based purely on skin colour.

---

When we consider rights and freedoms the state plays a significant role in what is permitted and what is policed. As the body which draws up legislation and then acts to ensure that it is followed, the state has a key role to play in setting the context for the rights that we all have, or those that we do not have. However, we did say much earlier that the state is not apart from society, that it is a part of society, and because of this we should recognise that rights are always established or lost within social and political struggles.

---

**Pause for reflection**

There is also a more philosophical question regarding rights which is very relevant to studying children and families. Let's start by thinking about whether we think that as individuals we should have rights. Take the issue of freedom.

Stop for a moment or two and think about your position regarding this question: should we be free? In western countries such as the UK we often talk about how important it is to have freedom. Can you state some reasons in support of freedom? Now, consider what you mean by freedom? Freedom to do what?

So, let's ask a further question, a more specific question: is slavery acceptable?

---

We are going to say no, slavery is not acceptable, but you do not have to agree with us. For us it is not acceptable, but there have been times when slavery has been acceptable. It also still exists, although in the UK there is legislation that applies to the treatment of others that may constitute slavery. Think about what it means for a society if slavery is permitted. In a society in which slavery is permitted it must be that within that society it is acceptable for some individuals to be denied freedom, to have no rights. What this means is that the right to own slaves must be accompanied by the right to take away another person's freedom alongside an acceptance that some individuals can be denied the rights that others enjoy.

Now think about freedom, and the extent to which it might be socially acceptable to deny freedom. It is possible. It has happened in the UK in the past and it does happen now.

---

**Pause for reflection**

Stop for a moment again and try to make a list of the characteristics or behaviours which could be, or have been, justifiably used to restrict an individual's rights.

You might find this easier by taking a historical or cross-cultural approach to do this. For example, any activity which breaks laws is something that could, and indeed often does, lead to a removal of rights.

---

Hart (1997) makes the important point that it may be possible to claim that all individuals should be free as the default position but then asserts that some characteristic or type of behaviour on the part of either an individual or group makes it possible to deny them their right to freedom. This is quite an accurate statement of what it means to live in the UK right now. Think about how it is that this can be possible.

However, it is also possible to see how activity which is not illegal can result in the restriction of rights. Actions by the state to restrict behaviours or activities by individuals which are not necessarily illegal can be seen in the introduction of the Anti-Social Behaviour Order, commonly referred to as the ASBO (Edwards,

2015). ASBOs had far-reaching powers with respect to restricting an individual's rights. For example, an ASBO could make it illegal for an individual to enter a defined area or neighbourhood or to socialise with certain other individuals.

ASBOs were introduced by Tony Blair's Labour government and can be seen as a challenge to the individualism that is central to neoliberalism, especially the idea that 'there is no such thing as society' as was claimed by Margaret Thatcher (1987). To explain, if we take the individualism of neoliberalism to its logical conclusion then no one can be anti-social, on the grounds that society does not exist. What the ASBO legislation does is to re-establish that there is such a thing as society, we live in it, and that the actions of some individuals can be detrimental to the lives of others. The ASBO can also be seen as emphasising how Blair's Labour government was able to argue that individual rights always come with responsibilities.

When the Labour governments of 1997–2010 were replaced by a Conservative-led Coalition government the new government set about replacing the ASBO. In place of ASBOs were two new remedies for problem behaviours, Civil Injunctions and the Criminal Behaviour Order (Ireland, 2011). Civil Injunctions are very relevant when studying children and families as they are aimed at preventing nuisance and annoyance by individuals who are under 18. Criminal Behaviour Orders are deemed to be aimed at the most seriously anti-social individuals. Both are intended to prevent an escalation of problematic behaviours that impact on others and thus on society. Brown (2020) provides a good account of ASBOs and the replacement approaches, focusing on how it is that the ASBO captured public attention and why the successors to the ASBO have been much more low key.

Following from this, after 20 October 2014, the Anti-Social Behaviour, Crime and Policing Act 2014 created a range of approaches to dealing with anti-social behaviour including wide-ranging powers for police officers and police community support officers to 'disperse' members of the public from a particular locality. Similarly, Public Spaces Protection Orders (PSPOs) are open-ended powers, which allow a single council official to ban activities in public spaces (O'Brien, 2016; Heap and Dickinson, 2018).

Although not specifically concerned with what this means for children, O'Brien (2016) provides examples that indicate how such orders may be used which could have significant consequences for them. Cockcroft et al (2016) are more specific and show how PSPOs have been used in ways which prevent young people meeting in public places and even which appear to prohibit the wearing of hooded tops, commonly referred to as hoodies.

---

### Note

Children are subject to these, and other, measures that restrict young people's access to public spaces, and even what they wear. Consider how these approaches shape how children are seen in society and even reinforce a negative view of young people regardless of whether they have behaved in a criminal or disruptive way or not.

---

So, should an individual have his or her right to free movement curtailed in this way? Should it be acceptable to remove an individual's rights when they may not have necessarily broken the law? It is obvious that we do live in a society which does accept that individuals should have their rights removed because of criminal behaviour as is evident by custodial sentences. This can be understood as necessary in terms of keeping wider society safe; however, we need to consider whether such measures are necessary when safety is not the issue but it is about particular behaviours that some in society don't like. What is more, we often hear calls from individuals and groups that more people should have their right to freedom removed.

## 4.9 Removing rights because of who, or what, you are

If removing rights because of anti-social or criminal behaviour is somewhat obvious we might also want to consider that one aspect of removing rights is linked to punishment. Punishment is often associated with creating pressure on individuals so as to encourage change in their behaviour or lifestyle, or even their ideas. An example of this might be how further legislation has been introduced recently to restrict individuals' right to protest. Protest has long been seen as a democratic right but this has been increasingly restricted in recent years.

But now it may be useful to think about removing rights because of characteristics that we cannot change. Historically, and globally, it is evident that rights are often denied to groups based upon some particular characteristic. You should be able to recognise a number of examples, such as people with special educational needs, sex, skin colour, sexuality or because an individual belongs to a particular religious group. What this means can vary from receiving lower pay to losing the right to live.

What is maybe the most important issue for us, though, given that our key concern is with children and families, is to accept that age is a characteristic which reduces rights. Think about the way in which children are compelled to attend school. We might agree that children need to be educated but think about the extent to which children are compelled to do this regardless of the child and their individual circumstances. This raises some tricky questions because if we were to make schooling optional, we would in effect be saying it is acceptable for some children not to be educated and very few people would support this. However, we have to acknowledge that for some children school doesn't work.

There is also a generally accepted argument that children do not have the capacity to make rational decisions, and this is often put forward as one reason why children and young people may not have the same rights as adults in life. It fits with the generally held view of children as becomings rather than beings. As was established in Section 2.4, if we see children as becomings we see them primarily in terms of what they will be in the future, and this ignores what they are now and what they are capable of now.

The state tends to take the same view; in general, the state is concerned with children in terms of the types of adult that children will grow into. If that is the case, though, what it also means is that children, as children, are inevitably seen from a deficit perspective; because they are considered to be not yet fully formed they are seen as lacking. Additionally, we could consider how it is that for the state they are a problem that has to be addressed in some way. This limits the way children can be seen as beings: humans with rights and something to contribute to society.

---

**Pause for reflection**

We usually presume children will make bad decisions if they are given a choice. However, do they?

When children are given information and a choice, why would they make a bad choice? We should note that adults also make bad choices. And if we sometimes make bad choices, or mistakes, isn't that just part of life and something to learn from? We become more resilient through failing and making mistakes and learning to overcome this.

---

Academically, there have been arguments put forward which aim to merge both perspectives suggesting that children are both becoming and being (Uprichard, 2008). However, although the possibility of academic theories which merge the position of children as beings and becomings may be encountered, we feel that you should consider that outside of academic debates it is the view of children as becomings that is dominant, and this can be seen in parenting, education and wider society.

This acceptance that children do not have rationality commonly impacts upon the rights that children and young people enjoy (Cassidy, 2012). So, if you talk to parents and/or practitioners it is likely that they would often resist the idea that children's rights give children and young people the right to self-determination in respect of their lives. For example, we can recognise that children often want to be able to play and, although research supports the idea that play is good for children's development, there is a strong discourse within the UK that is concerned with formal learning. This focus on learning tends to dominate provision for children especially within the early years and because of this we can see that children may not always get what they want (Davey and Lundy, 2011).

Further, in terms of learning, Bessant (2014) provides a good account of how children are denied freedom in the context of education, but we can also see how children are very often denied freedom in respect of what they wear to school or how they style their hair (Creasy and Corby, 2019). It is maybe ironic to note that, although schools universally promote messages about the importance of education and learning, many seem very comfortable in denying education to children when they do not comply with regulations about uniform. So, we deny education to a child because of the wrong colour shoes, or the wrong hair style. This reiterates what we said about policy and legislation earlier: there is no legislation regarding what children must wear to school, but most schools adopt policies relating to clothing and hair which they often police rigidly. The thing is, they don't have to have uniform policies, and there is no evidence that it impacts on education, but it is a choice schools make which impinges upon children's rights.

---

### Pause for reflection

Do an internet search for stories about children being sent home for wearing the wrong clothes and/or having the wrong hairstyles.

Now look for stories which emphasise the importance of full attendance at school.

How do schools which exclude children for uniform matters justify this, given the arguments about the need for children to be in school to learn? Could it be that policies about uniform are more concerned with power than with children's learning?

---

The development of ideas which argue that children are beings and that they should be afforded rights has contributed significantly to the ways in which childhood has changed over time. One important example of this is the decision of the Scottish Parliament, in October 2019, to ban the smacking of children, a policy that was followed by Wales in 2020. This is a very good example of why rights are important when it comes to childhood because in England and Northern Ireland, the other countries of the UK, it remains perfectly legal to hit people who, because of their physical size, are among the weakest people in the country. Think about this. As an adult you would not be legally permitted to hit any other person, but in England you are permitted to hit your children. In Scotland and Wales, that is no longer the case.

---

### Note

You may be reading this and be thinking that parents should have the right to hit their children because, as the argument goes, this is a way to teach children right from wrong and to be able to control children's behaviour.

However, consider what message this gives about children. If parents feel they can hit their children, that it is their right, this places the child in a vulnerable position that may go some way to explaining why some parents go beyond punishment and physically abuse their children.

---

This demonstrates how some hold power over others in society and how that power changes as society develops in that what is seen as normal or acceptable is challenged. In summary then our social practices are dynamic. They are constantly changing. Ideas about how we should live our lives and treat others contribute to this change.

So, the idea that children should be treated as beings acts to change the experience of childhood. But that does not mean that there is no resistance to change. Clearly, while some countries see that it is wrong to hit children there are individuals in parts of the UK who do not want to change behaviour that has been acceptable for years. It is important for you to consider that very often both sets of ideas exist at the same time. So, while society is increasingly accepting of the idea that children are beings with rights, there still exists the view of children as becomings, and this view continues to exercise power and influence.

To accept the child as a being we have to start to recognise the child as an individual and to acknowledge that they have rights as children. We can see how over recent years much has been made of children's rights as a result of the United Nations Convention on the Rights of the Child (UNCRC) (UNICEF, 1989) and the African Charter on the Rights and Welfare of the Child (ACRWC, 1990). However, while we can see advancements in children's rights from the time when children were seen as the property of their parents (in the same way that wives were once seen as being the property of their husbands!), we need to be careful in presuming that age is no longer a barrier to rights.

The UNCRC is a globally important development aimed at ensuring the rights of children but that does not mean that children always benefit from such rights (Baraldi and Cockburn, 2018). For example, the government of the US contributed to drawing up the UNCRC but it has yet to ratify it. This means that it has not yet formally agreed to the provisions of the convention. It is worth considering that although the UNCRC is often referred to within England, English children are not able to benefit from the rights that the UNCRC establishes because English children are subject to English law (Lyon, 2007). It is also worth noting that the UNCRC can often be said to draw attention away from more general issues by foregrounding individual rights. This is evident in the way that, within the UK, the serious extent of child poverty and a limited or restricted level of freedom over their own lives can be said to undermine children's rights in a more general sense.

At this point let us consider how these ideas fit with the state. Rights and freedoms are clearly important, but we could say that the state itself is not the driving force in terms of the rights and freedoms that we enjoy. Instead, it is maybe best to say that it is the government which shapes rights and freedoms within the context of the state. However, governments do not exist in a vacuum. Although you may hear it said that politicians are all the same, political parties are not; they differ in the ideas that they hold. Governments are formed by the political parties who win general elections. What they then do, though, is shaped by their ideas about what society is, what it should be and, maybe, what it can be. For that reason it is important to discuss political ideologies. Ideologies are best understood as a generally coherent group of ideas, and they are important in understanding the policies and legislation which are introduced as well as those which are replaced. It is also the case that in the UK we, as individuals, have some input into who the government is; we can vote. For that reason, the following section provides a brief discussion relating to some ideas about voters, with Chapter 5 then providing an explanation of a number of relevant political ideologies.

## 4.10 Democracy and populism

When it comes to matters of participation and influence over the state, the ability of individuals to have a political voice is often of interest. There are two basic positions: democracy and oligarchy. Democracy can be defined as government by the people, oligarchy as government by an elite or powerful group who hold power and thus control the country. In respect of democracies this does not mean that the people are directly involved in making the decisions but rather that voters are able to elect representatives of different political parties to make decisions on their behalf, such as by voting in a general election. This is generally referred to as representative democracy. The UK is a representative democracy.

---

**Pause for reflection**

Think about what you know in respect of elections within the UK.

You would expect that to become the member of parliament (MP) for a constituency a candidate would need to get the majority of the votes cast.

Similarly, would you expect that the government is in power because they have received a majority of the votes cast across the country?

This would seem logical and fair; however, systems are not always fair.

We need to stop and think about what is needed to become an MP and what a political party needs to become the government so that we can consider how representative our political system is.

---

To become an MP within the UK it is necessary to win what is called a simple majority of all the votes cast in an election. What that means is that a candidate only needs to secure one vote more than the next nearest candidate to be elected.

So, in the election let's say that you stand as an Independent and get 10,001 votes, the Conservative candidate gets 10,000 votes and the Labour candidate also gets 10,000 votes. You win. You have a simple majority and become the MP, even though many more people have voted against you than for you. Many European countries use a system of proportional representation, in which the number of MPs reflects the proportion of votes that each party gets so as to represent the country as a whole. The UK does not use this system, and in the vast majority of general elections the government is elected with around 40 per cent of the total votes that are cast.

In addition to general elections, it is also possible to have a referendum. This is where voters are able to have their say on a very specific matter. It is very rare for a referendum to be held within the UK but they have happened. In the UK a referendum was held in 2016 which led to the UK withdrawing from membership of the EU: what is usually referred to as Brexit. This saw a significant rise in claims that the people had spoken and that this meant that Brexit had to happen. However, that was not the case. Governments are never compelled to act in accordance with voters' wishes, especially when the results are as close as they were in the Brexit referendum. One of the weaknesses with the administration of the Brexit referendum was that the government did not set a threshold number of votes required to trigger leaving the EU. The proportion of votes cast was 51.9 per cent voting to leave with 48.1 per cent voting to remain. This is a very small margin and it is important to note that 27.8 per cent of eligible voters did not vote. This means that the decision to leave the EU was based upon a minority of voters voting in favour of leaving (Electoral Commission, 2022).

A further issue relating to the 2016 referendum is that it led to an increase in what is referred to as populism and this is something that is useful to know about. Populism is another one of those terms that we can describe as contested or slippery (Mudde and Kaltwasser, 2017). It is hard to pin down because what it means may have changed over the years or it may be a rather broad or imprecise concept which is used to describe an approach which is itself a little varied (O'Byrne, 2019). Here, though, we need to consider the ways in which populism is most commonly used within the UK now.

In a simple sense, populism describes the actions and claims made by political parties or by individual politicians who claim to represent or reflect what people want (Heywood, 2021). In other words, they are presenting a view that is seen as being what is popular. Populism is usually recognised too as something that is not really beneficial for society because it tends to promote simple messages or simple solutions to issues. These messages or solutions rarely stand up to scrutiny because social life is very complex and simple solutions do not take this complexity into account. One of the biggest problems for politicians is that the things that they have to deal with are often complicated and they very often have to take decisions which might not be popular or put forward solutions that will take a long time to address a problem effectively.

Populist politicians always try to present issues as being simple and therefore as things that can be solved by a simple action. As an example, we can consider the slogan used by the Conservative leader, Boris Johnson, during the 2019 General Election campaign, 'Get Brexit done'. It was simple and it was popular with many, but it wasn't really accurate. It was not accurate because it was focused on the simple act of leaving the EU. It overlooked the vast amount of work that then had to be done as part of leaving and it was this work, work which could take years to resolve satisfactorily, which is important in terms of our everyday lives because it establishes the terms of leaving. This can be seen in how the Johnson government wanted to renegotiate the agreement that it had put forward regarding customs borders in relation to Northern Ireland within a year of having proposed it, because of the problems that it caused.

So, the UK may have left the EU in that it is no longer a member state, but at the time of writing Brexit has not been done in a satisfactory manner and is unlikely to be done for a long time. Brexit has led to significant disruption within the UK because all the ways we have of running the country and operating in a global world were linked to being an EU member and these now need to be renegotiated. Furthermore, the cost and complexity of exiting the EU are very likely to make things worse for those individuals who believed exiting would make their lives better. The independent Office for Budget Responsibility has detailed the negative economic consequences of leaving the EU (OBR, 2022), demonstrating that the UK is now in a poorer economic position as a consequence of Brexit.

A key issue that characterises populism then is the way in which it acts to construct simple positions regarding any issue. This can be seen in the idea of 'us and them' or the way that issues are seen to have two sides and that these two sides are set in opposition. This ignores the fact that there can be multiple positions; it is not always a dichotomy. Therefore, it leads to ideas of there being other groups who are not like us, or groups holding different values or ideas that are posing a threat to our way of life (O'Byrne, 2019). As part of this emphasis on different values being some sort of threat you will often come across the idea that political representatives (MPs in the UK) act in ways which fail to represent voters' wishes and even that they act to oppose what voters want (Kaltwasser et al, 2017; Gandesha, 2018).

It has also been argued that very often the thing that drives populism is rapid change (Eatwell and Goodwin, 2018). Populism, its rise or its popularity, is explained by referring to large groups of voters who feel that society has changed and conventional politics and politicians do not share their values and do not work to benefit their lives. This is the idea that groups within society feel left out or left behind.

---

### Pause for reflection

We often feel that we have little control over how our country is run. Sometimes it seems too complex or just not very interesting. However, consider how who runs the country impacts on the everyday lives of children, young people and families. And on you.

If you are not sure what you believe or how you want your country to be run, then take some time to consider this and consider using your vote. Voting for the right party can make the difference in how children are treated and live their lives; and you would not be reading this if you did not care about children.

---

## 4.11 Making use of this chapter in an assignment

As a student on a family and/or childhood studies course it is very unlikely that you will be given an assignment purely focused on the state. It is likely, however, that you will have assignments which cover policy issues, and policy often seems complex or difficult, so it is always going to help you if you have an understanding of the state. This chapter will be useful for you to support points that you make within assignments, and you should dip into it as fits your task.

It is important to say, however, that when it comes to marking assignments, the marker is looking for evidence that you understand the issues involved in the assignment. Students often make the mistake of focusing on content, including things that have been talked about in lectures or other classes, when what is more important is demonstrating understanding of these things. To demonstrate understanding you often need to be able to explain and use the concepts that shape the context within which children and families live.

But, if we were to see this as an essay, accepting that you are unlikely to write such an essay, we opened by using the winter floods and the COVID-19 pandemic in the early 2020s as illustrating why we need a state. This is on the grounds that there are some things that individuals cannot achieve and that a body with power at the national level can achieve more. We also introduced the idea that the state, as this body, has particular views about how society should be and that these views are strongly influenced by whichever government is in power, but this means that it is important to distinguish between the government and the state. In doing this we also distinguished between governments that are socially liberal and those that are socially conservative. This is something that you might find very useful when you are being asked to analyse policies, so always consider whether a policy is liberal or conservative and try to understand what that means for children and their families.

Having done that, though, we felt it important to provide a more in-depth discussion of what the state is and made some comparisons between types of states and even how states can be subject to higher powers such as the EU. This also saw a discussion of how the state regulates our lives and how those who are critical of what the state might do in restricting rights come to define the state in particular ways such as by referring to it as the nanny state.

Always be careful; it is too easy to fall into the trap of seeing the state and the government as being the same, so a brief sentence or two which shows that you understand the difference will always give the marker more confidence in you. Take note, though, of the argument that the state is not easy to pin down and that it can be seen as quite a slippery concept. We also emphasised the importance of seeing the state as regulating the lives of children and families rather than controlling them. This is a subtle difference, but it is differences in explanations such as this that can help you to come across as stronger and that will always help you to get better marks.

Having explained what the state is in more detail, we introduced a discussion of power so as to explain further how the state exercises power and how it regulates the lives of children and young people. To develop the idea of the state having the ability to regulate our lives through the exercising of power we provided a discussion of rights and referred to anti-social behaviour and age as examples of how rights can be curtailed or restricted, sometimes even removed. As part of the discussion of rights we drew attention to some philosophical issues which underpin the ideas that we have about rights and how these may feed into the legislation and politics that we have at any given time. We also used this to explore how some societies point to certain characteristics as justification for the denial of rights, including the characteristic that is of most relevance to us – age. This provided an opportunity to comment on the UNCRC and the African Charter on the Rights and Welfare of the Child.

In some ways this could have been sufficient, but we also thought that it might be useful to provide a brief discussion of democracy and populism to close the chapter. If you were marking the chapter, you might say that we needed to remain focused and mark the paper down, but we hope that you find this a useful discussion, given that we live in a world where a number of influential politicians find it beneficial to suggest that they have simple solutions to complex problems and that they may ignore evidence because it suits their cause.

When you write assignments you always want to be moving beyond description and towards analysis. You need to do more than just describe what policies are, or what they are for. You should always be trying to explain the ideas and values which underpin them. As a pointer to some of the key concepts covered within this chapter and which could be very useful within your assignments consider the following:

- The government is not the state, and the state is not the same as a country; the state represents the wider framework of bodies which are engaged in the administration and running of the country.
- The state is not separate from society, it is a part of society.
- The government is the part of the state that governs the direction of the country by shaping policy and legislation.
- The state acts in ways which regulate the lives of children and families.
- Power can be exercised by the state through legislation and policy, but it can also be exercised through the discourses adopted by the state.
- The rights that we have are shaped within social and political struggles with the state.
- Legislation and policy can be used by the state to restrict or curtail our rights.

---

**Further thoughts**

Give some thought to the idea that the state is more than the government and think also about how the state can act to reduce the rights that citizens have.

Think about rights as systems which protect you.

The UNCRC is referred to as shaping children's lives. Look this up and consider all the things it says about how children should be treated. It is usually said to offer rights of provision, protection and participation. Are these rights evident in society?

---

## Further reading

Read the UNCRC. It is easily accessible online. Think about the values that underpin it and consider what it means for children.

# 5

# The relevance of political ideologies

This chapter will help you to understand:

- what political ideologies are;
- why understanding political ideologies is relevant to the lives of children and families;
- how you can make use of political ideologies within your assignments.

## 5.1 What do we mean by political ideologies?

You will often come across people writing or talking about political ideologies. This chapter will show why an understanding of political ideologies is important by discussing what they do in relation to the ways in which we experience our lives. To be fair, there is a lot to say about political ideologies and there isn't the space to do more than provide an outline of some of the main political ideologies that are relevant to our discussion. This is so that you can understand children and families in the UK in the context of the political ideologies that have shaped their lives.

It is important to state that it is not the case that any one ideology is correct or right and that others are not. You may favour a particular ideology, but an ideology can never be said to be right just because it has support.

First, though, what you need to know at this point is just what an ideology is. Taylor (2007: 1) sums it up as follows: 'Ideologies ... describe social reality and suggest ways to change it.' When you see a gap with full stops in a quote, as above, it means that the quote has had some words deleted. We have deleted some words so as to make the point more succinct. So, think about an ideology as a set of ideas which link together or are related to one another in ways which explain the world that we live in. They also offer us ideas about how to make changes which are proposed as being for the better. The changes that are suggested will generally take the form of social policies and/or legislation. Policies can be understood as plans which shape the services that we provide or the way that we practise when working with others. So, to summarise that and to reiterate why you really should have a working understanding of political ideologies: political ideologies shape the social policies and legislation that governments bring in, and social policies and legislation shape the context of our social and working lives.

For example, imagine that we value communities and because of this we see parents as needing some support because we believe that support will benefit not only their children but society as a whole. This can be seen as an ideological position. In turn this influences us to develop a policy relating to the provision of services which support children and families. Let us say that this new provision of services is in a dedicated building within each community where families can access help and advice. We then provide funding for this, recruit staff and set about putting the idea into practice.

You may recognise this as being Children's Centres. The ideology that underpins this approach is that if we support families more when their children are young it will help with or eliminate problems for families in the long term. Although that is one particular example of our ideology, if we also make changes in a range of social issues we can say that we are putting our ideology into practice. The ideological position here is that the state should support families.

So, for Taylor (2007), ideologies represent how we can understand society, and how we can change things. This rests upon our values in terms of what we believe society is like and what it could and should be like.

---

### Pause for reflection

If we place greater value on social cohesion and believe that we should all enjoy equal rights, we are likely to promote ideas about inclusion and ensuring that everyone is provided for.

If we place greater value on individual rights and/or believe that some people have characteristics which make them less deserving – for example, skin colour, gender or physical ability – then we are unlikely to be concerned about tackling inequalities and will see services that provide support and/or help people as expensive and unnecessary because someone has to pay for those services and we may feel that it is not our responsibility to support others who we are not related to or who we do not know.

---

So, as a simple definition we can see ideologies as a combination of how we understand the reality of society, how society should be and what social values we hold. That means that we have to ask the question of how we see the world and what sort of society we want to live in. For example, do we believe that we are naturally competitive and only concerned about ourselves or do we see people as deserving of help, are we community-minded and do we think that we should look out for one another?

When ideologies are shared by others then we start to see how people may act together in ways that are aimed at putting their ideological views into practice. These shared ideologies underpin political parties and can lead to political change. However, politics is always about power, not about doing good or changing things because it is seen as the right thing to do. A political party will always seek power because it is only by having power that they can change society in ways which correspond to their ideological position. We will consider this further when we discuss the ideas about need and about who is deserving and who is underserving later.

---

**Note**

You are very likely to hear or read about an ideology being said to be hegemonic. This is quite straightforward in the sense that it means that an ideology is dominant to the extent that we do not really question it; we just take it for granted.

The term hegemony is typically associated with the Italian Marxist social theorist Antonio Gramsci. You will be able to find an explanation of hegemony in many sociology textbooks, especially books covering theory. *Welfare Words* by Garrett (2018) is very good.

Garrett is particularly effective in demonstrating how hegemony fits with politics and social policy, showing how groups who have power act in ways which maintain and perpetuate hegemony.

---

At this point you might consider that there is a significant overlap between the concept of discourse and of hegemony. Do not be too concerned about this; just bear in mind that to be dominant an ideology has to promote a particular discourse to the extent that it appears normal, natural even. Consider how we see apparent differences in the way women and men behave; we may know people who see it as natural that women are perceived to be homemakers and men are the breadwinners. By promoting the idea that this is natural any criticism can be shut down or marginalised to a large extent because the term natural carries a strong message.

## 5.2 Making sense of Left and Right in politics

To begin our discussion of political ideologies it is useful to start with the basic distinction of Left and Right, followed by a few comments on the main political parties. This helps with the key distinction between political ideologies. This is a simplification, but it helps us to grasp a general understanding of dominant ideologies in politics and it is very common to hear people talk about political parties being left-wing or right-wing.

---

**Note**

Right-wing parties reflect neoliberal and/or neoconservative ideas. Underpinning right-wing politics is a general belief that inequality is natural.

---

They tend to be concerned with individualism, free markets and nationalism. They are critical of social welfare and are critical of, or resist, immigration as well as tending to favour punishment rather than prevention with respect to crime. Right-wing parties do not support ideas or actions referred to as 'woke', such as acknowledging social injustice: for example, the Black Lives Matter movement. They also tend to deny the reality of the climate crisis.

Left-wing parties are underpinned by a general belief that society can be changed so as to make it fairer.

They tend to see a greater role for the state in promoting wellbeing through social welfare, are critical of free markets for increasing inequalities and tend to favour prevention rather than punishment in respect of crime. Left-wing politics also tends to be more accepting of diversity and of critical ways of understanding society. Left-wing politics is more accepting of 'woke' ideas and of taking actions to make society fairer.

---

As always, though, things are never as simple as they seem, and it is maybe better to see political parties on a continuum from extreme or far right through centre right to centre left and far left, but where the position that any party occupies is subject to movement in either direction and it is not unusual to see certain policies as appearing to contradict the ideological leanings of any government.

For example, consider how the Conservative Party that was elected in 2019 under Johnson introduced policies such as the furlough scheme which would generally be seen as left-wing in response to the COVID-19 pandemic of 2020. This scheme saw the government paying 80 per cent of people's wages so as to support individuals and businesses. Similarly, in 2022, the Conservative government under Liz Truss acted to cap energy costs, though this was revised later. It could be said that these policies acknowledged the shortcomings of free markets because in a truly free market the state would not help businesses or families, but it could also be recognised that such policies prevent the collapse of the market system.

It is also the case that the Conservative government under Boris Johnson increased taxes for most people and businesses to an historically high level: again, something that is usually associated with left-wing governments. Right-wing parties usually present themselves as supporting low taxation whereas left-wing parties recognise that if society is to provide services then taxation is required to pay for them. Consider also, though, how under Tony Blair's leadership the Labour Party introduced some policies which could be seen as right–wing, such as introducing fees for higher education. These seem contradictory, but the important thing to consider is not specific policies but the general direction of a government.

This chapter is not really about the political parties, though; it is concerned with the political ideologies which shape what political parties do. However, as we recognise that students are unlikely to be studying children and families because of a strong interest in politics, we think that it will be very useful to provide a short outline of politics within Great Britain. Remember that Great Britain refers to the countries of England, Scotland and Wales. The UK refers to Great Britain and Northern Ireland. If you are reading this outside of the UK you should still be able to see how political parties within your country are also shaped by left-wing or right-wing ideologies.

Politics within Great Britain generally involves a contest between Labour and the Conservatives in England with the Liberal Democrats occasionally having a bigger profile, as was the case in 2010, when they chose to join with the Conservatives to form a Conservative-led Coalition government rather than joining with Labour. That government saw a return to explicitly neoliberal politics under the umbrella term 'austerity'. The austerity policies since 2010 are important when considering the lives of children and families as austerity has created significant problems for poorer groups. This is within a country, the UK, that has greater levels of inequality than most Western European countries. For real-life accounts of inequality read the books by O'Hara (2020; O'Hara and Thomas, 2014).

In Scotland, Labour had traditionally been the strongest party, but in recent years Labour has been replaced by the Scottish National Party which argues that Scotland should become independent from Great Britain. This is similar to how the United Kingdom Independence Party (UKIP) wanted the UK to leave the European Union. Brexit was not well supported within Scotland, nor is right-wing politics in general, and there has been increased support for the Scottish National Party since 2016. In Wales, Plaid Cymru have some influence on Welsh politics, but calls for independence have been much weaker than in Scotland. Labour tends to be the strongest party in Wales. Politics in Northern Ireland is organised to a much greater extent in line with the religious divisions in that country. As this chapter is about key political ideologies the examples that will be used will reflect the Labour Party and the Conservative Party. This also reflects the parties that have been in government for the previous 70 years and which have shaped the policy landscape of the UK.

In general, Labour are often referred to as being a left-wing party, as opposed to the Conservatives, who are seen as right-wing. Neoliberalism is without question right-wing. We have previously claimed that neoliberalism has shaped the landscape of UK society for the last 40 years and it is generally accepted that neoliberalism was introduced to the UK by the Conservative Party under Margaret Thatcher. Since 1979 the Conservative Party has actively promoted neoliberalism and has reconfigured UK society along neoliberal lines. However, the Conservative Party has not been in power for all of those 40 years. Between 1997 and 2010 Labour was the party of government, first under Tony Blair and then under Gordon Brown.

So, back to the problem that is raised when we say that neoliberalism has shaped UK society for 40 years yet for 13 years we had a Labour government, and we would expect Labour not to be neoliberal. The solution to the problem is to recognise the importance of the prefix 'new' in the term 'New Labour'. So, in a nutshell, in the early 1980s, under Michael Foot, we could say that Labour was positioned to the left in terms of politics. But, under the leadership of Neil

Kinnock then John Smith and finally Tony Blair in 1994, the Labour Party moved away from the left and towards the right so as to become a centrist government.

This is something that happens in politics, especially with the two main political parties, the Conservative Party and the Labour Party; they sort of sway from left to right, and they have tended to follow each other. Blair recognised that during the 1980s and 1990s many of the policies of the Conservative Party were popular and therefore argued that if Labour were to regain power they had to move further to the right. Think about what this means in terms of ideology though. It means that ideology does not restrict political parties. Parties may adapt ideology to suit.

Always be aware then that, like most social issues, political ideologies and political parties are not fixed. Governments may introduce policies which seem to be out of step, as we have illustrated. It is not unusual to see developments leading to changes and, as will be demonstrated, sometimes there are contradictions and compromises. Do not see these as problems; see them as grey areas rather than being black or white.

## 5.3 Neoliberalism: individuals, free markets and inequality

In thinking about the most relevant political ideologies of recent years we start with neoliberalism. Many books and articles point to the impact and consequences of neoliberalism within social policy, and it can be argued that this has been the most influential political ideology for over 40 years. All UK governments since 1979 have adopted some of the basic ideas that are found within this political ideology. This is especially the case with respect to how they have promoted the idea that society should be organised in a way which reflects how businesses operate in terms of markets, competition and choice (Jenkins, 2006). Further explanation of these terms follows. If you do not read anything else in this chapter, read this. It is almost inevitable that at some point you will read something or be told something that is said to be, or to reflect, neoliberalism, and therefore it is very important to have a basic understanding of this political ideology.

You may well come across the idea that neoliberalism is an ideology that is focused on economics. Economic issues are certainly embedded within neoliberalism, but to say neoliberalism is only about economics is insufficient and it should be recognised that there are social and cultural issues that are bound up with neoliberalism also.

To begin with, neoliberalism promotes individualism, and this is always accompanied by ideas relating to self-responsibility. From a neoliberal perspective, individuals should be concerned about, and take responsibility for, themselves. This idea is quite seductive in that many of us would agree that self-responsibility is important. What follows from this idea about individual responsibility is the argument that society works best when individuals are free to act in their own interests by choosing goods and services which they pay for within a free market. Goods and services refers to food, clothing and the things that we buy. However, it also refers to things that are necessary for our welfare or wellbeing, such as housing, education and health or care services.

In promoting the idea of individuals exercising choice within a free market as positive, though, we can see how neoliberals are able to construct a negative narrative about the provision of goods and/or services by the state. Because of this belief, governments that are influenced by neoliberal ideas will usually aim to cut services or aspects of social support which are provided by the state. This is because they consider that what we might call social or welfare services should be obtained by individuals paying for the services that they need or taking out insurance to cover them as required. For example, during 2021 there was a debate about whether or not the state should provide children from disadvantaged households with free school meals when schools were closed because of the COVID-19 pandemic. The Conservative government at the time, led by Johnson, initially resisted calls to provide school dinners when children were not in school irrespective of need. This fits comfortably with neoliberalism as from this perspective the feeding of children is a matter for families rather than the state.

---

### Note

In general, individuals who promote neoliberalism are against the provision of services by the state. From a neoliberal perspective the focus is always on the individual and they would argue that the best way to provide for everyone's individual needs is within a free market.

A free market is a shorthand way of referring to the ways in which we buy the goods and services that we want or need from private companies in a system where private companies compete with other private companies for our custom.

The term laissez-faire is associated with this position. It means that the free market should be left alone, that the state should not interfere or regulate it.

---

Free markets are often criticised on the grounds that they inevitably result in increased inequalities. It is important to establish, however, that from a neoliberal perspective this is not necessarily a problem. The Thatcher governments introduced neoliberalism to the UK at a time when the UK was becoming more equal, but from a neoliberal perspective this was seen as problematic (Dorey, 2015). Neoliberals do not deny that inequalities exist within free markets but what they will typically do is argue that inequalities are natural; that they are an inevitable result of the choices that we make throughout our lives or because of the ways that some of us either have more ability or possess the sorts of skills and talents that the market requires. So, if we are more skilled, or more able, and if there is a demand for the skills and abilities that we, as individuals, have, then we are likely to be able to obtain greater rewards than others who are less skilled, or less able. This is often presented as a common-sense argument; inequalities are just a consequence of the fact that some of us are naturally more able than others. The discussion of cultural capital in Section 5.7 demonstrates some weaknesses with this argument.

You can probably see why this is referred to as an individualist explanation. The focus is on the difference between individuals and how this leads to social inequalities. In addition, from a neoliberal perspective, the presence of social inequality in a financial sense can be seen as being good for society as it encourages individuals to work hard and to make the most of their abilities. The consequences for individuals who do not work hard will be a lower income and a lower standard of living, which in neoliberal terms is generally presented as being a result of individual choice and/or poor decision-making.

### Note

The opposite approach to an individualistic approach is a structural approach.

With respect to inequalities, a structural approach considers how belonging to a social class, a particular gender or a particular ethnic group often leads to personal inequalities.

Structural explanations point to the ways in which individuals from some social groups are disadvantaged whereas membership of other groups provides advantages in ways which reinforce and reproduce social inequalities.

Inequalities then exist as a result of structures which advantage those with power and which exclude or disadvantage those with less or no power. Arguments which focus on structural explanations such as class, gender or ethnicity are generally rejected by right-wing commentators.

So, the starting point in understanding neoliberalism is that it is focused on individuals, looking after their own interests, within a free market and that it downplays ideas which link disadvantage to characteristics such as ethnicity, gender or social class. A key neoliberal argument is that in a free society anyone can be successful if they make the right choices in life and make the most of their talents and abilities. This is linked to aspiration. For example, when becoming prime minister in 2022, Liz Truss claimed that she would transform the UK into an aspiration nation. In doing so she was suggesting that existing problems are the result of the nation as a whole not being sufficiently aspirational. We will say more about aspiration when we discuss social mobility in Chapter 12.

### Pause for reflection

We generally believe that anyone can be successful; however, consider how success is harder for some to achieve than others.

Can you think of ways in which characteristics such as skin colour, sexuality, gender or social class disadvantage individuals?

If you can, does this support or undermine neoliberal arguments about inequality?

Now it is time to go a little deeper and time also for a bit of a warning, so read carefully. You will often come across texts which use the term neoliberalism as though it is unambiguous or self-evident. That is not the case. Neoliberalism is an ideology that is not as clear cut as it first seems (Mirowski and Plehwe, 2009; Robson, 2011; Turner, 2011; Davies, 2014; O'Byrne, 2019). It is important to recognise the basic ideas of neoliberalism, but to understand it more fully it is useful to see it as a loose collection of ideas rather than as a hard and fast rule. With this in mind, some writers have presented neoliberalism as being a thought collective (Mirowski and Plehwe, 2009; Dean, 2014).

This is a very useful approach to take. What they mean by this is that neoliberals tend to share ideas but some will place more importance on some things rather than others. This means that it can appear inconsistent at times. This also means that the term neoliberalism works well as a general guide rather than as a rule. So, because of this, some aspects of what we expect neoliberalism to promote may not always be present or it may be that some actions or ideas put forward by neoliberals could appear to be contradictory. What is obvious, however, is that neoliberalism has been a strong and influential ideology for over 40 years (Jenkins, 2006; Lee and Beech, 2008; Mirowski, 2014).

The roots of neoliberalism can be seen as a form of criticism of the way in which the role of the state grew from the late 1940s (Peck, 2010). The relationship of neoliberalism to the state illustrates how we can see it as a guide rather than a rule and how there are times when neoliberalism does not seem to follow its own arguments. So, you will often read that neoliberalism is characterised by a laissez-faire approach that promotes reducing the size or the role of the state, when in practice the opposite can often be seen to be the case. As such this reinforces the argument that neoliberalism represents a thought collective and shows how the actions of governments since 1979 have generally been driven by ideology. Some modern states, such as the UK, can be said to reflect neoliberalism while not representing a laissez-faire approach towards markets at all.

Many politicians who advocate neoliberalism talk about shrinking the state. By this they mean reducing the range and extent of services that are provided by the state, but this does not mean that those services should not be provided at all. Since the 1980s this has led to many state-run services being privatised, such as water, gas and electricity. We have also seen private companies playing a much bigger role in services such as education or within the NHS and in social care.

Neoliberal ideas about organising social services as though they are businesses has had a real impact at all levels of education with some serious, and negative, consequences (Creasy, 2018). For example, academy trusts are private companies that are encouraged to take over the running of state schools in a way that introduces an element of privatisation to the education system. This also introduces risk; in Wakefield the collapse of a multi-academy education trust demonstrated how education funds provided by the state to educate pupils can be lost (Perraudin, 2019).

The fact is that in many areas of life free markets do not work in a way that is beneficial to society (Olssen, 2016). This means that it is necessary for neoliberal governments to intervene in a way which makes markets appear to work. Take note of the emphasis on making markets appear to work. We can see this, for example, in the way that the state bailed out banks in the banking crisis of 2008 and in the way that the government provided funds to pay salaries to workers during the COVID-19 pandemic of the early 2020s. In a truly free market environment businesses would have gone bust and workers would have lost their jobs in both cases.

However, although the state may have reduced what it does in terms of providing services, it still has a strong role in how society operates. In practice the UK state has been changed significantly because of neoliberal ideology but that does not mean that the state does less now. The state is still very powerful even though it can be seen to provide less for people in a direct sense (Gamble, 1988; Clarke, 2010; Hayek, 2013 [1973, 1976, 1979]).

As such the laissez-faire approach that is often portrayed as being a key aspect of neoliberalism is a myth. In practice, the idea of a laissez-faire approach in which governments do very little is replaced by an active state which seeks to create competition and which often intervenes to provide support for private enterprises when they fail so as to support or maintain the market (Davies, 2014). You may hear politicians refer to the need for the state to act in cases where the market is broken, but can the market actually be broken? In reality this just demonstrates that when markets are allowed to be free then there will be problems.

There is, however, one aspect of modern neoliberal states that does reflect a laissez-faire approach and that is towards amassing wealth. Before 1979, taxation in the UK was progressive. That meant that the more you earned, the more tax you paid. That has changed. The changes to taxation introduced by the Thatcher governments of the 1980s had the effect of reducing the taxes paid by the richest in society and raising taxes for poorer people (Cronin and Radtke, 1987). This was the result of lowering direct taxes such as income tax rates, especially for those with higher salaries, and increasing indirect taxes such as value-added tax, which we all pay when we shop.

It is also important to note that the state taxes earnings much more than it taxes wealth and that this contributes to widening inequalities. For example, income from investments such as shares are taxed at a lower rate than income from earnings and income from inheritance is tax-free at the point that it is received. So, we tax the income that we work for at a higher rate than we tax income that comes from investing our existing wealth, and this is taxed more than income which we do absolutely nothing for in the case of inheriting wealth.

In addition to taxation being reconfigured in ways which benefit the better off, welfare support has also been changed significantly since the Thatcher governments, with the value of benefits being reduced. For those who are unable to work, are without work or, as is often the case, where wages from work are insufficient, the support that the state has traditionally provided since the late

1940s has been reduced. The welfare system has become much more focused on claimants meeting certain conditions. This has led Prendergast et al (2017: 26) to argue that the 'neoliberal state is more laissez faire at the top – enabling the wealthier to amass more wealth without restraints, but is interventionist towards the poor'. This means that systems have been developed that can be said to rest on the idea that some are deserving of their wealth while others are not deserving.

What is evident then is that in spite of significant weaknesses, neoliberalism has been globally significant for over 40 years. In the UK it has shaped the way that we have organised and provided for society since the election of Margaret Thatcher in 1979. It is worth reading more about neoliberalism because it is the key political ideology influencing numerous aspects of our lives. Dorey (2015) provides an excellent account of how the governments led by Thatcher adopted an approach which has widened inequalities. We say governments rather than government to be precise. This is because Thatcher was elected three times and so ran three governments. Albertson and Stepney (2019) provide an accessible evaluation of Thatcher's policies in a range of areas. Larner (2000) also offers a good discussion of neoliberalism and Thatcherism, showing how they have shaped social policy and changed the ways in which we look at the provision of social policy. This is important because support for families should be understood as being in the form of social policy. Both Albertson and Stepney and Larner are easily accessible online.

One thing that does stand out, however, is that although neoliberalism can be seen to have had many negative consequences for many children and families, it is not enough on its own to explain the way in which the state deals with and provides for children and families. At this point in the book, then, we need to consider another political ideology, that of neoconservatism.

## 5.4 Neoconservatism: morals, culture wars and nationalism

### Note

What we can see in the social policies that have been introduced since 1979, especially, but not only, by the Conservative governments is the influence of two ideological perspectives which appear to be irreconcilable: neoliberalism and neoconservatism.

Both of these are distinct ideologies in that they are concerned with different aspects of society, and both are different to the preceding forms of liberalism and conservatism. This is why we add the 'neo' to the beginning of each. Neo means new and they are new or revised forms of liberalism and conservatism.

A simple distinction is that neoliberalism is focused on economic issues such as markets and welfare.

Neoconservatism is focused on cultural and moral issues such as how we live our lives and who should have rights.

During the 1980s it was argued that the Conservative Party was adopting a dual approach to policy and government. On the one hand it was said to be promoting neoliberal ideas such as arguing for restructuring and reducing the role of the state and introducing free markets into a range of services, but at the same time it was developing policies which reflect neoconservative ideas focused on social, cultural and moral issues.

---

**Note**

Many social policies relating to children and families reflect ideas such as a concern with naturalness or how families should be. We can call these ideas conservative.

It might be useful at this point to make a distinction between conservative with a small 'c', and conservative with a capital 'C'.

When anyone uses conservative with a small 'c' they are referring to being socially conservative. This is to be concerned with traditions, accepting things as they are and a resistance to change, especially rapid or radical change. Being socially conservative tends to reflect a general acceptance of how things are on the grounds that this is natural or normal.

When we see Conservative with a capital C we are referring to the Conservative Party. Always be aware of this distinction. The Conservative Party will usually reflect ideas that are conservative with a small 'c', but not always.

---

From the 1990s, neoliberalism came to dominate how we talk about politics; however, to focus on neoliberalism and to ignore neoconservatism is a mistake, especially when it comes to ideas about families. Although discussions of right-wing politics has often focused on neoliberalism this overlooks the part played by neoconservatism (Levitas, 1998) and this is very significant in respect of families, especially those deemed to be failing, and with the presentation of some family types as less deserving of support.

This approach is particularly evident in relation to what have been called the 'culture wars' (Duffy et al, 2021) and that is why it is just as important to understand neoconservatism as it is neoliberalism. We introduced the idea of being woke earlier but more will be said on culture wars later in this section.

Texts which illustrate and explain neoconservatism are not as plentiful as those about neoliberalism and you must be careful when searching online because many texts have a strong American focus. This is important because neoconservatism in the US differs slightly from the UK.

Where neoliberalism emphasises the importance of individuals operating within free markets, neoconservatism places much greater emphasis upon tradition, hierarchy and authority. In respect to the family we see this in the work of Patricia Morgan (2007) and Almond (2008). Both Morgan and Almond can be said to be conservative because of their concerns that changing family forms and practices represent unwelcome developments. Whereas in Chapter 2 it was suggested that it is problematic to refer to 'the family' as a consequence of the diverse nature of families within the UK, we could expect that both Morgan and Almond would not have any problems with referring to 'the family'. For them, the family is obvious; it is unambiguous. As such, from their perspective, not all families are legitimate because some do not correspond to the model of the family which both Morgan and Almond see as proper families.

One theme within neoconservatism that is very relevant is that of morals (Cain, 2016; O'Byrne, 2019), especially with respect to culture (Elliott and McCrone, 1987) and the family (Cain, 2016; Cooper, 2017). A key part of this moral theme is a concern with the emergence of the permissive society in the 1960s (Whitaker, 1987). This is said to have introduced a relaxing of moral values in the UK. This feeds into concerns relating to sexuality and family structure, especially single-parent families. Single-parent families are often viewed in relation to morals.

Mount (1982) provides a clear neoconservative account. He argues that the family is a natural unit, praising the family for resisting what he considers to be unwelcome invasions by the state, concluding that neither state support nor radical change is necessary. Ferdinand Mount is influential because Thatcher appointed him as head of the Family Policy Group, and the family was important within Conservative policies and rhetoric during the 1980s.

What is evident in the social policies of the Thatcher administration governments is that they tended to be based upon the idea of the family as having a very particular form (Douglas, 1990). As such, social policies could be seen as having been aimed at reconstructing a particular type of family behaviour (David, 1986). David argued that the aim was to re-establish motherhood as a central full-time role for women, thus locating fatherhood within the economic sphere on the grounds that this is in the best interest of economic growth. David backs this up with a quote from Patrick Jenkin that is used in many texts: 'Quite frankly I don't believe that mothers have the same right to work as fathers do. If the good Lord had intended us to have equal rights to go out to work he wouldn't have created Man & Woman. These are biological facts' (Douglas, 1990: 413).

What we see in this quote from Jenkin is a key idea in neoconservatism, the idea that we are not all the same. We are different, and this makes social differences, including inequalities, natural. For neoconservatives class, gender and/or ethnicity reflect real differences which mean that there are inherent qualities which make inequality natural and inevitable. This argument can be criticised as biological determinism, but it feeds into what is often referred to as populism in respect of the idea of culture wars. For neoconservatives, differences are also to be found within culture.

Such cultural differences may easily form the basis of an inevitable racism in that some cultures are presented as being superior to others. The approach that underpins a cultural form of racism, though, reflects the more general theme of 'us and them' that is evident within neoconservatism and can be seen in similar arguments about 'scroungers', single mothers and failing families, in that each has been presented at different times as not having the same cultural values as 'us'. This idea can be seen in television programmes such as *Benefits Street* which reinforce a populist or common-sense view of difference.

Values are a key issue for neoconservatives, and they can be seen as underpinning what has come to be referred to as the culture wars. In a nutshell, the culture wars originated within the US in respect of the civil rights movement which was focused on tackling racial discrimination, but can now be seen to represent tensions around establishing certain values as dominant. A basic approach positions progressive or liberal values against conservative values (Duffy et al, 2021). Progressive or liberal positions are active in addressing inequalities and injustice and in promoting equality, whereas conservative perspectives will usually resist the social changes that are necessary to achieve equality or tackle injustice.

### Pause for reflection

Within the UK culture wars can be seen to circle around issues such as Brexit (Koch, 2017) Black Lives Matter (Joseph-Salisbury et al, 2021) and the debates around statues, especially those representing historical individuals known to have benefited from the slave trade (Habib et al, 2021).

The culture wars are strongly associated with the idea of wokeness. Neoconservatives are strongly critical of ideas that are seen as woke. Wokeness refers to an awareness of social injustice or discrimination, and is something which seems to be particularly worrisome for right-wing commentators when this awareness is voiced, to the extent that wokeness is often used by right-wing commentators as an insult.

This is also often represented in claims that wokeness, or political correctness, has gone too far, something that Duffy et al (2021) argue is felt by the majority within the UK. However, it can be suggested that the resistance to wokeness is because addressing inequalities and/ or discrimination requires social change.

It is important to recognise that not all neoconservatives will adopt extreme positions; like neoliberalism, neoconservatism encompasses a range of ideas. Belsey (1986) succinctly illustrates the relationship between neoliberal ideas and neoconservative ideas by identifying five key principles which encapsulate each ideology but where the importance for each is seen to be the reverse of the same five principles for the other:

| Neoliberalism | Neoconservatism |
| --- | --- |
| the individual | strong government |
| freedom of choice | social authoritarianism |
| market society | disciplined society |
| laissez-faire | hierarchy and subordination |
| minimal government | the nation |

It is important to recognise that these ideologies are irreconcilable but that, at the same time, there is an amount of crossover between them. Right-wing political practice involves developing social policies which accommodate both, as is illustrated by Thatcherism.

It is also worth considering that when Thatcher was replaced as leader of the Conservative Party John Major became prime minister. Although Major is very often overlooked in books on social policy, one of his key concerns was to reinvigorate what he referred to as the need for basic values which underpinned his calls for UK society to go back to basics. There was a strong moral aspect to this, and it clearly falls in with concerns about single mothers at the time followed by New Labour's concerns with anti-social behaviour and with later concerns with troubled families. What is clear then is that, although neoliberalism is very important in establishing the economic context of families, neoconservatism is equally important in terms of policies about morals and culture.

## 5.5 Social democracy: equal opportunities, social inclusion and the Third Way

We are focusing this section on social democracy on New Labour because New Labour can be seen as a social democratic approach. It was also very important with respect to children and families. It is worth pointing out that New Labour was specifically associated with the Labour governments of 1997–2010 and the designation 'New' has not been used since.

A key issue within the redesignation of Labour as New Labour was the idea of the Third Way. This was a supposedly new approach to British politics which went beyond Left and Right, though it was never all that precise (Powell, 2000). However, as a simple summary to distinguish New Labour from the Conservative Party from 1979 onwards we can focus on one key issue, the approach to social inequalities, and how this relates to opportunities.

Under the leadership of Margaret Thatcher in the late 1970s the Conservative Party put forward the argument that the UK had become too equal. They considered that Britain's position within the world had declined and that this was associated with the strength of trade unions and with policies which were intended to address inequalities. Their solution to Britain's economic troubles was to be the introduction of neoliberalism. It was recognised that neoliberalism may increase inequalities but because of their neoliberal beliefs they took the position that if it was the case that neoliberal, free-market policies would have the consequence of increasing inequalities that was not a problem. If people were poor, then they were said to be poor because of their own failings. This type of explanation is an explanation which is said to pathologise poverty (Stepney et al, 1999; Thompson, 2017). It is a victim-blaming approach which blames the poor for being poor and has little concern for social divisions. The basic argument is that anyone can be successful if they work hard.

As we have stated, New Labour can be referred to as being shaped by ideas that reflect social democracy (Powell, 1999). This distinguished New Labour from both previous Labour governments but also from the Conservative Party. Unlike the Conservative Party under Thatcher and Major, the New Labour approach emphasised that some groups within society have advantages, and that some have disadvantages. If we think about the life-chances of children we can see that it is easier to become wealthy in adult life if you are born into a wealthy family and it is easier to do well if you are not held back by discrimination such as racism or sexism. However, what New Labour did was to adopt a strategy which turned attention away from a concern with equality and inequality in terms of outcomes as 'old' Labour had done, and which promoted a need for equality in respect of opportunities.

It is maybe important to reiterate that New Labour under Tony Blair was far less concerned about social inequalities than it was about equality of opportunity, and although inequality did not rise significantly under Labour between 1997 and 2010 (O'Hara, 2018), it did rise, and there was a sense that New Labour was not too concerned that it had done so. At the same time, some groups can be seen as having done better than others. Joyce and Sibieta (2013) illustrate how families and pensioners did well during the New Labour years, with workers without children doing less well.

**Note**

Historically, the Labour Party had been seen as a socialist party as illustrated by Clause 4 of the Labour Party constitution. Clause 4 established the goal of common ownership, or nationalisation.

Tony Blair can be seen as transforming Labour from a socialist party to a social democratic party by amending Clause 4 and committing to a dynamic economy rather than common ownership. This was not welcomed by left-wing members of the Labour Party.

Importantly, New Labour stopped arguing that we should all be equal, arguing instead that we should all have equal opportunities. This was important at the time because a concern for equality was often criticised as being socialist, especially where this involved state intervention or the provision of state services.

The British media in particular are always highly critical of policies which may reflect socialist ideas. New Labour avoided this criticism to an extent by arguing for equal opportunities.

Since 2010 Labour has moved further left under Jeremy Corbyn and then back to the centre under Keir Starmer, but it is still fair to say that it is more a social democratic party than a socialist party.

The concern for equal opportunities can be seen in the massive investment in children's services, and in education, alongside the promotion of the idea of social inclusion. So, when we consider the significant focus on the early years or increases in support for families under New Labour, it can be seen that this was to support their aims to make society more equal through increasing equality of opportunities. What was clearly evident during the period of New Labour was that there was a renewed concern with investing in public services, which included increased levels of support for services aimed at children and families (O'Hara, 2018).

Powell (1999, 2000) refers to the need for investment in people on a broad scale as being promoted by Giddens' ideas about the Third Way. It is also the case, however, that New Labour was influenced by the Commission for Social Justice which had been set up under the previous Labour leader, John Smith. John Smith was the leader of the Labour Party from July 1992 to May 1994 and Tony Blair became leader after Smith's death. Powell illustrates how Labour changed in its concerns by making a distinction between three positions:

1. the traditional Labour approach of focusing upon the redistribution of wealth but ignoring its production;
2. the Thatcherite approach to deregulation and the removal of public services; and
3. an approach based upon investing in human capital which sees social justice and economic efficiency as being two sides of the same coin.

Human capital is focused on the idea of individuals developing skills and abilities so as to be able to benefit within the world of work. It reflects the idea of meritocracy, which in turn presents the idea that hard work or high qualifications leads to reward and suggests that if we invest in ourselves to develop skills and qualifications then we will benefit from this. Human capital can be seen to underpin New Labour's concerns about education (Powell, 1999) but it also reflects the neoliberal-influenced idea of employability. This is the idea that it is your responsibility to make yourself employable.

In this third approach social justice is seen as being best achieved through ensuring that each individual has an equal opportunity to participate in an efficient economy. To reiterate the point though the key issue here is that New Labour rejects a concern with equality of outcome in favour of equality of opportunity (Powell, 1999).

What all this means is of course open to debate. The Third Way is presented as a more pragmatic approach to government. Powell (1999) notes that Blair refers to the Third Way as building a welfare state for the 21st century. No longer is welfare to be the safety net for the unfortunate; welfare is to be the springboard for all.

As such, the Third Way sets out to be more active at all stages of an individual's life. This changes the welfare state from being a passive system which acts as a safety net and restructures it as an active system whereby the state constantly supports people. New Labour argued that welfare should act proactively to prevent the individual having to call upon it. Central to this is the position of both education and work. This is because work is said to enable independence and it is education that enables us to work (Stepney et al, 1999).

New Labour worked to redefine the discourse of welfare and society in a manner that was similar to what the Conservative Party did in the 1980s. The concept of equality was replaced by that of social inclusion, resulting in a concern to tackle social exclusion rather than social inequality. The focus of New Labour then was not that we should all be equal but that we should all be included. Importantly, though, this was based on the idea that we can only be included if we participate within society and this is generally seen as meaning participation within the economy (Fairclough, 2000; Best, 2002). In other words, we must work if we are to be included.

By this stage you should have a feel for how social democracy under New Labour differed from the neoliberal-influenced Conservative governments that had been in power from 1979 to 1997. At this stage, however, it is also useful to consider two other concepts with respect to the ideas that underpinned New Labour: communitarianism and the idea of capital, which deserve a section to themselves.

## 5.6 Communitarianism

The roots of New Labour's Third Way may be found in ideas about communitarianism and the work of the British social theorist Anthony Giddens. A good introduction to politics is Best (2002). Best demonstrates that communitarianism is a reaction against particular types of lifestyle choice. Lifestyle is a term that tends to suggest that individuals have a choice how to behave or live their lives. In particular, though, it foregrounds the idea that individuals have too many rights and too few responsibilities. In many ways, though, it is the rise of individualism and the experiences of individuals and communities which are said to experience social exclusion that is seen as the starting point for the communitarian approach (Barlow and Duncan, 2000).

It is worth stating, however, that communitarianism is not critical of individualism per se; communitarianism is critical of what individualism can lead to if an inflated sense of individualism means that we do not stop to think about what our actions mean for others. As such, communitarianism argues that individual rights should not equate to the freedom to do just anything (Deacon, 2002). Communitarianism then is concerned with shifting public attitudes towards moral and ethical considerations and, importantly, with reintroducing the notion of responsibilities as accompanying rights. As Giddens has argued, there should be 'no rights without responsibilities!' (Powell, 2000: 47).

---

### Pause for reflection

Your neighbour has just bought a new HiFi and they aim to stream their playlist of thrash metal tracks at full volume. It will be loud.

They live in the apartment above you. Should their right to satisfy their desires mean that they should have the right to do this, or do they have a responsibility to their neighbours to play music at a level which does not impact upon their lives?

This may be a simple example, but it summarises the tension between rights and responsibilities which plays out within the communities that we live in because in this case your neighbour's right could make your life quite miserable.

Communitarians say that neoliberalism is wrong to promote individual rights while overlooking our responsibilities to others.

Within a neoliberal society, remembering that for neoliberals there is no such thing as society (Thatcher, 1987; Douglas, 1990; O'Hara, 2020), individuals may come to see themselves in isolation from others, with their focus being upon themselves as consumers. But consumers are only ever granted rights, never responsibilities. Consequently, social institutions such as the family have declined in importance in terms of providing mutual aid and support. Think about families who do not share mealtimes, or where technology results in fragmentation as each family member retreats to their own room or space, engrossed in their own phone, tablet, laptop or television. With this in mind read Smith (1997). Smith is easily accessed online. She shows how communitarianism presents a particular view of the role of parents with respect to children in terms of morals and family responsibilities, commenting for example on how time spent by parents with children in the US has declined.

### Pause for reflection

Think about how parents may resort to putting the television on or providing an electronic tablet with games to entertain children rather than engaging with them and playing with them.

Spend some time in a public place and look around. How often do you see children being ignored by parents as they interact with mobile phones rather than with their offspring?

How many adults and children are preoccupied with mobile devices and not socialising with others?

In terms of promoting communitarianism, Etzioni is probably the key social theorist and although communitarianism is presented as a new development some have suggested that it harks back to functionalism (functionalism is an old sociological theory which argues that if something, such as the family, exists then it must have a social function), and that there is a strong emphasis upon moral issues (Prideaux, 2005). This is something which Etzioni (2005) rejects as an incomplete reading. Etzioni recognises the problems of the functionalist model of society as reinforcing the heterosexual nuclear family with a clear division of labour and promotes instead a form of society which is more inclusive of diversity. There is a link here to New Labour in terms of how inclusion became a key theme of the New Labour project.

New Labour did much to argue that rights have to be accompanied with responsibilities and recognised that the social and economic changes brought about under the Thatcher governments meant that many individuals and groups lost out, becoming what are now often referred to as 'the left behind'. For New Labour we all belong to society, and we should all have a stake in it, hence the emergence of the phrase the stakeholder society during New Labour's time in power.

You should be able to find a number of useful accounts of communitarianism. Sage (2012) is very good. This is quite focused and applies communitarianism to ideas about the family as well as illustrating how Cameron's Conservative-led Coalition government tried to distance itself from the conservatism of Margaret Thatcher. A longer introduction to communitarianism which is aimed at students is Deacon (2002). This is a good book in that it covers other political ideologies too in relation to welfare and fits well with the theme of this book.

In summarising communitarianism it is useful to think about how it brings communities to the fore rather than individuals as is the case with neoliberalism. In doing so communitarianism promotes responsibilities rather than privileging rights, but when we think about responsibilities we are drawn to recognise that responsibilities are towards others. What we do as individuals has consequences for others. At first reading it may seem that communitarianism is adopting a critical stance, that it is working from the basis that what we do as individuals has the potential for negative consequences for others. Think, though, about how what we do as individuals can have positive consequences. This leads into Section 5.7 in terms of how communities can develop social capital and how this can be used to good effect to the benefit of all.

## 5.7 Social and cultural capital

To understand the idea of social or cultural capital it is first necessary to understand what we mean by capital. The economic view of capital is probably the best place to start. In economics, capital refers to wealth, including money or other financial assets. Think of it in terms of an investment which is expected to result in benefits (Lin, 2001). So, as a simple example, you invest a sum of money with the intention that you will get back more than you put in. The key point, though, in terms of what capital is, lies in the way that you have used that money to make more money. As such we can say that capital has a use value. Capital can be used in more ordinary ways to obtain something. So, if capital is money, then we can use money to obtain the things that we want by buying them. Keep the idea of capital having a use value in your mind.

### 5.7.1 Social capital

Social capital refers to the use value of the relationships and obligations that come about as we enter into social activities with others. In other words, as we enter into or form social networks, which may include families but can also include friends and associates made through social activities such as community groups, sports clubs and voluntary associations, we create a form of capital that we can draw on in times of need (Lin, 2001; Putnam, 2001; Putnam and Goss, 2002; Edwards, 2003; Fine, 2010; Field, 2017).

It is Robert Putnam who is generally credited with developing the concept of social capital, though he did not coin the term. Putnam credits the first use of the term to L. Judson Hanifan in 1916 (Putnam and Goss, 2002), though James (2004) demonstrates that the term was being used by economists before this. Since the early use of the term the idea of social capital has remained consistent in suggesting that disadvantaged and excluded groups and communities can be enabled to find a way to alleviate or even to overcome the problems that they face through developing social capital.

One example of this is the idea of voluntarism. This refers to voluntary work, and the role of such activity in the community. Although cynics may say that encouraging voluntary work is a way to get things done without payment, there are also benefits to be gained from a healthy voluntary sector. For Putnam, the real benefit of voluntarism is the way in which it fosters trust within social networks and the ways in which this type of social activity feeds into political activity. We might see that the idea of individuals having a stake in their communities and being active in working to make communities better is embedded in this idea.

It is worth pointing out, however, that although social capital has been presented as a useful way to think about communities and to counter the negative consequences of individualism, there are also criticisms. One important criticism of social capital is that it is often presented as being a way of tackling poverty, yet it ignores the material conditions and structures which create poverty. From the perspective of social capital there is a tendency to shift the blame for poverty away from individuals and onto the community, seeing the community as being deficient in some way such as in not demonstrating trust and reciprocity. Within this approach lies the potential for victim-blaming at the level of the community because we may look at poor communities and suggest that they do not do enough to improve their position. This is similar to arguing that poor people lack aspiration and that this explains why they are poor.

The idea of social capital is not really a political ideology but it is a concept that is often drawn on and it fits well with communitarianism. You are likely to come across it when studying families so it is definitely worth considering. Blair drew upon the idea of social capital to justify his approach to developing social policies and services. There is an implicit concern within the concept of social capital, however, that in some communities social relationships have declined, and this is where we can see an overlap with communitarian ideas. Communitarianism was concerned with the problems that individualisation creates. Social capital also addresses these types of issues.

As a concept, social capital has always been seen as a response to the fact that in some communities, some societies even, social activities and relationships have declined and communities have become fragmented. It is said that people have withdrawn from social groups and activities and that they have become poorer as a consequence. You can see this illustrated in the title of Putnam's book *Bowling Alone* (2001). The title refers to the decline of ten-pin bowling leagues in America and the emergence of people bowling alone rather than with others as part of a social activity.

Many discussions of social capital refer the reader to the work of Pierre Bourdieu, arguing that the concept can be seen as having its roots here (Johnston and Percy-Smith, 2003). On reading Bourdieu you will find that he refers to two very similar concepts, in name at least: social capital and cultural capital. Be aware also that Bourdieu's work on cultural capital was formulated as a critique of human capital theory.

### 5.7.2 Cultural capital

Goldthorpe (2016b) demonstrates why cultural capital is important by illustrating why it is that education is not as important in terms of upward social mobility as we might expect it to be. Be careful when reading this, because this is not to say that education has no value with respect to education; it is more that education on its own is not sufficient for explaining social mobility. This can be seen in two ways: firstly, we can see how intelligent and well-qualified young people from lower social groups are often not as successful in terms of upward social mobility as we would expect them to be if education was the sole determining factor; secondly, focusing on education does not explain why less intelligent or less educated young people from higher social classes do not experience downward social mobility to the extent that we might expect if social class position really reflected ability and merit.

To explain why this is we need to consider the role of the family. For both Bourdieu and Goldthorpe it is the actions of parents in higher social classes which give advantages to children with respect to upward social mobility and which also act as a safety net should their children not do well in education. This safety net works in a way which means that less intelligent children from higher social groups are less likely to experience downward mobility. What the work of Bourdieu adds to this argument is the idea that an individual is more likely to achieve a higher social status or position if, alongside human capital, he or she also possesses cultural capital. By this Bourdieu means the possession of cultural knowledge and networks which help in securing work and/or positions of a certain type. So, being involved in particular organisations or even knowing certain rules of etiquette may facilitate social progress. Sometimes it may be what we generally refer to as networks in that, if families have contacts, then it may be easier for children to find work in those areas.

## Pause for reflection

Consider the idea that ability is genetic, that it can be inherited.

The rich have often considered that their privilege is the result of having more ability and that this ability has been passed down through generations.

One way of demonstrating that cultural capital is more important than genetics is to compare top performers in two areas, football and entertainment such as showbusiness or the film industry.

If ability was really inherited, then we would expect to see that the top footballers would consistently be drawn from particular families. Yet this doesn't happen to any great extent. Now think about working in showbusiness, especially in the film industry. Look at top actors or directors and you will see that it is very common for so-called top actors to have family either working in the film industry or in the music industry. The important question is why.

Cultural capital provides an explanation. In football, to be a top-class player you have to consistently perform at a high level. You must really have ability. The children of footballers may be expected to be better, and they may have a better chance of getting trials with clubs because of their parents' contacts, or even because of what is expected of them, but this is an industry which scours the country looking for ability in very young children. If your child plays football for a junior team and they show some abilities, do not be surprised if they are invited for trials with a local club, yet very few make it as professional footballers and having parents who were professional footballers is of little help if your performance is not good enough. But if your child is into drama, how will they get their first break, no matter how good they are? Also, just how do we measure performance in drama? When we consider just how many individuals within the film industry come from families who are connected to that industry, we start to see how it is that cultural capital gives some children an advantage.

## Pause for reflection

In relation to children's success, you will probably come across arguments which suggest that children from lower social classes will be more successful in terms of achieving upward social mobility if they are more aspirational: in other words, if they want more.

What Goldthorpe and Bourdieu demonstrate is that aspiration is not enough. Other social and cultural factors are important.

In a study looking at recruitment practices by 'top' firms, which investigated the ability of young people from lower social classes to secure positions in such firms, Ashley et al (2015) emphasise the importance of what recruiters refer to as 'polish'. Weaver (2015) sums up this report in terms of the way that many firms adopt what he calls 'poshness tests'.

A more critical approach towards social mobility is to consider how aiming to provide for social mobility reinforces the idea that society is naturally unequal. Calder (2016) and Reay (2017) both argue that social mobility is not a solution to inequality and that it actually acts to reinforce the idea that society is naturally or inevitably unequal. If society was more equal we would be much less concerned with social mobility.

So, if you are faced with assignments which cover issues to do with social mobility or life-chances, you could find the concept of capital very useful. In summarising the different perspectives of capital, if we start with human capital theory, it is concerned with how, as individuals, we can be said to invest in ourselves for benefit. Social and cultural capital is less focused on ourselves as individuals and more focused on how we exist within social relationships and settings. If we want to make a distinction between cultural capital and social capital, we have to see that cultural capital is concerned with an individual's position within a social network and the benefits which follow for that individual from belonging to that network or community. Social capital on the other hand is much more concerned with the network itself where networks can be seen as communities, and the way in which a strong network benefits all.

## 5.8 What you can do with this chapter to make your assignments stronger

This chapter has focused on introducing some key political ideas and concepts that are very likely to have some use when it comes to understanding issues relating to the context of the lives of children and families as well as when it comes to writing assignments. In our experience it is the political issues which relate to families that many students find more difficult and less interesting. That is maybe not surprising. Students come to study children and families because of an interest in children and families, not because of an interest in politics. It is not uncommon for students to say that they are not interested in politics. OK, that's fair enough, but if you are interested in children and families, we are confident that we have already demonstrated why you cannot ignore politics.

Maybe the way to get around this is to think that we are concerned with ideas rather than with politics. We use the term ideology when we are talking about a set of connected ideas which in some way support each other. But if a group of people achieve the ability to impose their shared ideas (ideology) onto others, then that is really what we mean by politics. Politics is always about power.

That said, we do accept that for many students these political issues may not be the most exciting aspect of your studies, but if you look at them as tools that you can use to make your understanding of children and families better then that can help. The fact is, you just cannot avoid encountering politics because of the way that it shapes the context within which we live our lives. Remember Bronfenbrenner?

---

**Study tip**

Speaking as people who mark student assignments, writing about political ideologies can help you move from an assignment which describes policy issues relating to children and families to an assignment which provides an analysis of the context of the lives and experiences of children and families.

Writing about political ideologies is one way that you can move from what to why. By this we mean moving from describing what you see to explaining why something is.

---

Here is an example to illustrate this. Think about the Sure Start policy that was introduced by Blair's Labour government and which led to the setting up of Children's Centres across the UK to provide support for families. These have now either gone or the services that they offer have been significantly reduced. Based on research into Sure Start, it is generally recognised as having had a positive effect on children's lives and in terms of supporting the family (Barnes et al, 2007; Frost and Parton, 2009; NESS, 2012; Miller and Hevey, 2012; Longfield, 2020). The report by Longfield (2020) is clear in stating that the Sure Start system benefited children and families.

But if you were to write about the setting up of the Sure Start system across the UK you would be able to provide a stronger account if you were able to explain how communitarian ideas were embedded within the Labour Party at that time. You could also go further and use the material in this chapter to suggest that the Every Child Matters agenda can be seen as a direct response to neoliberalism. This is because Every Child Matters promotes the idea of inclusion and of providing for everyone whereas neoliberalism promotes an individualistic approach.

That could be your starting point, but you could also say more about changes to social policy and bring this in later. If so, you would need to say what happened to Children's Centres after Labour left power in 2010. After 2010 the Conservative-led governments which were in power changed how local authorities were funded and this saw Children's Centres across the country closing down. This change, the setting up then closing down of Children's Centres, did not just happen. Things do not just happen. Social policies do not just change. Each was the consequence of ideological beliefs which represent core values and priorities for different governments. You could usefully focus on differences in values to explain why services change.

So, we have governments led by different political parties. These parties have different ideas and values about what governments should do and we can say that these ideas and values can be understood as political ideologies. In the example of Sure Start, the ideas and values of the Labour governments of 1997–2010 led to policies which saw the setting up of extensive services for children and families. After 2010 the ideas and values of the Conservative-led governments saw changes to these policies or to these policies being scrapped. This resulted in a reduction in the services being provided for children and families.

---

**Study tip**

A key point here is not to think that one ideology is right and one is wrong. Instead, recognise that the services and support that are provided reflect the policies in place at any given time and that these policies can be seen as having been shaped by different ideologies.

So, it is perfectly reasonable for one person reading this to consider the setting up of Children's Centres as a good thing on the grounds that children and families benefit from having this support, with another reader thinking that it was reasonable to scrap Children's Centres because families should be self-reliant and should not be led to rely on state services.

---

In one sense, though, you also have to ignore what governments say because all governments will say that what they are doing is in the best interests of society. Instead, you have to look at what governments do and evaluate this in line with the evidence that you have. That is what being a student is all about: developing the skills to make sense of what you see and to determine what evidence is good evidence and then to assess and evaluate what the evidence tells us.

If you refer back to Chapter 2 you will recall that it was stated that the Conservative-led Coalition government claimed that the Troubled Families Programme would provide for social justice without ever establishing what it meant by social justice. Crossley (2018b) notes that the government has claimed that it was providing social justice as a consequence of family support workers helping families to access food banks. However, you could adopt a critical approach and question why some families are forced to turn to food banks in the fifth richest country in the world.

When we consider those families that are often referred to as failing families we can see that they tend to be poor families. We can see the effects of neoliberal policies in respect of inequality as since 1979 inequality in the UK has been increasing; more people are becoming poor. Compared to other European countries the UK is very unequal. O'Brien and Kyprianou (2017) report on research into families experiencing poverty in 2015 in Liverpool. They illustrate how the Trussell Trust was providing almost 26,000 food parcels in 2008–2009. Ten years later that had risen to 1.6 million (Trussell, 2019). This is in one of the richest countries in the world so we can say that it is not that the country is not rich enough to overcome this, the problem is how wealth is distributed, in that some people have very little and some people have a lot. It is your ideological position which will determine if you consider this to be a problem or whether you see it as acceptable.

So, when it comes to using this chapter, you need to see it as providing you with ways of making sense of a wide range of social policies in that you can look at any given social policy and think about how it reflects the basic approaches of the ideologies outlined above. The communitarian-influenced Labour Party has not been in government for a long time. Since 2010 the Conservative-led Coalition government and the Conservative governments that followed have often adopted neoliberal policies under the guise of austerity. Austerity was a term that was used to explain the approach to cutting services and public expenditure.

At the same time, although it would be reasonable to say that neoliberal ideas contributed significantly to making the UK less able to deal with the pandemic as a consequence of underfunding the NHS in the ten years before the 2020 pandemic and because of the social inequalities within the UK, it is also fair to say that the Conservative government's response was to adopt policies that would be more generally associated with Labour governments. In one sense the COVID-19 pandemic demonstrated the real limitations of neoliberalism.

So, as always, be careful: do not think that political ideologies always fit neatly with political parties. They don't. This is why we can say that Blair's Labour governments adopted some neoliberal policies and how it is that in 2020 Johnson's Conservative government adopted policies which went much further than previous Labour policies in terms of the state supporting individuals and businesses. It is also hard to say what politics will look like in the future. We can safely say, however, that now that the UK is outside of the European Union it will be weaker and poorer and that COVID-19 will have made this worse (Portes, 2021; OBR, 2022), but how that will translate into policies for children and families is yet to be seen.

In some ways then this is a chapter that may fit in with many if not most of your assignments. To help you with that here are some key concepts that you may find useful:

- Ideologies can be understood as a set of ideas which link together in ways which not only tell us about the nature of the world that we live in but that also tell us how to make changes for the better.
- Ideologies rest on values.
- Ideologies are said to be hegemonic when they are taken for granted as representing social life.
- Neoliberalism promotes the idea that society works best when individuals support themselves within a free market rather than when the state provides services for them.
- Free markets inevitably lead to social inequalities, but this is not a problem from a neoliberal perspective as inequalities motivate us to work hard.
- In terms of family life neoconservatism is focused on moral behaviour and often emphasises issues relating to sexuality.
- Neoconservatism tends to be critical of social change and diversity and promotes the heterosexual nuclear family as 'the' family.
- For neoconservatives we are not all the same; there are 'natural' differences.

- New Labour represented a social democratic form of government but it did adopt some neoliberal ideas.
- New Labour was very concerned with equality in opportunities and less concerned with inequality of outcomes. This underpinned many policies aimed at children and families.
- Communitarianism is an approach which promotes social inclusion alongside the idea that rights must always be accompanied by responsibilities.
- Communitarianism is focused on communities rather than individuals.
- Social capital reflects the idea that we can benefit from relationships and social networks.

## Further thoughts

It is important to be aware of political issues. For example, the UK is a very rich country but a very unequal country. You may not notice this if you and your family are managing and you feel you have a good life. However, the number of children experiencing poverty is increasing. To help with your studies, it is good to see both (or all) sides of an issue. Can you use ideologies to provide arguments both for and against the state doing something about poverty?

We haven't really addressed green politics in this chapter. You could find it useful to read about green politics and then consider why right-wing commentators tend to deny green issues.

## Further reading

Dorey (2015) along with Prendergast et al (2017) explains neoliberalism and neoconservatism very well. Heywood (2021) provides a good introduction to a range of political ideologies.

# 6

# Welfare, policy and the family

This chapter will help you to understand:

- how ideologies shape the policies that we have;
- the ways in which governments deal with need and who should get help or support;
- some of the ways that we may be critical of welfare services.

## 6.1 How is ideology put into practice?

We have previously outlined what the state is on the grounds that the state regulates the lives of children and families. This links back to Bronfenbrenner's (1979) ideas, especially with respect to the exo-system. Having defined the state, we then considered how the state may do, or achieve, things by considering power, following this up with a discussion of rights. This is because the rights that we enjoy can be understood as existing within a framework which the state shapes. That led to a consideration of why the state does what it does, and it meant making a distinction between the state and the government. It also entailed showing how governments are strongly influenced by political ideologies.

That brings us to this point and a consideration of how the state puts ideologies into practice. Jones (2016) is useful to illustrate how changes which the family has no control over can exert a significant pressure upon the shape of the family. In particular, Jones argues that many families struggled as a consequence of the deindustrialisation of the UK which started to happen during the 1980s, and that this can be seen in family, or even community, behaviours. What he then points out is that when it comes to unwanted social behaviours or social patterns it is the family that is seen to be at fault, not the context within which the family lives. In the election campaign of 2010 David Cameron often referred to Broken Britain and put forward ideas that he argued would mend what was broken. This is an example of rhetoric; rhetoric is the name that we give to language that is persuasive, language that shapes how you think about something.

If we stop to think about it, though, he explained the idea of Britain being broken in a very strange way (this does not imply any agreement on our part that Britain is broken!), but it is an explanation which reflects the neoliberal ideology that Cameron and the Conservative Party supported. Cameron first stated that

107

Britain is broken because the state had become too big, because it did too much and because, in particular, it did too much for families and individuals. By doing too much the state undermined individual responsibility. His argument was that if we are to mend Britain then the state must shrink, it must do less and the individuals who live in Broken Britain must take responsibility for their lives and their communities. What you should be able to recognise by now is that Cameron was drawing upon and reinforcing a neoliberal discourse relating to the nature and role of the state and how the state interacts with families. He was also providing a clear alternative to the extensive family services that had been established under Blair's New Labour.

What this does is to provide a set of ideas which made the shrinking of the state, which really means the reduction in state services, possible. This was then achieved through a series of developments under the umbrella term of austerity. In thinking about this you should consider how it fits with the general political ideology of neoliberalism. Neoliberalism always promotes a small state as beneficial. As such, we can see how Cameron used the rhetoric of Broken Britain to persuade voters that there was something wrong and that the way to put things right was to reduce the services that the state provided. This then shapes the context in which we live, in how services and support for families were reduced. Politics has real consequences.

**Study tip**

Policies and legislation make ideologies real; this is how ideologies get put into practice.

What this means for you as a student is that if you have a basic understanding of different political ideologies then you should be in a much better position to identify why political parties differ and why they introduce the policies that they do.

One thing that stands out in reading about neoliberalism and neoconservatism is that both were introduced into UK politics by the Conservative Party. As such, and given that it was argued that they cannot be reconciled, they make it appear as though the Conservative Party is a little contradictory. It is. The Labour Party is also. That is perfectly acceptable, but it is one of those things which always seems to trip students up. When it comes to students, they want things to be clear and they want things to be obvious. The problem is that things are rarely clear and/or obvious, especially when it comes to politics.

**Note**

To get your head around the inconsistencies that we see in politics think about a process with a number of stages and that at every stage after stage 1 something can go wrong, or something can introduce an element of change. Think of it as a game of *Chinese whispers*. We might find it useful to look at politics like this:

1. We have a political ideology. It doesn't matter which one but think of the ideology as being pure or perfect.
2. Politicians support the ideology and want to change things, but the pressures that they face as politicians mean that they have to make some concessions. They can't do everything that they would like to do. Imagine a politician saying, 'Vote for me, I will scrap the NHS.' They would be very unlikely to get elected. So now the ideology is getting a bit changed, a bit distorted, as it begins to influence the policies that are proposed.
3. Members of parliament propose policies but the House of Commons and the House of Lords are able to make some changes and the civil servants who draw up the policy may also have some input in terms of their advice. The policy might now be moving a bit further away from the purity of the ideology that influenced it.
4. The policy is introduced but it has to be interpreted, and staff whose job it is to work on the policy have to be trained. Trainers and training guides start to make the policy real but there is more scope for change from what was intended as people interpret what it means.
5. The policy is implemented and it is put into action but it gets even more distorted as the staff who put it into practice make their own interpretations and develop their own practice to some extent.

---

Can you see how the perfect, or pure, ideology gets changed and distorted when it starts to be turned into real social policies which real people put into practice? For example, the Early Years Foundation Stage provides a framework to work to, but it may be interpreted differently in each setting. As such, social policies might be seen as reflecting an ideological approach but might no longer be perfectly true to the ideology. That is why it is often a good idea to say a policy reflects ideology, that a policy is not ideology in itself.

So, this chapter will focus on issues concerning social policy and the idea of welfare. It will not dissect policies in detail, but it will provide an overview of academic debates about social policy, including a consideration of how different political ideologies may lead to particular policy approaches. Policy is the means by which the state acts on the family. Policies create the context within which families live. For example, they structure the support or otherwise that families get. This chapter also provides further insight into what shapes policies and will provide you with a stronger base for analysing and explaining policies. Once again, you need to see this chapter as giving you the tools to do more than just describe the things that you write about and to recognise that policies are socially constructed within a context of political ideology.

## 6.2 How does ideology underpin welfare?

It is useful to start by thinking that policies which seek to provide social welfare are best understood as a response to the idea that there is a social problem which needs attention. We have already introduced the idea that political ideologies shape the ways in which we understand the world so, to go back to the discussions relating to power and discourse, we can see how ideology and discourse combine to define what any problem is as well as constructing the possibilities in terms of addressing it. As such, the reality of any problem and the validity of any response always have to be understood as being rooted within ideology and discourse. Think about the example of Broken Britain used above. Britain is not a physical thing that can be broken, so to refer to Broken Britain is discursive in that it is only real in a linguistic sense.

The first thing is to explain social welfare and to consider why this is relevant to a book about children and the family. If we start by thinking about what the family does alongside ideas about reproduction and socialisation, we are also likely to come across the idea that the family provides both care and welfare for its members.

### Pause for reflection

Think about the range of services that a family might either want or provide.

Now consider who provides these or how they may be accessed.

Try to think about how these services would have been provided, or by whom, 100 or even 200 years ago.

How have things changed?

For example, individual family members often provide healthcare and education to others, especially in terms of older family members caring or providing for younger family members. As society has become more complex over time and as the level of things such as education and healthcare has become specialised so we can see how welfare provisions have developed to meet these needs outside of the family.

### Note

In the UK we often hear references being made to the welfare state.

What has come to be known as the welfare state was set up by the Labour government in the late 1940s (Lowe, 2005).

The term welfare state is maybe best understood as an approach to welfare wherein the state takes the lead in providing a comprehensive range of services.

However, it would be wrong to suggest that welfare only started in the 1940s. The Liberal reforms introduced in the early 20th century were the beginnings of welfare services as we know them now, but there were types of welfare available before this, as will be considered in Section 6.5 (Jones, 1991; Fraser, 2009; Beresford and Alibhai-Brown, 2016).

The welfare state was based upon an influential report carried out during the Second World War and published in 1942 – the Beveridge report (Beveridge, 1942). That is why you might see some commentators referring to the Beveridgean welfare state. The Beveridge report is easily accessed on the internet. The writers of the report (William Beveridge put his name to it but it was written by a team) justified the need for their proposals by looking back to the problems of the 1930s. The 1930s was a time of mass unemployment and of economic hardship for many. The Beveridge report set out a vision of how the state could intervene to improve people's lives by taking the lead in providing services.

This brings us back to the issue of ideas and values because the Beveridge report, the welfare state that was based upon it and the ways in which policies provide support for individuals and families can be seen to reflect very particular ideas about families. We can see this by considering how gender was positioned within the report. As a student you will often be asked to produce assignments which are critical, and we have already stated that being critical is about identifying weaknesses or problems. By focusing on gender we can offer a critical reading of the welfare state.

## 6.3 How have ideas about the family shaped welfare services?

The welfare state that was established in the late 1940s can be seen to rest upon particular assumptions regarding the roles of men and women in society, especially in the context of families. For the writers of the Beveridge report the family took a specific shape. Considering Chapter 2, we might say that what the report terms the family is inaccurate with respect to contemporary families. For the writers of the report, though, the family was unambiguous and meaningful. In particular, it was assumed that:

• all men would be fully employed;
• women would be mainly homemakers and carers; and
• marriages would be stable.

The family was also seen as being important in terms of the nation in a way that had important consequences for women. Consider this statement from the Beveridge report (1942: 53): 'In the next thirty years housewives, as mothers, have vital work to do in ensuring the adequate continuance of the British race and of British ideals in the world.' This statement positions women in terms of reproduction. Reproduction, in terms of having children, is seen as being important within the report, but this quote also reflects a particular view of Britain as a nation and of its place in the world.

Similar ideas that are current now are reported on by Walker (2020). He illustrates how the Russian state is encouraging couples to have larger families to secure Russia's position in the world and how right-wing governments in Hungary and Poland are encouraging larger families as a way of resisting immigration. Women are positioned as having a major part to play in these efforts. It is also worth considering some more general consequences for women in respect of the Beveridge report.

The way in which the Beveridge report positions women in terms of motherhood and with their place being firmly within the home serving their husband's and children's needs is reinforced by the following quote referring to women doing work that is said to be 'vital though unpaid, without which their husbands could not do their paid work and without which the nation could not continue' (1942: 49). It seems clear from this quote that the position being taken is that a woman's place was in the home. This is an example of how the state regulates family life and how particular views and values come to be formalised in policies, which then have the effect of shaping what families are, what they do and how we understand them. Women are not prevented from working outside the home, and many working-class women always did, but there was an expectation in the Beveridge report that women's first priority would always be the home.

What can also be seen within the Beveridge report is that it rests upon a view of women as being dependent on men after marriage. Consequently, the original social security provisions often provided lower benefits for women than for men. The term 'social security' has fallen out of use in recent years. It referred to a range of benefits that the state would pay out to individuals and families, such as unemployment benefits, so as to provide a degree of security. It has been replaced in recent years by the more negative term 'welfare'. Consider how lower benefits for women were justified in the following quote from the Beveridge report: 'In sickness or unemployment the housewife does not need compensating benefits on the same scale as the solitary woman because, among other things, her home is provided for her either by her husband's earnings or benefit if his earning is interrupted' (1942: 50). This follows a statement in the report which makes the point that women have a legal right to be supported by their husbands.

What stands out in these quotes from the Beveridge report is that it offers a very good example of how values and ideas underpin social policy. Remember, social policy is important, but it doesn't just happen; it always reflects ideas and values about society. As a student you will always be in a stronger position if you have an understanding of this.

One early feminist writer on social policy and the welfare state, Elizabeth Wilson (1977), argued that social policy can be understood as the way in which the state organises domestic life. Domestic life means family life. Wilson, like many feminist writers, stresses the patriarchal nature of the post-war welfare state. By this she means that the welfare state was set up in a way which reinforced a social structure within which men have more power than women. One key aspect of this is that women were seen primarily in terms of their role within the home rather than the workplace. What we should all be aware of, though, is that since the 1940s the position of women, and of families, has changed significantly.

If you are asked to adopt a critical approach to social policy and the family or provide a general critical approach towards the welfare state, it is very useful to consider feminist critiques of welfare. There are also right-wing critiques of welfare and left-wing critiques of welfare (George and Wilding, 1994; Taylor, 2007; Fives, 2008), but we are focusing on feminist critiques because they have greater relevance for a consideration of the relationship between children, families and the state.

---

**Study tip**

You may need to do a bit of reading around feminist theory but this will only make you a stronger student so it will be time well spent. Try the following: Freedman (2001), Scholz (2010), Hannam (2012) and Finlayson (2016).

In a nutshell, feminist theories (there are a number of different forms within feminist theory) focus on the way in which, within society, men in general have more power than women. This is generally referred to as patriarchy.

Patriarchy might seem difficult to explain at times so think about what this means in everyday life and think about how sexism and/or misogyny (the hating of women) acts to disadvantage women. For example, in spite of the England women's football team being European Champions in 2022, many schools still prevent girls from playing football.

So, to consider the family and social policy from a feminist perspective means critically assessing how women are disadvantaged as a consequence of how policy is set up and operates.

---

Feminist critiques of welfare issues often provide a critical focus upon the area of social reproduction and then illustrate how this underpins much social policy. These are not only in relation to the processes of bearing children but also the emotional and physical processes involved in caring for others (Williams, 1989). During the responses to the COVID-19 pandemic in the early 2020s significant numbers of parents had to work from home, but women were much more likely to take on responsibility for home schooling and other childcare duties than were men (Adams, 2020). Rather than simply accepting that women inevitably provide nurturing and unpaid caring for others, though, feminists ask: why is it women that do this? Why is it that women are expected to be responsible for caring? Women may choose to have children, but must they rear them as well? What about men providing care? What about the rights of women not to care?

Feminist writers have often provided a critique of the ideology of the family for the ways in which it privileges the institution of the family and how this reinforces women's dependency on men and their confinement to the home. Although neoconservative politicians and commentators have often sought to reinforce traditional family structures, this is far from the modern-day reality of the family. By the 21st century it is obvious that many women work, divorce rates are high and many children are born to unmarried parents.

Importantly, it can be seen that the growth of the welfare state has actually contributed to some of these changes. We previously commented upon how families have changed to such an extent that it is problematic to refer to the family. This is because of the diverse forms and structures that we can now recognise as being types of family.

## 6.4 Deserving, undeserving and the problem of need

Thinking about how the writers of the Beveridge report viewed families, and women, provides us with an insight into a key aspect of the thought and deliberation which goes into setting up the provision of any service – namely, is there a need? However, once a need has been defined, the question of who is deserving of support arises. Jupp (2017) provides examples of how the Coalition and Conservative governments since 2010 have often talked about strivers and skivers in a way which casts some families as deserving and others as undeserving. Crossley (2017: 6) considers the thoughts of George Osborne, the chancellor of the exchequer in 2012, in a way which moves a discussion of desert (a term referring to who deserves assistance and why) and of need into a consideration of the welfare state as being of questionable fairness: 'Where is the fairness, we ask for the shift worker leaving home in the dark hours of the early morning who looks up at the closed blinds of their next door neighbour sleeping off a life on benefits?'

There is little doubt here that Osborne is proposing that receiving benefits is something that has been chosen and that it is something to be critical of. This fits in with the strivers versus skivers discourse that has become a shorthand way of characterising those on benefits as in some way morally lacking (Coote and Lyall, 2013; O'Hara and Thomas, 2014; Valentine and Harris, 2014; Jupp, 2017). Shildrick (2018) argues that the poor in society are often depicted in ways which reflect a sort of poverty propaganda. Poverty propaganda obscures the factors that lead to poverty and makes it easier to accept that some are poor because of individual weaknesses or failings.

Consider, though, that a focus on being deserving or undeserving draws attention away from a concern with need (Shildrick, 2018). Desert and need are very different concerns, but each has consequences for the policies that we put in place and the support that individuals and families receive. As such, this section addresses the issue of need followed by a section that considers desert, showing that it is an idea that has a long history in British social policy.

If we start by asking the question what are our individual needs, then we could see how as individuals we all claim that we need different things. This emphasises that when we are discussing welfare policies, we are not concerned with the specifics of individual need at all. We are concerned with social needs. When we consider social needs then we are generally considering the needs of identifiable groups, but the idea of need itself is somewhat contested (Taylor-Gooby, 1991). One important question is whether or not it is possible to establish a justifiable level of basic needs (Hewitt, 1992). Needs are hard to define and agree on, though there is some acceptance of certain basic human needs such as food and shelter. What this points to then is that social welfare is somewhat different to individual welfare. Jordan (1987) illustrates this, arguing:

- Each individual's welfare depends on having needs satisfied but which they are not capable of meeting through their efforts alone.
- Social welfare depends on co-operation and social solidarity.
- Social welfare is therefore something more than, and different from, the welfare of individuals.

Jordan's first point is very important, especially in relation to family matters. In the discussion of the Beveridge report it was pointed out that the report assumed that a woman should expect to be provided for by a man. Let us now consider that the welfare state is based on the assumption that in some circumstances individuals will not be able to meet their own needs and that in these circumstances the state accepts the responsibility.

### Pause for reflection

Having young children makes it difficult go out to work for a number of reasons. For example, children need some degree of care that parents are unable to provide if they are at work.

Childcare is available, but this can be expensive so workers on low to average wages may find that it seems to be not worth working if the costs of childcare are high. If they are not working, they are not paying tax but might be claiming benefits.

So, this raises a question: should the state step in to make childcare more affordable?

Think back to the chapter on political ideologies. Which ideological position would support the state stepping in and which would argue that it should be left to the market?

It is not that easy to answer this question. If the state subsidises childcare, then childcare providers might raise fees. Here is another tricky question: what about the problems faced by single parents? Most single parents are women (ONS, 2019), so who should be responsible for supporting the child if we accept that having a child makes it difficult to work? The problem is that if the state steps in to provide support, then this it makes it more possible for men, the fathers, to withhold support. That does happen; some men will go to great lengths so as not to provide financial support for their children when they are separated from the child's or children's mother.

There is also an argument that the introduction of the welfare state has contributed to changes in family structures, especially the rise in single-parent families (Morgan, 2007; Griffiths, 2017). This is based on the idea that, if legislation makes it easier for couples to divorce and if the welfare system in place will provide support for each individual within a couple that splits up, then splitting up becomes more possible. Think about how we might make decisions regarding our lives. We might not be happy in a relationship, but can we survive economically outside of it? If the state will effectively subsidise our decision and the consequences of our decision, then we may choose to break up. If there is no external, financial support available then it may not seem nice, but we may feel compelled to stay.

So, on the one hand, it may seem perfectly reasonable for the state to provide financial support to a single parent based on need, but the provision of such support may be the very thing that has increased the number of single parents. Looking at it like this, we can see that the issue of defining need can be tricky. The cost of single-parent family benefits can be high, and governments have often tried to reduce the support that they provide. One way to combat this was the introduction of the Child Support Agency, replaced in 2012 by the Child Maintenance System. The aim is the same, though: to ensure that absent parents provide financial support for their children rather than the state providing support.

## 6.5 How can we ensure that welfare only goes to the deserving?

The issue of need has been something that is central to social policies for a very long time. What often accompanies a consideration of need, though, is the issue of who is and who is not deserving of having their needs met. It is interesting to consider how the state has responded to this.

### Pause for reflection

You might stop to think at this point about who you feel should or should not receive welfare support.

Think about why you come to these decisions.

Should welfare support perhaps be the last resort?

This might appear to be going off at a tangent but we can use a discussion of 19th-century concerns to demonstrate that some issues are very persistent. In considering desert, who deserves to be provided with support, it is useful to consider some historical approaches to dealing with need caused by poverty. The first legislation aimed at tackling poverty dates back to 1598, closely followed by another in 1601 (Jones, 1991; Fraser, 2009). These are usually referred to as either the Elizabethan Poor Law Acts or the Old Poor Law. They provided a basic system whereby the parish in which someone lived was responsible for providing relief to the poor, though this was very limited. What came to be known as the New Poor Law is of much greater relevance.

This also reflects the idea of the deserving and undeserving poor. The Poor Law was intended to act upon the undeserving poor, with the deserving poor being dealt with by charitable organisations (Harris and White, 2018), though this did not always happen in practice. Charities could also be harsh in their solutions to the problems that were experienced by the poor. Thane (1996) offers the example of able-bodied widows finding that that some or all of their children were removed from them and taken to the workhouse so that childcare was no longer an obstacle to obtaining work.

As a national system the New Poor Law introduced two key principles for receiving relief, or what we would now call support. Firstly, to obtain support under the New Poor Law (Poor Law Amendment Act 1834), an individual or family had to enter the workhouse, something that was referred to as 'indoor relief'. This abolished the previous practice of providing support for the poor in the community, hence the distinction between indoor relief provided for inside the workhouse and 'outdoor relief', provided for outside the workhouse, by which we mean in the community. The intention was that relief (support) would only be available within the workhouse.

Secondly, the New Poor Law reflected the general belief that if support was available then this would discourage people from working to support themselves. After all, why work when you can get money for doing nothing? (Think about the discourse around an underclass, or of strivers and skivers, and this starts to sound familiar.) This 'problem' is probably still central to social policy today. The New Poor Law 'solved' the problem by introducing the principle of less eligibility (Jones, 1991; Fraser, 2009). To us this maybe does not really make much sense but that is probably because of how the term 'eligible' is now used compared to what it once meant. If we translate 'the principle of less eligibility' into 'provision that is the least attractive' it makes more sense (eligible meant attractive at the time).

The guiding principle of what was provided in the workhouse was that the living conditions of the lowest-paid labourer working in the community were to be more attractive than those of anyone who enters the workhouse. Welfare was available but it was designed to be unattractive. Such an approach may be said to be present within the current welfare system. What has been suggested by some is that the state has taken a punitive turn in recent years towards those families who rely on welfare benefits. Since 2010 the British social security system, originally established to support families experiencing hardship, has been reconfigured to put individuals off claiming and to punish those that do (Fletcher and Wright, 2018; Wright et al, 2020).

So, to receive welfare after the New Poor Law was introduced, it was necessary to enter the workhouse. If families entered the workhouse they were split up;

workhouses had a very clear separation policy, with male dormitories and female dormitories. Once inside, welfare was provided but it is important to remember that it was designed to be harsh. The aim was to provide a quality of life that was of a lower standard than that experienced by the lowest-paid worker on the outside. The workhouse was meant to act as a deterrent to claiming support.

Out of interest, many workhouses still exist, though not operating as workhouses: it is possible to visit one in Southwell, Nottinghamshire; some students at York St John University are accommodated in the old workhouse; and one of the authors, Creasy, was born in a hospital that was once the workhouse in Rotherham.

What we can see from this discussion of the New Poor Law is that the concerns that the state was dealing with in the early 19th century may not be too different from concerns that are still being discussed today. A concern with identifying who is deserving of welfare support and who is not has been a perennial problem within social policy. There is often a moral dimension to this, with some benefit claimants being cast as immoral (Romano, 2018), something which casts doubt on their claims of being deserving. Lyndon (2019: 603) provides a good account of how poverty affects families and emphasises how contemporary discourse presents families as either hard-working or 'a parasitical, pathological, underclass', in a way which draws on ideas that are clearly evident within the New Poor Law of 1834.

## 6.6 How the state shapes family life

One consequence of the development of a range of welfare services is that this has contributed to more women working and to changes in family forms. The welfare state itself creates a paradox in the way that the development of welfare services led to the expansion of many job opportunities in areas that had traditionally been seen as women's work, especially in what can be called caring work. When we say paradoxical, we mean the way in which we can see a contradiction in what is happening. So, it is paradoxical in that the Beveridge report positions women within the home but then increases job opportunities which are typically seen as reflecting the sort of work that women are traditionally expected to undertake. In this way, the welfare state creates what economists call pull factors which contribute to an increase in the number of women going out to work as welfare jobs pull them into work. As more women go out to work we might recognise that very often this means that more welfare services are required to fill the gaps left in terms of caring within the family.

Whether you live in a nuclear family or a single-parent family, there has been an increasing trend towards parents working. This can be used to highlight the tensions between the different concerns of the state in that the need for a dynamic and active economy leads to increased economic activity, which in turn reduces the care available at home. As such, initiatives that were introduced under Blair's Labour governments such as extended school opening times, including breakfast clubs or homework clubs, can be seen as a response to parents working as well as providing support to make it easier for parents to work.

The state also influences other parts of society or the economy. So, consider how the state may have an impact on how and when some people work. One key aspect within neoliberalism is the idea of deregulation. This means reducing regulations such as policies and legislation which restrict what individuals, organisations or businesses can do. During the 1980s neoliberal policies aimed at deregulation can be seen to have led to changes in respect of how people work (Hegewisch and Gornick, 2011; Vincent and Neis, 2011; Rönkä et al, 2017). For example, deregulation in the retail sector has led to many more shops being open on Sundays. This changes the working patterns of shop workers, which then has an impact on the ability of some parents to care for their children. Traditionally, it was women who formed the bulk of shop workers and so this means that this example of deregulation had particular consequences for women.

Alongside this, there have been changes which have increased the requirement for workers to work during what were once referred to as unsocial hours, such as evening, night and weekend work, times when children are at home rather than at school. At the same time neoliberal policies have seen the additional payments that workers were once paid for working unsocial hours being reduced or removed as this type of work has become presented as normal. Such developments inevitably influence our experience of family life.

What these changes mean is that it has now become a normal practice for young children to experience care outside of the home and by individuals other than family members. This has been supported in particular by policies that were introduced by the Labour governments in 1997–2010 (Smith, 2013). What is evident is that the Labour governments of this period were very concerned to make it easier for parents to work, especially as work was, at the time, seen as a way of getting out of poverty.

Childcare is one reason for parents to leave work, so providing support for childcare in the early years such as funding for two-year-olds can be seen to help parents with low incomes to access training or work (Gibb et al, 2011). This is not to say that children in the early years are solely cared for outside of family relationships. Many will be, but it is still the case that young children are also likely to experience care that is provided by family members alongside family friends and paid staff. However, as Dermott and Pomati (2017) point out, the UK has very high childcare costs compared to other European countries and this acts to make full-time work in particular unattractive on the grounds that for many parents it is just not worth it.

## 6.7 So what?

Having considered lots of ways in which the state intervenes in family life, it seems relevant to ask why. From a theoretical position the work of Foucault is always useful, especially with respect to how and why it is that the state has come to be concerned with the population (Hewitt, 1992; Wells, 2018). This concern with population extends to families and children, including what has been called the governance of childhood (Smith, 2014). We can say that the state is concerned about governing the lives of children because of something that was established earlier: that is, the way in which the state has a particular view of what childhood should be and with what children will become. In Creasy and Corby (2019), we argued that the state has a primary view of children as becomings; by this we mean that children are always seen in terms of their future, in terms of what they will become. In one sense then the state intervenes in family life so as to produce what it deems to be desirable outcomes.

---

**Note**

Service providers such as teachers and social workers often talk about outcomes in relation to children.

Think also about how service providers often emphasise outcomes being measurable such as exam results but that families may be concerned with other outcomes such as children's happiness.

Now consider how a concern with outcomes reinforces a view of children as becomings. Does it ignore what children are now?

---

We can see how the idea of outcomes feeds into social policy. Sure Start, as was introduced by Blair's Labour governments, was set up with the aim of changing the lives of children from poor or disadvantaged families for the better. It fits with a discussion of life-chances as well as reflecting a discourse of childhood as being a process and viewing children as becomings. In particular, though, policy approaches such as Sure Start, as well as associated approaches such as the Every Child Matters framework and the Children Act (2014, 2004), illustrate the ways in which the state acts upon families and childhood as a consequence of seeing them as something that can be shaped so as to achieve specific outcomes.

In evaluating the family from the perspective of social welfare then it is clear that it is one thing which we all have some experience of, though often in very different ways. Clearly some state support is necessary but again we are drawn to questioning the extent of such support and the form it should take. Should this be a carrot or a stick? The contradiction is between, on the one hand, wanting to support families where parents can stay home and care for their children, and on the other hand, a desire to lessen the burden of parents on the social security system by encouraging them to seek paid employment.

So, as was said at the start, this chapter discusses issues that underpin social policy or social welfare rather than being focused on particular policies. As such, you can use it in your assignments to pick out some key ideas. For example, we can see some of the key concepts as follows:

- Ideologies are experienced through legislation and social policies but in the process of implementing policies ideologies often get distorted, so the policies which we experience may not always 'fit' perfectly with ideology.
- Social policies reflect a particular view of the world and in doing so identify both problems and solutions.
- Social policies often reflect views about social differences and divisions such as gender, social class and ethnicity.
- Policies often define issues about need and entitlement as can be seen in ideas about who is deserving and who is undeserving of support or assistance.
- In respect of needs we are usually concerned with social need rather than individual need.
- Legislation and policy can be slow to change.

Of course, you may only use certain sections of the chapter to help you with assignments. That said, consider how we approached the chapter by being focused on how ideologies are put into practice and how this means engaging with some philosophical ideas about society and how it may be criticised.

We started by briefly discussing how politicians may use rhetorical language to shape how we understand society and use this to justify a policy approach. So, Cameron's arguments about Broken Britain and Osborne's use of the phrase 'strivers versus skivers' encourage us to think that there is a problem and that we need to introduce policies, or to change existing policies, to address the problem. You might use other examples that you encounter in your studies. What this rhetorical language did, though, was to make sense of the policies that Cameron and Osborne introduced which came to be known as austerity.

We then noted that ideologies are rarely clear when they end up as social policies and talked about a number of ways in which the policy that is put into practice may not fit neatly with an ideological view.

The discussion of the Beveridge report and the welfare state was to show that policies always have ideas about society embedded within them. The example that was used was of women's social role and the way that motherhood and reproduction are presented as explaining and justifying the policy that is introduced. This then led into a discussion of need and desert because all policies have to take into account the issue of meeting a need and then of who should be provided for. This allowed the opportunity to demonstrate that establishing desert and need can be tricky.

After this we provided some examples of how the state has addressed these problems and provided the historical example of the workhouse to show how the state can create a harsh environment that is designed to put people off from seeking support. This raised the issue of the way in which the state is involved in children's and families' lives and how the state, through social policies, shapes the context within which children and families experience life.

Having covered some broad issues relating to children, families and the state, including the ways in which social policies are shaped by political and philosophical ideas, we now turn towards some contemporary issues that we see as central to understanding and working with children and families. This sees the following chapters being much more focused on adopting a critical approach towards wellbeing, vulnerability, resilience, risk and safeguarding before returning to a broader discussion of inequalities and the life-chances of children.

### Further thoughts

Listen to some politicians and try to identify examples of rhetoric in what they say. Do they use terms or phrases as though they are unambiguous?

If you work, do colleagues and/or line managers adopt a similar approach at all?

### Further reading

Bates (2014) and David (2016) are both good books if you want to understand what girls and women experience as part of everyday life. Read Chapter 4 of Bates in particular.

The Beveridge report is easily accessible online and reading this will give you a good insight into how the state might want to achieve something and what sorts of values are embedded within the approach being taken.

# 7

# Wellbeing

This chapter will help you to understand:

- how wellbeing differs from being well;
- the importance of subjective wellbeing;
- how children's wellbeing tends to be dominated by what adults want for them.

## 7.1 What do we mean by wellbeing?

If you are studying any course linked to childhood or to children and young people, you will inevitably come across the concept of wellbeing. Wellbeing has become increasingly important in relation to understanding and working with children and young people. This can be seen in how it forms a major part of a range of policies and services. In addition to its importance to practice, the issue of wellbeing can be seen within many academic papers and books (Ben-Arieh, 2006; Taylor, 2011; Knight et al, 2014; La Placa and Knight, 2014; Bradshaw, 2016; Children's Society, 2018; Moore, 2019). However, as is often the case with concepts that you will come across in your studies, wellbeing is something that tends to be presented as though it is unambiguous.

In reality this is very far from being the case; wellbeing has different facets to it (Dickerson and Popli, 2018). Wellbeing can mean different things to different people and can be incorporated into practice in quite different ways. Importantly, Street (2021) draws a distinction between child wellbeing and human wellbeing, arguing that we cannot understand child wellbeing without first understanding childhood, or childhoods. Street also takes us back to the idea of children as beings or becomings when making this claim.

So, when it comes to writing your assignments you will look better informed if you can talk about wellbeing as something that is socially constructed and which is not as clear cut as it sounds. This chapter will give you a basis from which to question what we mean about wellbeing, and it will help you to be more precise in how you write about it. Later, if you end up working with children, young people and families, being able to understand the complexity of wellbeing will help you to be more effective in terms of setting objectives and evaluating your work, and the work of others. For example, Moore (2019) suggests that how we understand wellbeing is dominated by psychology. This might be the case for psychologists, but that doesn't mean that everyone who is concerned with wellbeing is focused on psychology. Moore asks the reader to think about this.

As a starting point you might want to think about why we even use the term wellbeing especially as it is something that has not really been in common usage for all that long. It is important to note that the term wellbeing came into use to refer to something that differed from a medical view of being well (La Placa and Knight, 2014). When it comes to childhood this is important because very often children have been seen primarily in terms of their health, as can be seen in the key role that health visitors play in the lives of infants. This brings us back to the work of Foucault. In Chapter 2 we talked of how Foucault draws attention to the place of discourse in social life and how this can help us to understand the world. Foucault also considered the idea of how professional groups look at people as if looking through a lens. He originally talked about the medical gaze (Foucault, 1989). This means that we are guided by our profession to understand people in terms of what that profession sees as important. So, medical professionals look at health, educationalists look at education and so on.

We can see this in terms of the way in which health visitors are charged with assessing a child's development in the early years. What the health visitor service does is to remind us that a concern with physical health has often been seen to be of prime importance when it comes to children. When considering child mortality and infant health concerns in previous generations this can be seen as understandable but a focus on health often persists when it is less of an issue to be concerned with. For example, when writing about wellbeing in the early years, Roberts (2010: 3) states that 'health and happiness are needed to underpin the kind of childhood that is *every* child's right'.

This is the sort of statement that is very difficult to argue with. Most of us wouldn't want to argue with it but as undergraduate students you are expected to be developing a critical understanding of childhood, so it is worth looking a little closer at what Roberts is saying here. To begin with, we can say that Roberts is suggesting that wellbeing is a characteristic of good health. At the same time there is the implication that a child who experiences poor health will not therefore experience wellbeing. In stating that this is every child's right Roberts may also be guilty of taking rights for granted. We have already considered the ways in which children are very often denied rights in Chapter 4, so it is worth thinking about what Roberts means and whether or not he is being a little idealistic.

For a definition of wellbeing that works in relation to children and young people we have previously argued for an understanding of wellbeing as individual experience, or what we might call subjective wellbeing (Creasy and Corby, 2019). The Children's Society (2018: 9) states the following: 'Subjective well-being can be thought of as a positive state of mind in which a person feels good about life as a whole and its constituent parts, such as their relationships with others, the environments that they inhabit and how they see themselves.' Drawing upon this claim you might be able to see that subjective wellbeing provides the scope to adopt a broader way of conceptualising wellbeing. Moore (2019) is also useful in how he links wellbeing to the person.

Establishing a working definition for wellbeing is important because like a good number of concepts within social sciences it is a concept that can be said to be slippery. Remember, we say that it is slippery because of the way that what it means is not always agreed upon or because it has no obvious and unambiguous definition. This becomes evident when you read studies that are concerned with wellbeing. For example, try to read the following: Sixsmith et al (2007), Ecclestone and Hayes (2009), Spratt (2016), Fava et al (2017), Wellard and Secker (2017) and Street (2021). You will often come across concepts being used in your studies and must always be careful not just to assume that they are obvious or clear. Always try to grasp just how the concept is being defined in the study that you are reading about. Problems can arise if we present social issues as straightforward because many social issues, such as wellbeing, are not straightforward at all; they are complex and multi-dimensional (McNaught, 2011; Fava et al, 2017; Street, 2021).

What is really important to understand then is that wellbeing is not simple. It will not be the same for everyone. Also, wellbeing is not a fixed state. It is not something which individuals should seek to achieve and then forget about. Because wellbeing is multi-dimensional in nature it is always something that is going to be dynamic. It will always be changing in both objective and subjective terms.

## 7.2 Does wellbeing represent individualisation?

There is little doubt that wellbeing has come to take on an increasing importance within services and practice (La Placa and Knight, 2014). However, when we think about how services for children and young people are provided, we are drawn into considering the policy context. Policy often seems a bit dry to students and sometimes seems a bit remote from the actual issues regarding childhood and how we might provide for children, but previous chapters should have demonstrated how important it is. If you take a module on policy issues and the focus is on the wording and details of each policy or how it changes from a previous policy, it will be dry. What is always much more interesting and useful is to understand why we have the policies that we have and what it is that influences changes in policy. What you always need to keep in mind is that what, and how, we provide for children and young people is always rooted within policy. This could be at the level of organisations which provide for children, such as local authorities or nurseries, but it can also be at the level of government. What we can say then is that both policymakers and practitioners are bound up with policy.

So, wellbeing is a rather slippery concept. It is often a concept that is taken for granted as being obvious but which, in reality, is not at all obvious. Consider that for policymakers, and for practitioners, the fact that wellbeing is a slippery concept could make it very useful. This is because with wellbeing not having a clear and unambiguous definition policymakers and practitioners can find it easier to claim that what they are doing is increasing or enhancing wellbeing for children and young people. Alongside this, as was stated at the beginning, wellbeing is a concept that is difficult to reject. Who wouldn't want to improve wellbeing? This takes us back to issues that were raised earlier, though, in terms of thinking about who it is that defines what wellbeing is or what is in the best interests of the child.

---

**Pause for reflection**

How would you define wellbeing and what does it mean to you?

How would you see wellbeing in respect of children and what might that mean?

Do you think that children and young people might see wellbeing differently?

---

What we tend to find is that wellbeing comes to represent the aspirations that adults have for children. How children understand wellbeing often gets overlooked (Anderson and Graham, 2016). With this in mind, studies have demonstrated that there are differences between what adults see as important for children's wellbeing and what children may see as being important (Fattore et al, 2007; Sixsmith et al, 2007; Spratt, 2016; Street, 2021).

---

**Note**

The concept of helicopter parenting is relevant here. Parental involvement in a child's life is usually accepted as a good thing but helicopter parenting sees this involvement being taken to extremes.

Helicopter parents make decisions for their children in the belief that this will advantage those children (Creasy and Corby, 2019).

LeMoyne and Buchanan (2011), however, report that wellbeing is reduced in children who experience helicopter parenting as a consequence of the behaviours and strategies that are adopted by these types of parents because they exert too much control over children.

---

In addition to policy relating to wellbeing it is also worth considering a much broader context. This is another example of how we might find it useful to consider wider social forces or conditions when we assess and evaluate matters relating to children, young people and families. It may seem a long time ago now, but in 2008 there was a significant economic downturn. Basically, the global banking system had become increasingly unregulated, and this had led banks and other financial institutions to engage in a number of practices which were very risky. In 2008 it all went wrong, and this caused some problems for the UK government that was in power, Labour, as it did for many governments around the world.

In the UK in 2010 there was a general election and a new government, the Conservative/Liberal Democrat Coalition government. Chapter 5 noted that since 1979 the Conservatives have been very critical of providing social services (this is because they go along with neoliberal ideas, and neoliberals argue that social services should be provided by private companies rather than the state), and the financial crash of 2008 provided an opportunity to change policy direction by introducing a series of measures that came to be known as austerity. What austerity politics meant for many people and for the UK as a whole was cutting back or scrapping services such as Children's Centres and a worsening of finances for many families (Churchill, 2013; Jupp, 2017; Lehtonen, 2018).

It was also the case that wages stopped growing. For many people, wages are no higher now than they were in 2008 when inflation is factored in (ONS, 2018). For example, people working in the public sector such as education, the NHS and social services were restricted to pay rises below the rate of inflation for almost ten years. At the same time many people now rely on insecure jobs in what has been called the gig economy (Gerrard, 2017; Gross et al, 2018; Choonara, 2019; MacDonald and Giazitzoglu, 2019). The name gig economy reflects the way in which bands play gigs. These are one-off events rather than regular bookings. So, jobs in the gig economy are one-off jobs characterised by insecurity rather than stability in that there is no certainty of any follow-up job. They are often based around the idea of self-employment and do not come with benefits such as sick pay or pensions. The economy has changed and the growth of part-time and insecure work for some is also accompanied by underemployment or unemployment for many others.

In some ways this seems to be unrelated to wellbeing, but at the beginning we asked you to think about why it is that the term wellbeing has started to be used so much in recent years. It is possible to take the view that giving greater prominence to the idea of wellbeing can be understood as turning attention away from financial or economic matters and, instead, focusing upon individual experience. This is not to say that wellbeing is not important in its own right, it is, but at the same time it can be seen to have come to the fore as a concern at the same time that economic conditions for very many people have been deteriorating.

So, from a critical perspective what appears to be a concern for wellbeing might be seen as a strategy that is being adopted by a government that is unable to improve economic conditions, or even has no motivation to do so. If this is the case, might we see wellbeing as the re-emergence of an old idea, namely that we might be poor but that doesn't mean that we cannot be happy? There again, this is not something that is without merit. Who wouldn't want to be happy?

## 7.3 Inequality and wellbeing

Happiness is something that has been considered in recent years, especially against a backdrop of children and young people reporting that they are unhappy with their lives (Children's Society, 2018). However, it would be wrong to suggest that economic wealth is the key factor with respect to being happy. Happiness is not simply the consequence of being richer (Layard, 2011). It is difficult to assess happiness, and what tends to be the case is that researchers who are interested in wellbeing consider the extent to which the numbers of children and young people experiencing problems can be assessed. So, although the Children's Society has stated that fewer children report that they are happy now, it may be more useful to consider the rising numbers of children with mental health problems.

This is a good way of also demonstrating that the social lives of children and young people are important. For example, we could ask why it is that increasing numbers of children and young people are reporting problems with their mental health. We either have to say that there is something about children and young people that has changed, or to consider that something about the lives of children and young people has changed.

This brings us back to a consideration of the social context within which children and young people live and the pressures that they face. Wilkinson and Pickett (2018) illustrate how inequality can impact upon wellbeing or on mental health. Earlier studies have also suggested that inequality is not good for mental health (James, 2009). This is relevant because the policies introduced by the UK Coalition government from 2010, which are usually referred to as 'austerity', have seen a significant increase in the number of children that are experiencing poverty (Churchill, 2013; Jupp, 2017; Lambie-Mumford and Green, 2017; Tunstill and Willow, 2017). Be careful, though; inequality is not in itself a measure of how well off we are. It is a measure of comparison.

So, what Wilkinson and Pickett (2010, 2018) are suggesting is that inequality is a major problem in terms of what it means for society and in terms of what it means for wellbeing. What can also be seen is that those groups who were already the poorest within the UK are those that have experienced the greatest falls in their incomes since austerity policies were enacted, and that this contributes to inequality widening. As children and young people are far more likely to be dependent upon others when it comes to their economic position, this inevitably means that their position is weakened. Alongside this it is important to remember that the austerity policies introduced by the Coalition government of 2010 and continued by subsequent Conservative governments have seen major funding cuts to services which support children, young people and families. For example, the extensive and successful system of Children's Centres developed under the Labour governments from 1997 to 2010 has now pretty much disappeared (Ryan, 2019).

So, as we end this chapter you might want to consider that wellbeing can be affected by the environment that children and young people grow up in. This idea is at the heart of the ideas put forward by Bronfenbrenner (1979) that were introduced in Chapter 1. As such you can say that something such as poverty has an effect upon the material world that children live in. We say material because it is concerned with real things, material things. If you still aren't clear about this think of what we mean when we say that someone is materialistic or ask parents and grandparents just why it is that Madonna claimed to be a material girl! When we consider the lives of children and young people we can also see that they are influenced and affected by things that are not real in the way that a warm home is real, or that clothes are real. Children and young people's lives can be shaped by the ideas that people have about them. If clothes are material, then we say that ideas are abstract. Some ideas seem very real because they seem so obvious, but what Chapter 8 will demonstrate is that ideas can be understood as being developed within social contexts. For example, what makes children vulnerable?

## 7.4 The key ideas that really should be in an essay

OK, so you have read to this point and you have been introduced to a range of ideas that are related to the issue of wellbeing. Some of these ideas were more obvious than others and some will have been easier to understand than others. That's perfectly normal. We still read things and struggle with what is being said. Hopefully, though, most of this chapter will have been fairly clear. However, assuming that you have an assignment on wellbeing, let us end by picking out some ideas and issues which we would expect to have a place in it:

- Wellbeing is something that is socially constructed and although it may sound obvious, it usually isn't. We can say that it is a slippery concept and that it is not a fixed state.
- What we mean by wellbeing has often been dominated by health or by psychology, but a social understanding is just as important because saying wellbeing sets it apart from health. Health is concerned with being well.
- Always look to provide a working definition for your assignment. A good approach is to define wellbeing in terms of individual experience, or what we might call subjective wellbeing, because this is a broader way of understanding it (Creasy and Corby, 2019). The Children's Society (2018: 9) says the following: 'Subjective well-being can be thought of as a positive state of mind in which a person feels good about life as a whole and its constituent parts, such as their relationships with others, the environments that they inhabit and how they see themselves.' You can also link wellbeing to the person (Moore, 2019).
- In respect of children and young people, very often wellbeing comes to represent the aspirations that adults have for children.
- It is important to consider the social context when looking at wellbeing. For example, inequality can be seen to impact upon wellbeing.

It is not that you have to follow these in the order listed, but this order makes sense in terms of how you build up an argument. If you end up with the social context then you have scope to bring in other issues that may be relevant to the module or course that you are studying. One thing that is related to this, and which leads into Chapter 8, is the idea that some children and young people don't experience wellbeing because they are vulnerable. Of course, that should lead you to ask the question, vulnerable to what? What do we mean by the term vulnerable? Chapter 8 will say more.

## Further thoughts

Be clear that wellbeing is different from being well in a health sense.

People often talk about their wellbeing. What do you think they mean?

Give some thought to how social media can construct an idealised context within which children and young people live their lives.

Consider the ways in which highly positive social media posts might impact upon the wellbeing of others.

## Further reading

Street (2021) is useful. Note that when you want to find journal articles you should always use your library search engine rather than a generic search engine.

# 8

# Vulnerable children

This chapter will help you to understand:

- how vulnerability is socially constructed rather than being natural or inevitable;
- how the discourse of vulnerability undermines children's abilities.

## 8.1 A discourse of children as naturally vulnerable

**Note**

It is quite easy for us to point to things which underpin children's vulnerability.

Children are smaller and weaker. They are less worldly wise and may not understand situations fully or in the same way that adults would. Because of this, children are seen to lack power. They are weaker and they are, for the most part, dependent on others.

It can sometimes be useful, however, to consider how children can be empowered so as to mitigate what may be seen as 'real' weaknesses such as size.

What we want you to think about then is not just about children's smaller size, which makes them physically weaker. Similarly, don't just think that their lack of understanding is a sufficient explanation for them being vulnerable; after all, many adults also display a real lack of understanding about many aspects of their lives. Instead, try to think that children, and young people, are vulnerable because adults organise the world and determine what children can do, in ways which make children more vulnerable.

It is very common to see discussions about children and young people which associate them with the idea of being vulnerable. Because of this it is often said that there is a discourse of vulnerability that is strongly associated with risk. This can be seen to be linked to debates about wellbeing when it comes to children (Turnbull and Spence, 2011; Turnbull, 2016; Wellard and Secker, 2017). As such we can say that a discourse of risk has come to shape both practice and policy with children and young people, especially in the context of concerns about wellbeing. A fuller discussion of risk together with ideas about safeguarding is covered in Chapter 10, but what you really need at this stage is to make sure that you understand what is meant by the term discourse, because if you are not comfortable with what is meant by discourse then a number of academic arguments and texts will not make as much sense as they could do. Discourse was introduced in Chapter 2 but a short refresher could be useful.

---

**Study tip**

Remember, we mentioned above that discourse comes from the work of Foucault. It is bound up with language in terms of how language shapes meaning, but also how this fits in with a way of understanding the world.

So, think of a discourse as a set of ideas which operate in a way that structures what we can know and understand about anything within society. The result of this is that we see some things as normal and natural but at the same time this makes other things unthinkable. What this means is that what we know about something (such as childhood) only exists as part of discourse.

Therefore, what we know is not real in itself, it is only real in the way that the language that we use acts to construct reality. It is the way in which language is used which makes something appear real and natural.

---

So, the understanding of all children as naturally vulnerable can be seen to be formed within a particular discourse that has emerged in recent years. They haven't always be seen as vulnerable. Try to think that children are not naturally vulnerable but come to be vulnerable because of the language that we use about them and the way in which this then causes us to understand children and relate to them in a particular way.

There is a discourse about children and childhood which presents children and young people as vulnerable, albeit some more than others. As such, it is fair to say that all children are at risk of harm; however, some children are more vulnerable due to their environment or due to factors that are unique to them, for example:

- being non-mobile: babies under one year old are at most risk and the homicide rate for this age is much higher than for older children;
- disability: if we fail to recognise the additional vulnerabilities faced by some, but not all, disabled children, then we are unable to promote resilience;
- being different in a way that means exposure to prejudice or unwanted attention;
- those already considered to be a problem, such as young offenders or children in care. This is not to say that we think that these groups are necessarily a problem!

Following from this, vulnerability often becomes linked to types of need and the idea of children in need comes to be seen as somewhat obvious. That said, needs can be categorised in different ways. This means that we might talk about universal needs, or we might refer to complex or even acute needs. This, however, is another example of how it is important to establish just what we mean when we use a term, because although the term vulnerable will often be drawn upon, it is often done so in a way which suggests that it is obvious and unambiguous (Coram and Coram International, 2017).

---

**Pause for reflection**

Take a moment to list how children and young people are said to be vulnerable.

Is vulnerability natural or could it be that social conditions make children more vulnerable?

---

We generally see children and young people as being naturally vulnerable because of their age, especially in terms of physical, sexual or emotional abuse. However, we often see children being said to be vulnerable as a consequence of some level of deprivation that they experience, and politicians and commentators commonly refer to vulnerable children when they mean children who experience poverty. Of course, this could be seen as a way of recognising the problems that are caused by poverty while not referring to poverty itself – the cause of the problem. As such, poverty becomes normalised.

## 8.2 Policy and need

In the discussion on wellbeing in Chapter 7 it was established that poverty and inequality are relevant when we seek to understand the lives of children and young people. We could also say that the fact that governments from Elizabethan times have introduced policies which seek to deal with poverty, or to respond to the consequences of poverty for society, is also evidence that it is important. The issue of need is very relevant to understanding how we provide for people. It seems obvious to state that the types of welfare provided by the state will rest upon an understanding of what people's needs are. At the end of the 1940s the UK, led by a Labour government, set in place a series of policies that came to be referred to as the welfare state. As with any state system, though, things do not stay the same for ever, and the services and support that are provided by the state are and will be subject to change. This is inevitable because society changes, so what is provided to support society also has to change.

Consider also that it is possible to construct a discourse about social matters which makes it easier to affect the changes that we want to see. For example, around the time of the 2010 General Election in the UK politicians started to refer to 'hardworking families' (Cain, 2016). This can be said to act to distinguish these families, families who work hard and do the right thing, from those families who are different. The families who are different are those families who are not working hard, though just how hard work is defined is left unsaid. What this does is to set up a situation whereby it becomes easier to gain public support for cutting support to families who are not in work. It draws upon an older discourse within UK policy about deserving and undeserving.

Welfare policies in the 21st century have seen a move towards the idea of support being targeted. The idea here is that support is aimed at those who need it the most, something that rests on the idea that there are maybe some who claim benefits who do not really need them. So, think about the idea of children in need. This means that we can identify children who do need help compared to those who do not, and target help to the right children.

The idea of vulnerability fits easily within this approach. It is difficult to provide an argument against targeting the most vulnerable. What often happens within such discussions, though, is that poverty comes to be seen as synonymous with vulnerability. It is then a small step to claim that children and young people who experience poverty are naturally, or inevitably, vulnerable. Remember what was said previously, though, about being critical of what you read. You might well accept that children and young people who experience poverty are vulnerable, but can you say what they are vulnerable to? Typically, it refers to the additional needs that they have or the barriers that such children face which may make them less likely to live healthy, happy, safe lives, or that they are less likely to do well at school or to have successful transitions to adulthood.

The concept of vulnerability is quite firmly embedded in what is written and said about children and young people. Their vulnerability is very much taken for granted. In a society which places so much emphasis upon individuality and individual difference it does seem to stand out that we find it very easy to accept that all children are vulnerable. Once again, we can say that this is another concept that is taken for granted as being somehow obvious and unambiguous. The practice of identifying some individuals and groups as being vulnerable has come to be seen as something that is beyond thinking about, it is something that is natural. But is it? Maybe to answer that a bit more fully we need to consider the social context in which children and young people come to be seen as vulnerable.

## 8.3 What is the social context of vulnerability?

It may well be the case that when we look at babies and infants we can draw upon ideas about natural vulnerability, but this natural vulnerability decreases as children grow. We cannot say that a 17-year-old is as vulnerable as they were when they were 17 months old, but both have no input into many aspects of their lives because of policy and legislation. Policy and legislation are created by adults. At the moment, in the UK, we are all considered to be children until we reach the age of 18 years old. This can be used against us. Look at the criticism that has been directed towards Greta Thunberg for seeking action with respect to the climate crisis. Many adults find it easy to belittle Thunberg on the grounds of her age. This is in spite of the fact that the scientific evidence of a climate crisis cannot be disputed and that she is campaigning for something that would benefit everyone.

So, what we want you to consider is that with respect to being considered to be vulnerable, although we tend to see the characteristics that groups or individuals possess as the thing that creates vulnerability, for example, living in poverty or having a disability, what we should also be thinking about is how we fit into relationships with others. So, if we remain focused on the idea that children are vulnerable because they are children, we then have to assess who gets to be defined as a child.

---

### Pause for reflection

How times change ...

Corby's father left school and went to work at the age of 14, as did most of his peers. This seems young, but although Corby continued at school until she was 16 she worked at weekends from the age of 13 and was expected to buy her own clothes from that age.

Creasy also worked from 13, as a golf caddy and delivering papers. He left school at 16 and went to work as an apprentice electrician. He was 15 when he first paid for and went on holiday with a friend without adult supervision. They rented a caravan at the seaside for the first two weeks of year 11.

There were no mobile phones, and their parents didn't have a phone in the house. There was no easy way of contacting parents.

Does any of this happen now? Were they vulnerable?

---

What you might consider then is that social, political and cultural factors combine in ways that shape what it means to be vulnerable (Brotherton and Cronin, 2013; Brown, 2017). For example, in the UK there is a legal requirement on local authorities to provide services for children deemed to be in need or at risk of harm. New Zealand is very explicit in having a Vulnerable Children Act. If we think about how this happens within discourses which shape how we understand the world that we live in, then we can start to see how children and young people may come to be vulnerable because of more general ideas about their place within society and what is best for them. McNamee (2016) illustrates this using the words of a young girl who says that she is vulnerable to the actions of her parents but that this is because of the way in which the legal system insists that a child's best place is with their family and insists that she lives with them. In this case it is not the girl's age that means that she is vulnerable, it is a more general belief regarding childhood and families.

Although in this example the issue is a general social belief in families always being best, we can also see how in recent years there has been a growing belief in the benefits, and need for, providing support to children and young people such as counselling or other forms of therapy. The two things can be seen to fit together. As a society we have come to believe that children and young people are vulnerable and this feeds into the belief that they require support so that they may be better able to handle the pressures that are encountered within contemporary society (Furedi, 2004). What is ironic is that, the more that we provide these types of therapeutic intervention, the more it is accepted that children and young people are vulnerable. A comparison of the extent of therapeutic provision within schools, colleges and universities now and that of, say, 50 years ago is evidence of a growing concern to respond to the problems that children and young people are said to experience (Ecclestone and Hayes, 2009).

A further consideration in terms of vulnerability and wellbeing is that if we assume that children and young people are naturally, or inevitably, vulnerable then the consequences are that as a society we may act in ways which prevent them from experiencing issues and situations which contribute to developing resilience. This is something that is considered in Chapter 9. An absence of resilience is reflected to some extent in the term snowflake. Snowflake refers to children and young people who are said both to lack resilience and to be hyper-sensitive. The idea of snowflakes points to a growing concern with children who are becoming more vulnerable and less resilient (McElwee, 2007; Creasy and Corby, 2019).

In conclusion, then, although it seems obvious to say that vulnerability follows from being weaker or from being dependent on others, it is also important to consider how it should always be understood as being shaped within social relationships and within discourse. As such it is more useful to understand vulnerability in terms of social context and not to see it as being something that is wholly rooted in individual characteristics. For example, think back to what was said about children who experience poverty or deprivation being assumed to be vulnerable. This can be said to link wellbeing with vulnerability. It seems reasonable to suggest that children and young people who are vulnerable are at risk of not enjoying wellbeing but, if the social context of their lives is important, it is therefore pertinent to consider this further.

## 8.4 What might you use in an essay out of this chapter?

We end this chapter by thinking about the key ideas which really should be present in any assignment about vulnerability. So, let us say that you have an assignment that is either focused on vulnerability or vulnerability comes into it. Your job is to convince the marker that you understand the issues. Developing a clear argument within an assignment does that, and to do that there are usually some key issues which are needed. Based on this chapter we think that the key issues about a critical understanding of vulnerability are as follows:

- Children and young people are often seen as being naturally vulnerable, but we should question this.
- Vulnerability is not necessarily an individual characteristic; it exists as a product of relationships where some groups have less power than others.

- Vulnerability can be seen as being socially constructed and is embedded within the way that we understand childhood and in how this intersects with the policies that are created to provide for children.
- How we understand vulnerability shapes the ideas that we have about children's and young people's needs: for example, vulnerability is often associated with ideas about risk and this leads to children's freedom being restricted so as to safeguard them.
- Social, political and cultural factors combine in ways that shape what it means to be vulnerable: for example, children who are seen as experiencing poverty come to be automatically accepted as vulnerable.

Overall, vulnerability is another of those concepts that seems really obvious but once you start to scrape below the surface it can be seen that it rests on ideas and assumptions which are not as clear cut as we might initially think. Discussing vulnerability in an assignment will often provide you with an opportunity to consider discourse. Although a discussion of discourse is not always necessary, you might look stronger if you can talk about it in a way that makes sense. It is always a good idea to drop references in to show that you have read around this. If we think of the ways in which social, political and cultural factors combine to shape what it means to be vulnerable, then this also provides scope to explore why it is that children who experience poverty or deprivation are seen as vulnerable and this then gives you an opportunity to consider the material about life-chances that will be discussed later.

## Further thoughts

Can you make a good case for vulnerability being socially constructed rather than natural? Say how or why.

Does the idea that all children are vulnerable overlook the fact that some children might be vulnerable to others? Can children also be a threat?

Do some parents do too much and, in doing too much, make their children vulnerable?

Think about how ideas that children should be, and are, innocent contribute to their vulnerability.

## Further reading

Coram and Coram International (2017) provide a short account of how policymakers have tried to define and measure vulnerability. Furedi (2004) offers a critical account of how the rise of a therapy culture promotes the idea of vulnerability.

# 9

# Resilience

This chapter will help you to understand:

- why resilience should be seen as a process rather than a thing;
- how resilience might be developed;
- why overprotecting children can prevent the development of resilience.

## 9.1 Why is resilience important?

Chapter 7 discussed how in recent years a concern with wellbeing has become very important. But if we want children to experience wellbeing then we also have to consider what contributes to that. Chapter 8 explained how it is that the broader context of childhood can act to make some children more vulnerable than others, something which can obviously have an impact on wellbeing. However, one key aspect of achieving wellbeing is the ability to be resilient, and that is what we turn our attention to now.

At a basic level, resilience can be seen as being any individual's ability to deal with adversity. That might be dealing with problems as they happen or it could be overcoming them as we move forward (Frydenberg, 2008; Garrett, 2018). In looking at resilience in this way we can see how being resilient is important for our everyday life as we all encounter adversity in different shapes and forms just by being part of the social world.

---

**Pause for reflection**

It is really difficult to imagine that any of us will not experience some problems at some point within our lives. We could list a number of issues that have affected our lives.

Consider difficulty or adversity that you have encountered and have overcome. Think about how you achieved this.

---

It is important that we are able to cope with adversity; we all need to be resilient, and childhood and youth is a key time in our lives when we have experiences which contribute to how resilient we are. Very often, though, experiencing adversity is presented as something that is not good. Instead, and recognising that some adversities and situations can be unpleasant, try to consider how it is that experiencing some form of adversity is a crucial part of developing resilience. Look at it the other way around; if we never experience adversity, never experience things which cause us a problem, then we can never really learn how to deal with the problems that we will inevitably face in our lives.

## 9.2 What do we mean by resilience?

We have to be careful when thinking about resilience because just like lots of other concepts relating to social life we can see how it is a very slippery concept (Ecclestone and Lewis, 2014; Taket et al, 2014; Martínez-Martí and Ruch, 2017). As individuals we might know what we mean by resilience but being confident that we all agree what we mean is not so easy. Because of this you might often find that some people use the term in slightly different ways. Don't worry about this. Just make sure that you always establish what you mean and then use it consistently.

---

**Note**

Traditionally, ways in which people talk about resilience have been dominated by ideas concerning an individual's character. This is a trait approach. The trait approach used to be very popular with respect to explaining why some of us are more resilient than others. Resilience was seen as something that we either had or didn't have.

More recent ideas about resilience, however, reject the idea that there is some inherent trait which means that we either are resilient or are not. Instead, it is better to see resilience as being the outcome of experiences, which means seeing it in terms of being a process (Fletcher and Sarkar, 2013). By adopting this approach we can see that practitioners work to promote resilience (Hamilton, 2011).

---

Adopting the approach which sees resilience as a process also means accepting that unless individuals experience some type of adversity it is hard to develop resilience.

---

**Pause for reflection**

Consider the way that we are protected against diseases by being given inoculations. Inoculations involve vaccinations which give us a mild dose of a disease so that our bodies can develop resistance to it.

As we go through life and have experiences we develop coping skills that build our resilience which help us to deal with bigger problems.

But what if we avoid doing things and never encounter challenges?

---

As you would expect with something that is so important, a number of writers have explored issues to do with resilience and it is always useful to read a few sources to develop your own understanding. For example, Olsson et al (2003), who are focused on adolescence, are useful in showing different ways in which we can understand resilience. Importantly, though, they also consider how wellbeing fits into our understanding of resilience. In addition, they also show how important it is to take social factors into consideration. In doing this they draw attention to the differences that are evident if we see resilience as an individual characteristic or trait that we can be said to possess compared to seeing it as a process.

When we start to see resilience as a process then we are drawn into understanding it in a broader sense. So, if we see resilience as a process rather than a characteristic, we have to also recognise that it is not fixed. Instead, we have to see it as something that is dynamic (Hamilton, 2011). If something is said to be dynamic, it simply means that it is constantly changing. That doesn't mean that it is changing a lot, just that it is changing to some extent. By recognising resilience as being dynamic we start to see how the extent to which we are resilient is always changing. So, if you think about yourself, by seeing resilience as a process you may recognise that there are some times and some situations where you are more resilient but there are other times when you are less resilient. This is a much better model than saying that we either have or do not have resilience. At the same time we might start to see how individuals can become less resilient over time.

With this in mind, we then have to return to a consideration of what it is that might support our development of resilience or which may maintain the resilience that we have. This means that we have to think about the factors which can contribute to the ways in which we are able to build resilience (Taket et al, 2014).

---

### Pause for reflection

We have said that as we go through life and engage with experiences this helps us to develop resilience, but what we might call support systems or networks can also help.

Take a few minutes to think about the systems and networks of support that are available that help you in your studies.

---

Very often this can be seen as the outcome of the effect that three factors have on us. These three factors can be summed up as the individual, the family and the community. As always, though, a word of caution is appropriate.

These three factors may be the most influential of the factors which affect us in terms of developing and maintaining resilience, but we don't experience them in a vacuum. We are also subject to other things which can have an impact upon us, such as social policies at any given time, or the media. For example, think about how children and young people today are subject to pressures from social media that older people such as their parents or grandparents never experienced. This can create adversity, but it can also enhance support. So, if we take a broader view of the context in which any child or young person lives, we should be able to have a much better understanding of why it is that some children will cope but that others will seem to struggle, even though the adversity that they face may appear to be the same.

## 9.3 Can parents help to develop resilience?

What is not really in doubt is the importance of both developing and maintaining resilience. However, in Chapter 8 it was argued that children are very often seen as being in some way naturally vulnerable. If this is the case, then we should also consider the role of parents or carers in understanding resilience because children and young people tend to rely on parents or carers to provide for them. Note that not all children and young people live with parents and that some adults who take on the role of parents are not technically the parents of the children that they care for. For the purposes of simplicity we will refer to parents to mean parents and/or caregivers.

What parents do, particularly when it comes to what they do in the early years of a child's life, will have an influence on how children develop. As such it may not be surprising to see that types of parenting styles that are controlling or restrictive, such as helicopter parenting, are associated with leading to children displaying low levels of resilience (Taylor et al, 2013).

There are many factors which influence how a child develops. One factor is the extent to which a child is able to exert agency because this will influence their individual experience and have some impact upon the extent to which they are able to develop and maintain resilience (Hamilton, 2011). Remember that when we say agency in social science we are referring to any individual's capacity to act. To link back to Section 9.2, though, we should be aware that the political concerns of any government may increase or decrease the extent to which they are concerned with what happens within families, as well as greater or lesser concerns with the conditions within which families live.

## 9.4 Why we need adversity

You always need to be careful to consider how the concept of resilience is being defined and/or used in anything that you read. It is clear that we all need some degree of resilience. We will all experience some form of adversity at some time and it is important that we are able to deal with it. There is a tendency at the moment, however, to foreground adverse childhood experiences and to present these as the cause of later problems in adulthood. As always we have to remember that child development is not simple. It is never a case of cause and effect. As an issue, adverse childhood experiences have become quite important as a way of explaining why some children display social and emotional problems. However, not all children who could be said to have experienced adverse experiences have problems (Fergusson and Horwood, 2003). Always avoid falling into the trap of being deterministic. This means seeing that any event always has consequences. We agree that experiencing adverse childhood experiences can have an effect on children in later life but this is not bound to be the case.

The danger is in seeing adversity as both uniform, always the same, and of always being of major significance (Fletcher and Sarkar, 2013). The key thing is that all children will experience adversity and it is important that they do. In reality, then, children will experience a range of adversities which we could classify as being low level.

So, instead of seeing adversity as being present or absent, and always bad, see it as something that is experienced as a continuum. Recognise that there are adversities that are quite minor and there are those that are much more significant.

---

### Pause for reflection

Be careful not to make the mistake of thinking that everyone who experiences adverse childhood experiences will be harmed or display long-lasting behaviour as a consequence; they won't. Some may, but many others will deal with it, with or without support.

Further, think of the problems we experience in our lives as being on a continuum from minor to major.

Think about the saying 'first world problems'. This term refers to the sorts of problems that people who are generally fortunate might encounter. It is not that they are not relevant, just that they are minor compared to what some people experience.

OK, you couldn't find your phone this morning but is that the same sort of problem as not having access to clean drinking water? Both can be seen as adversities but not to the same extent.

---

We all experience adversities as part of normal life, and it is the case that for many reasons modern life can be stressful. We see evidence of what this means for children and young people in reports demonstrating increased levels of mental illness or decreased happiness. But think also about what you have read in this chapter. If we all need to experience adversity so as to develop and maintain resilience, we can recognise how having our encounters with adversity reduced will have a knock-on effect on our ability to be resilient. In other words, if we never face problems we never learn to deal with problems.

To end, then, think about the term that is often used with respect to your generation if you are the typical 18–22-year-old student: snowflake. The term snowflake is used to refer to young people who are said to lack the ability to cope with criticism or stress (Creasy and Corby, 2019). This is not to claim that the snowflake label is accurate. We would certainly not claim that young people cannot handle stress, mainly because it seems that the world is far more stressful now than it was when we were young. But, as a final thought, what if this is an accurate descriptor? What if young people cannot deal with stress or with criticism? Might it be because parents and other adults have sheltered them from it and therefore they have never learnt how to deal with it? Could it be that in trying to remove all adversity from children and young people's lives, as some parents seem to do, we have also reduced or removed opportunities to develop and maintain resilience? The chapters on risk and safeguarding that follow will be very useful if you want to explore this further.

## 9.5 What can I do with this?

The aim here is to provide a conclusion that illustrates how you might use this chapter. This will be done by picking out some key points that we think would be expected in an assignment on resilience. Bear in mind that your assignments may vary in what they are looking for and that the marker may be looking for something very specific. Always read your assignment guidance carefully and take advice about what is seen as a good assignment within your university.

We place a great deal of importance on writing because the real task of a student is to demonstrate that you understand the material that you have covered. If you can explain a complicated theory or idea in a clear and simple way you will always look better, yet students often make the mistake of thinking that the most important thing is to cover the right material. OK, you might get the content right but if you don't write clearly then a lot of your effort will have gone to waste, so get all the help that you can with writing and always make sure that you proofread and polish your assignments carefully at least three times before submission.

Of course, to be able to do this you have to recognise that the submission date of an assignment is not the date that you are working towards in terms of completing an assignment. You really need at least a week for proofreading and polishing.

But, with content in mind, an assignment on resilience really ought to make the point that:

- Resilience is important in that it contributes to wellbeing. This is important because you shouldn't just say that resilience is important; you have to say why.
- Experiencing some form of adversity or challenge is a crucial part of developing resilience, which means that if we remove all adversity from a child's life, we are not helping them to develop resilience.
- When we see resilience as being rooted in individual character, something that we either have or lack, then we can call it a trait.
- When we recognise that resilience is developed through experiences over time and that it has to be maintained we can see it as a process.
- If we see resilience as a process, we can recognise that it is not fixed, it is dynamic.

- Three factors – the individual, the family and the community – all contribute to developing resilience.
- Parenting styles can support or hold back the development of resilience.

When you write an assignment you will have to think about how you will introduce these points and make decisions about what order you cover them in. Think about the context in which you use them. So, what point can you make? In *Taming Childhood* (2019) we develop the argument that changes to parenting and practice that have been driven by worries about risk have meant that children and young people have fewer opportunities to develop resilience. You might think about how the points above fit in with this. You would then need to think about what you should read to be able to understand the issues. Use this book as the starting point and then think about how your reading provides you with the evidence (in the form of references) which will support your argument. Of course, what this also does is demonstrate how a concern with resilience is likely to mean that you also end up reading about risk. If so, then Chapter 10 will be helpful.

### Further thoughts

If we want children to develop resilience, should parents let children make mistakes? It has become a common parenting practice to prevent children from experiencing failure. This potentially means that children miss out on experiences because of parental fears of failure.

This can also extend to allowing children to avoid things that they think they may not like. How much should children be encouraged or permitted to avoid difficult experiences?

### Further reading

Creasy and Corby (2019) provide useful discussions of issues related to resilience such as helicopter parents and snowflakes. Olsson et al (2003) are good for linking resilience to wellbeing.

# 10

# Risk

This chapter will help you to understand:

- the ways in which resilience interacts with risk;
- how safety is prioritised over health in health and safety matters;
- how concerns with risk limit the lives of children.

## 10.1 Children, risk and resilience

As a student studying childhood or as a practitioner working with children and/or families you will be familiar, or will inevitably come to be familiar, with the practice of making risk assessments. You will also probably be aware of limitations that are placed on children's activities because of risk. There seems to be a widespread concern that children should not be subject to risks and that they should not experience harm.

This chapter takes a critical approach to understanding risk and proposes that risk is an essential part of growing up. That is not to say that we should allow children and young people the freedom to do anything. It is also not the case that we are suggesting that we allow children to come to harm. What is being suggested, however, is that the fear that adults have about risk can impoverish children's lives as they are often prevented from encountering anything that might be considered as risky.

This is important if we recognise that by removing all risks from children's lives we might also hinder the development of both self-esteem and of resilience. In making this claim you can start to see an example of what is meant by criticality within higher education. Remember, being critical is finding faults with theories or practice. It is about finding weaknesses in arguments and in showing what is wrong with them; it is not simply providing an opposing argument. So, it may seem perfectly reasonable to remove risk from children's lives so as to prevent harm, but by adopting a critical perspective it is possible to recognise that in doing so we may be undermining a child's capacity for development.

This critical approach is useful in illustrating how your studies in higher education often require a broad understanding of the issues. We can offer some simple definitions of some key ideas that are relevant to this book: what do we mean by risk, vulnerable, protective or resilient?

- Risk can be seen as something that can lead to harm; it may be a dangerous element or factor, but it may also be a hazard.
- To be vulnerable is to be capable of being physically, mentally or emotionally hurt.
- Protective refers to providing or being able to provide protection.
- To be resilient is to have the ability to recover from or adjust to adversity, the ability bounce back.

That seems straightforward but as a student you need to go further. You need to question the things that you encounter, to interrogate ideas. So, harm may be physical injury, but it may also be seen in low self-esteem in later life. Consider how health and safety relate to this. We tend to be very aware of an immediate risk of harm or to safety but are often much less aware of risks which impact upon health in the future.

---

**Pause for reflection**

Think of some immediate risks to children and young people.

Now think about things which cause problems for children in the future.

While we would never want children to suffer, some of the things we fear are very rare, but our actions to protect children can be quite intense and can have negative effects on their future.

For example, to protect children from possible abduction by a stranger, a very rare event, we don't give children freedom to go out independently. A lack of freedom to negotiate the world independently can lead to a lack of confidence to do so when we are older, and a fear of the world in general.

---

Think also about who is vulnerable. We have already demonstrated that we cannot take vulnerability for granted. We should not assume that all children are naturally, or equally, vulnerable. It could be reasonable to suggest that all children are likely to be at risk but that some are more vulnerable than others, as was suggested in Chapter 8.

One other word of caution is required. It is always important to see things as dynamic and to recognise that the risk of harm faced by a child or young person will not remain constant; nor will the child's ability or inability to deal with risks. For example, if, as we have said, the child is very young, then the risk is greater. As the child grows older so risk may be lessened. Think about the implications for children who are disabled, though, if achieving independence is important in reducing risks and if this is impacted by their disability.

It is also worth thinking about how we understand things as being risky or not. Calder (2008) draws on a number of studies to make the point that we are really not very good at assessing risk. This is because many of us struggle to understand probabilities. We consistently feel that activities over which we have no control pose a greater risk than those activities where we do have control. Calder points to driving a car compared to flying. Many people get very anxious about flying even though statistically it is far safer than driving. This is probably because we feel in control when driving, yet what we always fail to consider is that when we are driving we have no control over the actions of other drivers.

At this point it might be worth thinking about how ideas about risk have had an impact upon children's lives. Frank Furedi has introduced the idea that parents were becoming paranoid in respect of how they deal with their children's lives. Furedi (2001) provides examples of parents going to great lengths to oversee the safety of their children, such as following a school bus in case it has an accident while their child is on board. You will probably know of parents who refuse to allow their children to play in their own garden unless they are present to supervise them and watch over them constantly because of a fear of risk. You might even be that parent or have had parenting like this.

These examples illustrate how risk has come to influence parenting. Risk has also had an influence on government and organisational policies. For example, Turnbull and Spence (2011: 947) note that 'The documentary analysis supports the assertion that "risk" has underpinned UK Government policy across the field of children and young people since 1996/1997 but not in any consistent manner.' However, what Turnbull and Spence also demonstrate is that, although it is evident that some approaches see children and young people as *at* risk, other approaches see them as *the* risk! We can also consider that children and young people may be at risk from the actions of others but may also be at risk by engaging in risky behaviour themselves.

---

**Pause for reflection**

Can you give examples of concerns or behaviours which relate to the following:

- people who pose a risk to children and young people;
- risks children and young people pose to others;
- risky behaviour that children and young people engage in?

Consider which of these behaviours have the most serious outcomes for children, and which of these we have solutions to.

But also consider how solutions, such as not allowing children their freedom, can have unintentional negative consequences.

---

This means that there are three ways of thinking about risk:

1. Children and young people are at risk.
2. Children and young people are a risk.
3. Children and young people will do things which are risky.

As a student it is important to be precise when you write assignments. So, when you hear someone referring to risk or when you read about risk, especially in relation to children and young people, it is very important to be clear which of the three positions listed above applies. In listing these three approaches we can also start to appreciate that risk is not unambiguous. It is not always clear what is being referred to.

If you become, or if you are, a practitioner working with children and young people, it is important to focus on the types of risky behaviour that children and young people may engage in, but that does not mean that children and young people will see things the same way as you do. Children and young people are quite capable of understanding the world and of drawing conclusions. Be aware, however, that these might not be the conclusions that adults would draw. For example, we can be fairly confident that young people see rock climbing as risky even though we may argue that no harm will come to them because of the safety measures that are put in place. On the other hand, they may not see smoking as risky even though it is, and it can be easily demonstrated that it is.

Maybe in these examples it becomes evident that it is immediacy or delay in experiencing harm which impacts upon the ways in which we understand risk. Being aware of the immediate consequences of a fall when rock climbing intensifies the sense of risk about the activity, but the long-term detrimental effects of smoking reduce the understanding of the risk of smoking.

In thinking about how adolescents seem likely to engage in behaviours and actions which pose a risk to themselves it has been argued that this is because adolescents seek heightened sensations; they like the excitement. McElwee (2007), however, addresses the claim that adolescence is characterised by 'sensation seeking', and argues that this can be rejected as being too simplistic.

McElwee points to how adolescents can be seen to be:

> actively navigating risky behaviours such as not getting involved in potentially serious physical fights with peers that might involve the use of knives and baseball bats, not using needles to inject drugs, not walking around … unsafe locations, and, generally using their 'street knowledge' in avoiding situations or people that might pose a threat to them. (2007: 250)

This is important because McElwee is able to demonstrate that children and young people are not naïve, something that is often said of them; they are aware of risks. Coleman and Hagell (2007) note that 'for young people risk either involves a degree of chance, or it involves potential harm if precautions are not taken'. Importantly, Coleman and Hagell also argue that young people consistently refer to personal responsibility when it comes to engaging in risky behaviour.

In thinking about children, young people and risks it may be more accurate to say that at times they both underestimate and overestimate them. This idea can be seen in the work of Bond (2013) with respect to mobile phone use.

In reading Bond (2013) it can appear that children and young people display an unrealistic understanding of how mobile phones can offer protection. Think about children and young people as being in a situation in which mobile phones come to act as comfort blankets during a period when the young person is developing confidence in themselves.

However, just as we argued that we should not see all risks as the same, Coleman and Hagell argue that it may be useful to draw the distinction, as we have already done with risk factors, between those which are individual attributes, those which originate from within the family and those that depend on resources in the neighbourhood or community. Coleman and Hagell also argue that risk behaviours should be seen as exploratory. The notion of exploratory risk may be interesting and useful because what we really want is to see children and young people develop in a way which means that they can cope with risks. As has been established, this is generally referred to as resilience.

As was stated in Chapter 9 a simple definition of resilience is the ability of a child or young person to bounce back, to be able to deal with adversity (Frydenberg, 2008). In respect of the issues that are being covered in this chapter we can see how risks can help young people to discover their strengths, to enhance self-esteem through overcoming challenges and/or adversity, and, in doing so, this contributes to the individual's capacity to overcome adversity in the future.

In many ways the resilient child is the child that we would want to produce, the child that we would want to raise. By this we mean that when they have grown up, indeed while they are growing up, we would want to be able to reflect upon their development and say that we could be confident that they are able to cope. We must remember, though, that to develop resilience we need to encounter risk.

## 10.2 The move towards individual responsibility, reflexivity and choice

Giddens points to a concept that is seen as important in understanding social life: the concept or practice of reflexivity, a concern with self-reflection (Elliott and Lemert, 2014). This concept was first introduced in Chapter 2 and you will often come across it in respect of reflective practice. For Giddens, reflexivity is an essential part of social life. We naturally reflect upon the world that we live in and consider where, and how, we fit in. However, in contemporary society this process has been intensified. So, we can see that reflexivity becomes something that is not just what individuals do; it becomes a social practice in that we are expected, or even required, to do it.

What this means for society is that we come to see our lives as a project that we manage. We reflect on who we are, what our life is like, and then by considering the resources available to us we project manage our lives to achieve goals (Ferguson, 2003; D'Cruz et al, 2007). This sense of planning our own future is something that is very new.

---

**Pause for reflection**

As an example of reflexivity, think about how often you, as students, are advised to do things, or acquire skills and experience, such as to make yourself more employable.

Now ask older people if they ever thought about employability skills. It is likely that they would ask you what you mean.

We can see how this sense of reflexivity becomes embedded in all aspects of our lives such as reflecting upon the extent to which you are a good parent or a good friend and so on.

---

Within this reflective approach is an inevitable element of self-blame. It is individualistic; problems become your problems rather than being seen as resulting from social conditions. What we can see is that there has been a significant move towards reflexivity and that this is often bound up with ideas about accountability. In turn, this reflects a much more individualist account and can be seen as being something that is embedded within the political ideology of neoliberalism (Garrett, 2018). We can consider that this is an example of how a political ideology has real consequences for how we live our lives.

A key aspect of understanding how reflexivity shapes our concerns with risk can be seen by turning our attention to what we can call individualisation. By this we are saying that we become much more concerned with ourselves as individuals, something that we have already seen as being closely associated with neoliberal ideology. Our understanding of our self as an individual can be seen to have been heightened as things which can be seen as having bonded us together in previous generations have broken down. For example, we can see in the increase in single-parent households that the family has changed and, although we might still see the family as important, it is not as tight knit as it once was. Similarly, when we think about how social class impacted upon our lives in previous generations or how gender was experienced then we can see how social life seems much more flexible now. Old social bonds can be said to have broken down and we have become much more individualised.

This breakdown in more traditional forms of social systems is said to have increased both anxieties and responsibilities for individuals. Think about how it was that for a long time, working-class boys in particular would often be expected to follow their fathers into industrial occupations and women were always seen primarily in terms of being housewives. This sort of world has gone and the need to define our own future becomes the prime motive for many, but this often means that it is pursued at the cost of commitments to others, and this has the effect of further weakening social ties. It is supported by the increased practice of being reflective, of reflecting upon who we are and what we want our life to be. So, if we agree with Beck and Giddens that we have become much more reflective and come to call this reflexive modernity then, we can start to see how it is that contemporary society impacts upon our lives in a way that heightens our sense of risk.

Alongside this is the growing prominence in our lives of the idea of choice. The situations that we find ourselves in are often seen as being the consequences of the choices that we make but this is a poor explanation really. Lupton (1999) illustrates this by referring to debates around the case of in vitro fertilisation in Australia. She shows how, in contemporary society, social changes which have led to more women staying in education longer and pursuing careers, or marrying later, results in many women not wanting to get pregnant until they are in their late 30s or into their 40s.

However, what we do know is that it is harder for women to get pregnant at an older age. This is a biological reality. It is easier to get pregnant at 23 than it is at 43. When women cannot get pregnant, though, it becomes recast, not as the consequences of social changes which have led to many women deferring pregnancy, but as the consequence of individual life-choices or even as a problem relating to health. Please do not see this as an argument that women should not stay in education or pursue careers; it is simply an example of a particular consequence of social change.

Personal or individual choices often loom large in discussions of risk, but they tend to do so in a way which ignores the social context. So, what we find is that in any society there are some things which are understood as being risky and other things which are not.

---

**Pause for reflection**

Do an internet search for 'human towers'.

This Catalan tradition of building human towers ends with young children climbing to the top of the tower without a safety harness.

Now consider how many parents in the UK would let their children do this. But many parents will regularly strap their children into a vehicle that they will then drive at high speed, sometimes in a very dangerous manner.

Is this because parents feel control in one situation but not the other?

---

## 10.3 Are we protecting children when we remove all risks?

If you think back to what was covered earlier, it was said that to understand childhood it is important to consider the social, cultural and political context within which a child lives. That is because these three factors all act to shape how a child experiences life. It was also said that if a child is to develop and maintain resilience it is important that they encounter adversity so that they can develop approaches to deal with it. Now consider how young adults are often referred to as snowflakes and wonder if any inability of young adults to handle adversity or criticism could be a consequence of having been sheltered from it while growing up. Consider how children are being metaphorically wrapped up in cotton wool by overprotective parents and think about how parental fears about risk may be the one thing that makes their children more vulnerable and less resilient.

If you end up working with children and young people you will often be called upon to assess risks, and there is much evidence to demonstrate that concerns about risks have led to children being restricted in what they can do or in terms of what we provide for them. Wheway (2007) provides lots of examples about how health and safety concerns are employed to reduce risks. However, it is important to consider the nature of each because what we might recognise is that they have different concerns, concerns which may be contradictory. For Wheway, what stands out is that very often safety takes precedence over health. That is worth thinking about. What he is saying is that anxieties about safety lead to restrictions being placed on what children can do, but this very often means they live sedentary lives, in ways which may have significant consequences for their health as adults, as we have argued.

In terms of social, cultural and political issues you may want to draw upon the model that was presented by Bronfenbrenner (1979) in Chapter 1. In Bronfenbrenner's model the child is at the centre, but they exist within a series of contexts which Bronfenbrenner represents as concentric circles. This is a very useful model for getting us to consider the ecology, or the environment, of the child. The child's experiences are, to a large part, shaped by others. If the outer ring represents society and society is preoccupied with risk, it can be seen how the rings that are nearer to the child are influenced by what is happening in society in general. This takes us back to examples provided earlier of parents restricting what their children can do or where they can go because of anxieties about risk (Jenkins, 2006; Guldberg, 2009).

This may be a good time to revisit the debate within sociology between approaches that rest upon structure and those that rest upon agency. This is because on the one hand we have suggested that society has become more individualised and that this rests upon individual choices and behaviours, and on the other hand we have pointed to the ways in which social structures provide the context for this individualisation. We are, of course, concerned with what this means for children, young people and families so we will point to issues that are relevant to those.

## Note

In terms of structure, we can say that socio-cultural practices and policies, along with social divisions, act as structures within which the child lives.

In terms of agency, we are considering those behaviours that the child chooses, such as how they spend their free time and with who, although we might consider that this is not entirely free and that it usually changes with age and independence.

In considering how parents come to wrap their children up in cotton wool we inevitably look for influences upon their lives. One important factor is the media. Think what Lupton (1999: 17) is saying when she says that 'Blame is also often a key aspect of media coverage of risk.' Consider how accidents and tragedies seem to be approached by the media with a concern to apportion blame. Interestingly, she also comments that 'media attention to a risk issue does not necessarily translate into concern on the part of lay audiences' (1999: 18). In part this reflects the idea that ordinary people have become more sceptical about experts.

## 10.4 Where do I fit this in?

This chapter will end as others have done and pick out some key points that would reasonably be expected in an assignment about risk. As before, this is not to say that these are the only important points because your assignment might want something very specific. As was said previously, always read your assignment guidance carefully and take advice about what will attract higher marks.

### Study tip

You probably have marking criteria which try to define what an assignment will look like in any grade band, such as a 2:1 or a 2:2. However, marking criteria are very difficult to write in a way that is totally unambiguous, so you have to see them as guides rather than fixed definitions.

For example, if the criteria states that to be awarded a 2:2 mark your work has to be good, what does good mean? Does it mean every part has to be good?

What this really means is that the advice given previously about the need for clear writing stands. Always give lots of time to proofreading before submission.

Never see a submission date as the date when you have to finish your assignment; it isn't. The submission date is when it has to be submitted by. Always aim to give yourself at least one week before to proofread.

So, an assignment on risk really ought to make the point that:

- Risk refers to something that can lead to harm. This could be physical injury now, but it could be a problem that is only evident much later, such as poor health.
- Risk has come to play a major part of practice with children and young people.
- We need to experience risk as part of our development. If we remove all risks from children's lives, we will hold back the development of both self-esteem and resilience.

- Risk is dynamic. The risk of harm faced by a child or young person will not remain constant, nor will the child's ability to deal with risk.
- We often see risk as lower when we are in control and higher when we are not in control.
- Risk has shaped social and public policy relating to children and young people.
- We might see children and young people as being at risk, as being a risk and as doing things which are risky.
- Risk factors may originate in the individual, in the family and in the community.
- Risk society contributes to increased individualisation and a sense that we have to project manage our own lives.

Depending on the course that you are on, you might find that some of the issues covered in this chapter are more useful than others. Some courses will emphasise risk in more practical terms such as risk assessments whereas others will be more critical and will want to evaluate the ways in which risk shapes how we go about our lives and what this means in providing for children and young people. Be careful in what you choose from this chapter. Don't write an assignment to a different question! It happens. Considering context is important, but if you are asked for something very specific then provide something very specific. Chapter 11 will be useful if you have an assignment which asks you to explore the consequences of risk and the ways in which we may go about providing for children and young people facing risks in that it looks at safeguarding. Inevitably, though, it will draw a distinction between safeguarding and child protection and consider the political context in which this may change.

### Further thoughts

Does childhood obesity suggest we are much more concerned with safety than we are with health? Think about the ways in which safety tends to dominate discussions of risk relating to childhood.

Consider how children's freedom to play outdoors unsupervised has been restricted because of fears about risks, limiting their physical activity.

Then think about what we feed children. As a society we permit children to be fed very unhealthy food on a regular basis that contributes to poor health.

### Further reading

Wheway (2007) is very good in distinguishing between risks relating to health and those relating to safety. It is easily accessed online.

# 11

# Safeguarding

This chapter will help you to understand:

- the difference between safeguarding and child protection;
- how safeguarding and/or child protection are always socially constructed;
- how we can distinguish between a child in need and a child being harmed.

## 11.1 How culture and values define a child in need and a child being harmed

So far, arguments have been put forward which indicate that it is important for children and young people to have resilience so that they may cope with adversities in the future. It has also been suggested that a growing concern with risk has impacted upon the lives of children and young people in terms of what they are able to do and that this is counter-productive with respect to developing and maintaining resilience. That said, there are children and young people who do face adversities of a kind that they really should be protected from.

Because of this we now move on to consider a number of issues regarding how society safeguards children and young people from harm. The aim is to provide a discussion of issues related to safeguarding and child protection so that you may understand, and might write about, the ideas and concerns which underpin safeguarding more effectively.

We start this chapter by drawing a distinction between safeguarding and child protection. The first thing to establish is that safeguarding is much broader than child protection. So, it may be more accurate for you to recognise that child protection is an aspect of safeguarding. Safeguarding is concerned with keeping all children safe. Child protection is focused on protecting identified children from harm.

This returns us to something that was said before in that as a student it is always important to be precise when you write. Think carefully about the words that you use. This can be seen as returning to the importance of discourse, especially in terms of the language that we use to describe things and how this shapes our understanding. Consider the following example from May-Chahal and Coleman (2003: xv), who avoid the term 'child abuse', preferring instead to use 'child maltreatment' and 'significant harm'. They offer three reasons for this:

157

- Most European countries reserve the use of abuse for cases of sexual abuse, having other terms that approximate to maltreatment.
- The term child abuse suggests that there is a proper use for children, reflecting ideas about ownership.
- As a term, child abuse may be seen as too general as it has come to refer to a range of harms as well as to behaviours which sometimes lead to no harm at all.

It is worth reiterating that providing detailed descriptions of a range of terms is beyond the scope of this book. The aim of this book is to get you to think about principles and to introduce you to critical ideas about such principles. There are other books which are much more focused on the details (see 'Further reading').

When it comes to safeguarding it is accepted that safeguarding and/or protection is required in cases relating to the maltreatment of children and young people. Such maltreatment may range from physical or sexual abuse to neglect. The Children Act 1989 introduced the test of significant harm as being the trigger in respect of intervening to protect children. This sounds straightforward: if a child or young person is experiencing significant harm then there is a duty to protect them. As with some other concepts that were introduced previously, though, the act is not as clear cut as it first suggests. The problem is that the Children Act did not define what significant harm is and practitioners are required to make a judgement about the extent to which the child is likely to be harmed and the possibility of such harm continuing. Griffith (2009) and Holt (2014) both provide a good account of the Children Act.

May-Chahal and Coleman (2003) make a good point in relation to this. They draw attention to how we might distinguish between a child in need and a child being harmed. This distinction makes more sense by considering some previous guidance from the Department for Education and Skills (DfES, 2006) which identified three domains within which issues may arise that see the need for safeguarding actions to take place. This meant that practitioners at the time were being asked to consider information and analysis relating to:

- the child's developmental needs;
- the parents' or caregivers' capacity to respond appropriately to those needs; and
- the wider family and environmental factors.

---

**Note**

You will often come across the term 'toxic trio' in respect to safeguarding.

It refers to the way that children are deemed to be at greater risk if their home life involves parents with mental health issues, substance abuse, such as drug taking, and if there is violence such as domestic abuse.

The toxic trio is useful in demonstrating how concerns with keeping children and young people safe have moved beyond a concern with direct actions against the child. The toxic trio encourages us to consider the context within which the child lives in a way which acknowledges that the social context can shape the personal experience.

However, as Morris et al (2018) demonstrate, although the term toxic trio has become commonplace within social work practice, there is a danger that it restricts thinking about safeguarding to characteristics of the family and of the idea of toxicity itself rather than what is leading to harm. To consider the wider context read Morris et al (2018) and Featherstone et al (2017).

This is a good time to return to a point that was made previously about the way in which some things look obvious. We can look at the three domains, or three aspects, of a child's life as discussed and think that they are obvious, that they are unambiguous, but are they? We could consider the extent to which we really know what the child's developmental needs are, or consider the extent to which we can say that parents or caregivers are able to respond to those needs. Then we have to think about the wider family or environmental context. (Remember Bronfenbrenner's concentric circles?)

### Pause for reflection

Give some thought to what it is that means that some children may be at greater risk than others. Which children are at risk?

Do you think that some families pose a greater risk to children than others?

Now think about how difficult it is for practitioners to remain objective at all times, yet that is what is required of them. Fontes (2005) raises an interesting point relating to child abuse in the US which addresses this by raising ideas that can be understood as the consequences of racism. She notes that, although there are no significant differences in incidences of maltreatment between African Americans and White Americans, African Americans are more likely to be accused of maltreatment and to have this upheld in investigations. This then has the consequence of seeing greater numbers of children of colour being removed from the home.

Think about how this might be as a consequence of ideas that are held about some social and/or ethnic groups. For example, Fontes talks about how boundaries are established in families and how some families have very fixed or rigid boundaries and others are more flexible. Her discussion of the flexible boundaries that are said to be seen in many poor or ethnic minority families is interesting as it reveals how diverse practices can be understood within a cultural context. In a similar context within the UK, Featherstone et al (2017) point out that children from deprived communities are far more likely to be removed from the family than are children who live in wealthy communities.

With this in mind, think about your own values and beliefs. Can practice be separate from values and beliefs? It seems reasonable to suggest that practice cannot develop in a way that is totally separate from our values and beliefs and our individual values and beliefs may be very deep-seated. We can be critical of the society that we live in but it is not always easy. Some things just seem unquestionable. Practice changes because of factors such as policy change, political direction and funding. In turn, this will have an impact on our opinion of what is acceptable or not.

In relation to child protection, you may also come across the idea of thresholds. To define thresholds is to suggest that there is a point at which a child is more or less at risk. You may also be exposed to the term 'good enough' parenting. This again aims to define a standard of parenting that will ensure that a child develops sufficiently and will not suffer harm despite the absence of things that others may assume to be essential, such as a lack of material possessions or a lack of educational ability of the parents. It may also apply where there is the presence of behaviour that some would find difficult to tolerate, such as drug and alcohol use.

However, when we think about it there is often nothing inevitable about thresholds or about what is seen as being good enough. These come to be established within a social context and in a way which means that they act as tools which enable practitioners to operate in their jobs. They are not fixed, though. They can change.

So, as an example, consider practitioners working with parents where drug use is evident.

---

**Pause for reflection**

Imagine that you are part of a team at a multi-agency meeting, sharing information regarding a family and looking at how the child and family can be best supported. A decision has to be taken about the risk posed to the child by the parents' drug use. Illegal drug use can be seen as a major risk to the safety of the child. As a worker you may feel that any drug use suggests these parents are unfit to appropriately care for their child. You may be right; however, let's consider knowledge, values and beliefs.

How knowledgeable are you on the impact of drugs on behaviour? How knowledgeable are you on the habits and behaviours of those that take drugs?

Now think about alcohol and how many parents regularly drink alcohol. Alcohol use presents risks to children yet as alcohol is legal we often overlook its use.

---

Sometimes professionals have to develop the ability to set aside their own values and beliefs and accept that others can lead different lives from what they may experience and yet still be good parents. This is not to say that this is always true, but you should consider that it is possible.

## 11.2 Should we keep all children and young people safe?

Before 1997, the focus of child protection work was on identifying those children who were deemed to be at risk and working, or intervening, to prevent this. After 1997 and the election of the Labour government under Tony Blair, this focus on child protection can be seen to have been replaced by a concern with safeguarding. What you will often read is that this was as a consequence of one particular case relating to one particular child, Victoria Climbié. Victoria Climbié was murdered by her aunt and her aunt's boyfriend in February 2000. It was a case which came to dominate what was happening within children's services at the time and for some time afterwards, but it is not true to say that the shift to safeguarding was solely because of this one case. Ideas were changing and this case simply came to act as a focal point.

---

**Note**

In considering the move from a focus on child protection to a focus on safeguarding it is important to recognise that the ideas which underpin each also change.

From the position of child protection the child is at risk from the actions of specific adults. Very often this was seen as family members. The focus therefore is quite narrow. It is on particular children at risk from particular adults.

In safeguarding the risk is shared by all children. All children can be harmed, and all adults can be the threat. In this approach we all come to be seen as a potential threat and we all come to have responsibility for keeping children safe.

---

We can see this in the introduction of Criminal Records Bureau checks (CRB) and how these came to be used in ways that restricted how adults could interact with children and young people. Under this system adults were required to have a CRB check to work with children and young people. There was a further consequence to the introduction of CRB checks, though, in that they also came to represent safety in a way which simplified the issue of risk or threat. Having a clean CRB check came to be denoted as signalling safety. Note that CRB checks have since been replaced by the Disclosure and Barring Service check.

In the shift from child protection to safeguarding there is also a further aspect that is certainly worth considering. Child protection always seems to reflect ideas about others being a threat to children, usually adults. In terms of safeguarding there is a much broader approach being taken and this shows us how the introduction of new policies changes how we see things.

As we have said, the Victoria Climbié case is often presented as being the catalyst for change and can be seen to have been influential in the development of the policy framework called Every Child Matters. In 2003 the Labour government published a plan for a new policy approach that was aimed at improving the life experiences of children and young people: Every Child Matters: Change for Children. This policy document highlighted the need for a comprehensive revamp of the services available to children, young people and their families. Four key themes were at the centre of this initial green paper, which aimed to strengthen preventative services. These were:

- increasing the focus on supporting families and carers;
- ensuring that necessary intervention takes place before children reach crisis point and protecting children from falling through the net;
- addressing the underlying problems identified in the report into the death of Victoria Climbié, said to be weak accountability and poor integration;
- ensuring that people working with children are valued, rewarded and trained.

Every Child Matters can best be understood as a framework which shaped how practitioners working with children carried out their work. It strongly influenced the Children Act (2004). Overall, it did much to shape how practitioners engaged with and provided for children. Every Child Matters promoted five key outcomes with the aim being that every child (0–19 years), whatever their situation or background, would have access to the support required to:

- be healthy;
- stay safe;
- enjoy and achieve;
- make a positive contribution; and
- achieve economic wellbeing.

These five themes then were established as the principal goals that Every Child Matters set out to achieve. Consequently, agencies and practitioners could be seen to organise and evaluate themselves in terms of the five outcomes. In turn, this was encouraged by Ofsted inspections which assessed how schools and Children's Centres met these outcomes. Although Every Child Matters was effectively shelved in 2010 when the Conservative-led Coalition government came to power, it can still be said to have some influence today. A very good discussion of what Every Child Matters was can be found in Knowles (2009).

Importantly, the Every Child Matters framework had a significant influence on practice, especially with respect to safeguarding, epitomised in the outcome Stay Safe. The influence that this had, however, was very often on the way that practitioners turned their focus onto making the environment safe and how this included becoming increasingly aware of how children's own behaviours may serve to create risk.

## 11.3 Sex, technology and risk

In the last couple of decades in particular there has been a growing concern regarding the idea that children and young people need to be protected in respect of sexual activity, especially from adults; something that seemed to become much more prominent as the UK moved towards a safeguarding approach. This is not entirely new as the UK, in line with most countries, establishes an age at which young people are deemed to be able to give consent to engaging in sexual activity (Moore and Reynolds, 2018). In some ways the ideas that underpin a sexual age of consent reflect ideas about development and what can be called age-appropriate behaviour. Having an age of consent indicates a belief that children and young people either cannot make rational decisions regarding natural human behaviours prior to a particular level of development or that they constitute a socially vulnerable group who require protection from other members of society. Maybe it is both! However, one thing which demonstrates the extent to which these ideas are social in nature rather than being somehow natural or obvious is that there are significant differences regarding what the age of consent should be and what it is.

So, just as we have argued that discourse can shape our understanding of the world that we live in, we might consider that legal structures can do the same. How we approach protecting and safeguarding children may be shaped by values and beliefs which are found within discourses regarding sexual behaviour, and which underpin legal structures, but where the legislation often becomes taken for granted.

---

**Pause for reflection**

How times change …

To illustrate how social attitudes differ and change try to find out what age Elvis Presley, a revered entertainer, was when he met his future wife and how old she was.

In Shakespeare's *Romeo and Juliet*, how old is Juliet?

In 1969 the rock group Blind Faith released an album featuring a topless 11-year-old girl on the cover. It is still available to buy today.

Also, consider the Tate gallery. The Tate is a nationally renowned art gallery and many art galleries show nudes in paintings and photographs. In September 2009 the Tate removed a picture of the actress Brooke Shields posing nude. In the photograph that was removed she was ten years old.

Looking at cases such as these demonstrates that ideas about what is appropriate change. You might be able to find other examples.

---

Similarly, laws differ or change. Many teenagers may engage in sexual activity which is illegal because of the age of consent, but what is illegal in the UK may not be illegal elsewhere. In thinking about harm, however, it is possible to see consenting behaviour between two 15-year-olds as illegal but not abusive.

That said, look at how ideas about what is right or wrong can come up against the law. In 2015 a 17-year-old boy from Fayetteville, North Carolina, was charged with possessing child pornography when his phone was found to contain photos of himself naked. In 2014 Nottinghamshire Police warned under-18s that they could be placed on the Sex Offenders Register for distributing child pornography if they shared nude photos that they had taken of themselves (*Guardian*, 2014). Currently in the UK 16-year-olds can legally engage in sexual activity but cannot legally possess nude photos of each other as this constitutes child pornography. Now consider also that in UK law individuals can marry at 16.

The relevance of these examples is in the fact that typically we have tended to assume that children face risks from others who will treat them in ways that can cause them harm. What we must also remember is that children's behaviour may be risky in itself and therefore children and young people may pose risks of harm to themselves in varying ways. Alongside this the practice of sexting or taking nude selfies illustrates how the world that we live in may create new risks (Megele and Buzzi, 2018; Moore and Reynolds, 2018). The invention and mass adoption of mobile phones with the capacity to record still and video images, together with the possibility of instantly distributing such images, have created this new risk.

Our intention is not to be Luddites here and it is not to argue that new technologies have created new behaviours; rather it is to demonstrate that new technologies have the ability to change behaviours in ways which increase the risks that young people face even when based upon consensual behaviour.

---

### Pause for reflection

When you were at school did you know of anyone who had shared sexts?

The possession of indecent images and videos of minors can lead to imprisonment and to being recorded on the Sex Offenders Register.

If we consider the increase in practices such as sexting, we can see why it is that most sex offenders are under 25.

In respect of legal definitions of minors regarding indecent images, within the UK, a child is established as being below the age of 18 as a consequence of the Sexual Offences Act 2003.

Crown Prosecution Service information regarding indecent material is available online.

---

This act extended the Protection of Children Act 1978 to cover indecent photographs of children aged 16 and 17. The act also introduced a new set of offences specifically dealing with the exploitation of children through child abuse images, providing protection for all children up to the age of 18. Note that the definition of a child was altered from 16 to 18 years by section 45(1) of the Sexual Offences Act 2003, in force from 1 May 2004. Of course, depending on when you read this, it may have changed again. Always be careful to check details when it relates to the law.

The advent of mobile phones incorporating digital cameras and video recorders together with internet resources such as social-networking or video-sharing sites has also opened up new avenues for bullying and risks (Megele and Buzzi, 2018). Not only can indecent and/or embarrassing images and videos be posted on the internet, but mobile phones and social-networking sites provide opportunities for the posting of malicious texts and comments.

Although privacy settings and the ability to block numbers seem sensible ways of avoiding the experience of cyber bullying, it may be that the best approach is caution. Remember also that organisations such as schools, care homes and colleges have a duty of care to safeguard young people.

## Note

At this point it might be worth considering your own cyber presence.

Before we are critical of young people's use of the internet consider how you might have used the internet and what material someone might be able to find about you.

Now think also that employers have been known to search the internet in relation to applicants for jobs and that some people have lost their jobs because of the material that they have posted on sites such as Facebook.

As an example, consider the case of Rachel Burns from 2015 (McDermott, 2017).

In one sense cases about the internet and social media usage point to the way in which safeguarding can be seen as a more useful approach towards providing for children and young people than is child protection. If we only focus on physical threats then we are very likely to miss some children who are experiencing other types of harm. But, to repeat something that was said before, when we want to understand the ways in which we provide for children and young people and when we want to make sense of how children and young people experience their lives it is important that we take a broad perspective. If you are to write good academic assignments you are usually going to be drawn into considering the social, cultural and political contexts within which children and young people live. In one sense it may appear to be moving away from the actual issues that children and young people face, but it is very important if we are to understand childhood.

## 11.4 The social and political context

Earlier it was said that the case of Victoria Climbié was very important with respect to how safeguarding developed in the UK. We could ask why it was that this case changed things when there were very many cases of children being harmed and even killed before this. Parton (2004) offers a good account of how social change can be seen as the context for the shift from child protection to safeguarding by looking at an equally distressing case from the 1970s, that of Maria Colwell. In one sense, what is evident when reading Parton is that he is suggesting that particular cases come to be seen as emblems of particular social problems. As such they act as triggers or catalysts for changes to the existing system. What Parton also does, though, is to turn our attention to the social context within which systems such as children's services operate.

So, with this in mind, think about two aspects of change that are relevant. The first is social change and how this has had an impact upon the family. The second is political change and how this has changed the context within which we understand social services.

When it comes to the family, Parton demonstrates how the social context of families has become quite complex and diverse, something that was discussed in Chapter 2. With respect to the political context, politicians have done much to contribute to a reduction in trust in, for example, social workers and have contributed to changes to the way that they work. For example, in a paper about the death of another child, Peter Connelly, often referred to as Baby P, Joanne Warner (2013) talks about how social workers come to be seen as uncaring and as working to a tick-box system. However, it would be wrong of us to think that social workers have in some way decided among themselves that this is how they will work. It would be better to consider the extent to which the way that they work has been changed by others. One way of understanding this is to see how their work has been changed by something that is often referred to as a managerialist way of working. In turn, managerialism is something which is often presented as being closely associated with neoliberalism (Creasy, 2018).

Managerialism, sometimes referred to as New Public Management (NPM), is an approach that is concerned with how managers come to exert control over the work of others. It especially relates to the type of work that we may see as professional but which exists within the public sector, such as teaching or social work. It can be argued that managerialism is a way in which neoliberalism comes to shape public services (Ball, 2016). Managerialism promotes the adoption of business-like principles within social or public services. It adopts bureaucracy and form-filling as a way of exerting control over types of work that are not easy to oversee in a direct sense.

It is important to state, however, that the NPM approach which leads to managerialism existed before neoliberalism and that it is an approach that has been adopted by governments that would not be seen as neoliberal (Hood, 1991). So, Blair's Labour governments significantly increased the use of target-setting within public services alongside concerns about accountability, which may be seen to have increased bureaucracy and form-filling within public services. Hood (1991) identifies seven key features of NPM:

1. Greater hands-on management.
2. Explicit standards and measures of performance.

3. Greater emphasis on output controls.
4. 'Disaggregation' of units in the public sector.
5. Greater competition in the public sector.
6. Stress on private-sector styles of management practice.
7. Stress on greater discipline and parsimony in resource use.

These features will be recognised by many workers within social services and can be understood as a way in which the context of such services operate. In turn this has consequences for how individuals experience such services and how effective they are.

So, what we must always consider is that to understand something such as practice with children, young people and families, it is important to consider the social, cultural and political context at the time. As such, we might see how the Climbié case provided an opportunity for the Labour government from 1997 to establish that they had a different approach from the neoliberal-influenced Conservative governments led by Thatcher and Major. So, it might not be that this case is particularly different, or that it is particularly shocking. It might just be that it happened at the right time for a particular government: in this case, the Labour government.

During the 1980s and 1990s the neoliberal governments led by Margaret Thatcher and John Major were often accused of being uncaring because of the way in which they cut support for social services. The Coalition and Conservative governments made deeper cuts after 2010 but during the 1980s and 1990s funding cuts were a new, unwelcome development within social services. Thatcher in particular was criticised for a comment she made saying that there was no such thing as society (Thatcher, 1987). The turn towards safeguarding and the Every Child Matters agenda was the basis of another key difference between the neoliberal-inspired Conservative governments from 1979 to 1997 and the Labour governments under Tony Blair.

Think about this. Thatcher and Major were criticised for apparently not being bothered about many people in society, especially the poor. In one sense, the Labour Party under Tony Blair needed to demonstrate that it had an alternative vision for society, a society whereby the government was concerned with everyone. In terms of what we are concerned with in this book we can start to see how, under Blair's New Labour government, the policy framework which came to be presented as Every Child Matters promotes the idea that the government is bothered about all children. This suggests a much more inclusive approach and clearly responds to Thatcher in the implicit argument that there is such a thing as society. But, what also changes is that we move away from a system in which some children are at risk, as in child protection, and we see the introduction of an approach whereby all children are at risk and safeguarding is everyone's responsibility. What's more, risk itself comes to be a much broader concern and is no longer confined to threats to children which are rooted within the home and/or from family members.

In this way, the political perspective of the government at the time, in this case the Labour government, who adopted a much more inclusive approach than previous governments, is made real in the way that it establishes a policy framework which influences society in a wide-reaching manner. The key thing for you to take note of here is that things do not just happen with respect to how we provide for children, young people and families. It is always important to consider the social and political context within which developments can be seen to take place. So, from 2010 the move away from safeguarding and back towards child protection, with its greater concern about individual children, rather than all children, can be understood in the context of the change of government in 2010 and the return to power of a more explicitly neoliberal government with a much more individualistic outlook.

## 11.5 Making use of this in assignments

It is perfectly reasonable to imagine that you will take a module on safeguarding and/or child protection and find that you are being asked to consider very specific issues such as legislation and details about practice such as what to do if you suspect a child is being abused. In this book we have avoided that level of detail. Our concerns are always about developing an understanding of safeguarding overall. This will include how child protection fits in and the political dimension to this. So, as always, think about the key points that we would expect to see in an assignment on safeguarding but see them as suited to an assignment that is broad. If your task is very specific use what you need. That said, it will always be important to consider the following:

- Child protection is an aspect of safeguarding. Child protection tends to be very focused on children identified as being at risk of being harmed. Safeguarding is a much broader approach that covers all children.
- The Children Act 1989 introduced the test of significant harm as being the trigger to intervene to protect children but did not specify what significant harm is.
- The Every Child Matters framework did much to bring safeguarding to the fore.
- The toxic trio of parents with mental health issues, substance abuse and violence are important in safeguarding practice.
- Safeguarding practice will require an understanding of values.
- We may safeguard children from others and from themselves.
- As new technologies develop, they may create new risks which require changes to how we safeguard.

You can probably see how safeguarding follows on from risk but safeguarding could also be seen as more likely than other aspects of work with children and young people to be subject to political change. Think about how child protection emerged in a focused way and then became much broader as part of the Every Child Matters agenda. This means that you might have to be more careful when it comes to assignments because this is one area where you might be tied to particular aspects.

---

### Further thoughts

Does a clean Disclosure and Barring Service check guarantee safety?

Does the safeguarding agenda cast all adults as a potential threat? Might this impact upon men rather than women? What about men working in childcare?

In what ways do contemporary social media or file-sharing platforms pose risks to children and young people and how might we address such risks?

---

### Further reading

Holt (2014) provides a good account of the Children Act. Lindon et al (2016) provide a very accessible discussion of safeguarding, including good descriptions of the range of issues involved. Morris et al (2018) argue for a broader understanding of what may harm children and point to wider structural factors such as the harms posed by poverty and deprivation.

# 12

# Life-chances, inequalities and social mobility

This chapter will help you to understand:

- what is meant by life-chances and life-choices;
- why social mobility does not solve problems resulting from inequality;
- how changes to housing policy make life harder for poorer children.

## 12.1 How life-chances explain social inequalities

The term life-chances comes from the work of Max Weber, a German sociologist. It has come to be in widespread use in recent years. This is especially the case in relation to children, where ideas about life-chances are often to be found in arguments about social mobility and education (Goldthorpe, 2016b; Munro, 2019).

When we talk about life-chances we implicitly acknowledge the fact that children do not share the same opportunities in terms of their futures. These differences are rooted within their childhood environment in terms of how this provides either opportunities or obstacles to doing well in life.

---

**Pause for reflection**

Life-chances can be defined (simply) as any individual's potential to achieve that which is seen as socially desirable.

So, imagine that it is some time in the future and that you are, if you aren't already, a parent. If you want, you could do this exercise for yourself. Think about your children's future, or your own, and think about what you would want for your children, or for your own future. What would you desire?

Do you have a life-project plan? What is on it?

---

When it comes to desiring things for the future we often think about a good job, which tends to mean well paid and interesting. We also often think about owning a nice house, having a nice car and other things. When it comes down to it, we often want what we could call a good standard of living, to be happy and to have economic freedom.

We know that different jobs are paid at different levels. You will also be aware from previous discussions that in recent decades there has been a significant growth in precarious and insecure work in what has been called the gig economy. In addition to this we have already discussed how many workers have seen their wages fall in recent decades. But at the same time that wages have fallen for many, the value of welfare benefits in the UK has also fallen. What this means is that lots of people are not financially secure.

So, if we consider these changes, we can ask ourselves what sort of job would we want for ourselves or our future children. This is relevant when we think about children as we often see them in terms of what they will become. Would we want our children to have well-paid, secure jobs, or would we want them to have low-paid, insecure jobs? Put like that, the answer is obvious. It would be odd to hear anyone say that they would want their children to have low-paid, insecure jobs with no benefits. This is where the concept of life-chances becomes relevant.

In studying or working with children and families you will often come across ideas and issues related to life-chances and it is not at all unusual to hear for calls for improved life-chances for certain groups of children. Renaming the Child Poverty Act (2010) the Life Chances Act (2010) also suggests that life-chances are a current concern within contemporary UK society (Calder, 2018).

---

**Note**

Life-chances are an acknowledgement of social inequalities.

Think about this. There would be no need for improving life-chances if we lived in an equal society and it may therefore be possible to suggest that a focus on life-chances acts to reinforce social inequalities.

---

This is because by focusing upon life-chances we are effectively saying that we will accept that some children will experience poverty, and the disadvantages that come with it, but simply work to ensure that such children have the opportunities to escape poverty in adulthood.

---

**Pause for reflection**

Think about the sorts of things that will make it harder for children to achieve the things that are seen as desirable in life.

What are the advantages that help children achieve?

---

Importantly, when we speak of life-chances we are specifically referring to social factors which provide advantages for some and disadvantages for others. Importantly, we are not identifying the cause of differences as being rooted in individual characteristics. This is not to say that we do not have different characteristics or abilities which mean that some of us do better or worse than others but instead we are recognising that there are social factors which impact how our lives may turn out.

## 12.2 How life-choices explain social inequalities

At this point a word of caution is required. This chapter is concerned with illustrating how life-chances play a part in perpetuating or reinforcing inequalities; however, in recent years a similar-sounding, but very different, explanation has also been used: life-choices. It is important to recognise what is different about these explanations.

### Note

Life-choices as an explanation recognises that inequalities do exist but proposes that they can be explained as being a consequence of the choices that individuals make throughout their lives.

For example, you are reading this because you have chosen to study for a degree. We know that having a degree tends to improve your chances of both getting a job and getting a job with better pay. This means that we would expect that in the future you will be better off than someone without a degree. This is not necessarily the case but in general it is.

The term life-choices tends to be favoured by right-wing commentators. It is a seductive explanation but not a very good one, as we will explain.

As individuals we are always making choices. For example, we the authors haven't always been academics working within a university. When we decided, as adults, to become students and study for a degree, we each thought that this would enable us to get a better job. We made a choice within the context of knowing that some jobs paid more than others. Looking at it like this life-choices seems to be a way of explaining the differences which exist within society. It doesn't. In one sense life-choices reflects the idea of agency which we introduced earlier. Agency is important in lots of things but when it comes to inequalities structural matters are more important. If you live in a society where racist or sexist discrimination exists, some of you will face significant obstacles. You can work to change things but it could be very hard work.

### Pause for reflection

Another version of life-choices is what we could call 'wanting it'. Think of television programmes such as *Britain's Got Talent* or *The X Factor*. How often do contestants who are being voted off make a comment along the lines of their competitors wanting it more than them? Watch interviews with football players who have just lost a game and consider how often the loss is explained as being because the other team wanted it more.

But is wanting it enough? How often do you hear it said that as individuals we can do anything if only we want it hard enough, or if only we work hard enough? You probably hear this a lot, you might even say it a lot.

Creasy really wanted to play for Sheffield Wednesday Football Club. The only problem is that he wasn't good enough to get in a Sunday league pub team. Wanting it is not enough. Wanting something may provide motivation and working hard may help improve our abilities but they aren't enough to explain social inequalities.

---

A good way of demonstrating that life-choices is not a sufficient way of explaining social inequalities is to return to consider gender and pay. In spite of decades of equal pay legislation women's pay in the UK is around 80 per cent of what men get paid. It is not that men and women get a different rate for the same job but that on average, comparing all women with all men, women's pay is less than what men get paid. If life-choices were to be a sufficient explanation, then we would have to say that women in the UK in general choose jobs which pay less even though this does not happen in all countries. When we look at it this way, and when we consider that historically it has been possible to pay women less than men, we start to see that there has to be some social factor involved in this. In other words, inequalities exist but it is very difficult to claim that inequalities are the consequences of individual choices.

Within the UK in recent years the idea of life-choices fits in with wider debates about choice, potential and widening participation. These debates start by accepting that inequalities exist but provide explanations for inequalities that are often based on children, young people and families not being aspirational, not wanting more and not making the right choices because of this. In turn this is said to mean that some children do not achieve their potential. Of course, this ignores the fact that it is not at all possible to determine what anyone's potential is (Creasy, 2018). It is another of those seductive terms; of course, we would want children to achieve the best that they can, but a child's ability may be disadvantaged by social structures, and a focus on choice or aspiration ignores social structures.

This focus on choices ignores factors such as class, gender and ethnicity by providing an explanation which rests upon the idea of individual factors. This reflects a neoliberal view of society in which individual effort and hard work are said to be what matter alongside the idea that we can all overcome adversity if only we work hard enough and want it enough.

As was suggested earlier, though, these types of ideological ideas are not separate from what happens to us in our everyday lives. This is because ideas shape the sort of social policies which then have an impact upon us. For example, consider how the idea of aspiration fits with policy. This is the idea that as individuals we should all, naturally, want more.

This then gets applied to the fact that when we look at those young people who enter higher education (HE) there is a clear social class gradient (Emmerson et al, 2006; Hatt et al, 2008). You are more likely to enter HE if you are from higher social classes and you are much less likely to enter HE if you come from the lowest social classes. Politicians and policymakers then look at this and try to explain why. One response is that those young people who did not enter HE were not aspirational enough. They didn't want something that would improve their lives.

We can see the Aimhigher project, introduced by the Labour government in 2001, as a policy response to the way in which young people from different social classes enter HE in different numbers. The goal of the Aimhigher project was to see an increase in the numbers of young people from low-income families enrolling into HE.

Although the aims of Aimhigher can be seen as valid, the language that is used within the programme acts to locate the problem within young people from poorer backgrounds and does not recognise that there are social factors that impact why it is that so many do not do so. If participation in HE is simply down to individual aspiration or motivation we would not see patterns that reflect class in this way.

A focus on aspiration, though, just presents the issue as one of individual character and not as a consequence of structural features within society. As such, it seems obvious that social inequalities which arise from social structures have an impact on children and young people's lives in a number of ways.

## 12.3 What social inequalities, and what is wrong with inequality?

As an undergraduate student studying children and families it would be worthwhile for you to think about inequality a bit more and to consider if inequality is a problem for society or not. If you have taken A-level sociology you will have come across the theory of Functionalism. Don't worry if you haven't; it's quite straightforward. Functionalist theory says that if something exists in a society then it does so because it has a function. In other words, it does something for society.

With this in mind there is an argument that inequality in terms of income is beneficial because it generates motivation (Davis and Moore, 1945; Wrong, 1999; Hauhart, 2003). It gives us something to work for. Some jobs require more training or education than others, or some jobs are associated with greater responsibilities than others so individuals need an incentive to do those jobs. Greater levels of pay provide the incentive, but the consequences of this are that society is not equal.

From this perspective you might draw the conclusion that inequality benefits society. You might reasonably consider your own position and the fact that many young people choose not to find a job at 16 or 18 but instead choose to study further. This seems reasonable when we are led to believe that achieving a degree will lead to higher pay in the future. However, it does seem odd that young people from the poorest backgrounds, the ones that maybe know the most about the disadvantages of being disadvantaged, are the ones who are less likely to enter HE, even though this can be seen as something which will boost earning power. Given what functionalist theory is saying, we might ask why these young people are not motivated in the way that the theory suggests.

It is worth noting also that inequalities tend to follow patterns in that if we are to consider incomes then what we find is that other social characteristics come into play. Gender and ethnicity, for example, impact upon the types of jobs individuals get and the level of pay that they receive. Women and certain ethnic groups consistently earn lower wages. The ways in which class, gender and ethnicity play a part in educational inequalities are well documented (Farquharson et al, 1999; Reay et al, 2001, 2005; Breen, 2022). For evidence of the pay gap between men and women the Organisation for Economic Co-operation and Development publishes data which make it possible to compare different countries online. They show that gender differences in pay are much higher in some countries than in others.

There is a further aspect to this in terms of the extent of inequality. It is one thing to accept that inequalities in pay can provide an incentive to work hard, undertake more training or take on more responsibilities, but how unequal should the differences be? This is relevant because inequalities relating to income and wealth have a significant impact on our life-chances. Wilkinson and Pickett (2018, 2010) evaluate the impact that inequality has on society and argue that inequalities have a negative effect on society irrespective of how wealthy any country is. They argue that it is not the wealth of a country that is important as much as the inequalities within it. The UK is a very wealthy country, but it is very unequal when compared to similar countries. What is more, the inequalities are getting wider (Lyndon, 2019). We can see this increase in inequality when we consider that in spite of the vast wealth within the UK, the numbers of children whose parents rely on food banks is high and growing (Lambie-Mumford and Green, 2017; O'Hara, 2020). The problem within the UK then is not the lack of wealth within the country; it is not that the UK is a poor country. The problem is in terms of how wealth is distributed.

---

### Note

The usual way of illustrating inequalities within a society is to use the Gini co-efficient. The score using this is always between 0 and 1.

A score of 0 would mean perfect equality in that everyone in society has the same. A score of 1 would be perfect inequality with one person owning all the wealth.

As such, the score for any society is always somewhere in-between. By considering the value of the Gini co-efficient within the UK over time it can be seen that since the adoption of neoliberal policies in 1979 inequality within the UK has increased significantly (Clark, 2021).

Is this increase good or bad for society? Why?

Be aware also that Wilkinson and Pickett are not confining their argument to those who are poor. Their argument is that we are all affected by inequality.

## Pause for reflection

Is inequality relevant to you?

Many people do not believe that they are experiencing inequality such as poverty or deprivation. That does not mean that inequality is not problematic.

Marmot (2015) is useful here. Marmot provides a good way of understanding how inequality is detrimental to society as a whole. His explanation also links back to the discussion on life-chances.

Marmot's main concern is with health, but the way in which he explains inequalities and the effect of inequality can be used in a more general way. He does this by referring to inequality as a gradient. Think of walking up a hill. When the slope is gentle it is quite easy to walk up, but it becomes harder the steeper the slope gets.

Now think of the gradient as representing how easy it is to make the most of our abilities or be rewarded for our talent and abilities no matter where we start.

If we think about this model as being indicative of life-chances we can start to appreciate what Marmot means when he says that it is the gradient (the steepness of the slope) that is important (where the gradient represents the extent of inequalities, with greater inequality being a steeper slope). We might all agree that the lives of the poor are not good and recognise that it can be hard for the poor to escape that social position. The steeper the gradient, the harder it is. However, this is not the key point that Marmot is making. The key point is that a steeper gradient makes it harder for those who start at the bottom to get halfway up but it also makes it equally difficult for those who start halfway up to rise further also.

As such, all children are disadvantaged by a society that is more unequal. By looking at inequalities in this way we are also led towards a consideration of society in which those that experience poverty are not cast as being somehow different because of personal characteristics or individual failings. The poor are not a separate group who are different; they are just those who occupy a particular social position but, importantly, where it is the structure of society that makes it easier or harder to change position, to move out of poverty.

This approach also encourages us to conceptualise poverty in social terms. In recent decades there has been a discourse that constructs the poor as a group, or groups, which are different to those who are not poor: that is to say, the non-poor. We say the non-poor to distinguish them from the rich. Not being poor does not mean that someone is rich; in recent years the term 'just managing' has also come into general use. The poor are often claimed to be separated and distanced from the rest of society by virtue of their own behaviour and difference. Becker (1997: 159) has argued that it is useful to consider how poverty is reinforced and reproduced as a consequence of the cumulative effects of social reactions, social attitudes, institutional structures and professional practices. This is because these act to 'label people with little money and little power as "different"; which then devalue them, deny them equal opportunities and full citizenship, and punish them for being "poor"'.

To understand what is meant by structural factors read *Chavs* (Jones, 2016). This was covered in Chapter 1 and offers a good example of how individuals may end up in poverty because of things which happen to them rather than because of their own failings or deficiencies. Jones talks to families in Ashington, Northumberland, and shows how government policies that contributed to deindustrialisation had a real impact on families with many of them experiencing poverty as a consequence.

Now consider the lives of children and young people living in areas such as Ashington, where their employment opportunities have suddenly changed when compared to their parents' or grandparents' generations. Changes in the nature of the labour market and in family structures mean that young people face new risks and new challenges when making the transition from education to employment.

So, we can say that children's and young people's family of origin is an important determinant of their future success and that what happens to families is important, as Jones illustrates. However, for some of the most disadvantaged young people, a problematic family background may be part of their difficulties. It is always important, however, to distinguish between the problems that a family experiences and the factors which contribute to it.

What is also important is to consider just how many families experience poverty but where parents work (Hirsch, 2018). There has been a long-standing discourse within the UK of poverty arising from not working. In recent years, however, in-work poverty has increased significantly in the UK as the value of wages has fallen. More will be said about this in Section 12.5.

## 12.4 What can the state do about inequalities?

By this stage we have established that we live in a society that is clearly unequal. This inequality has an impact upon children's lives, and it means that some of them are more vulnerable to not achieving wellbeing than others. It means that some of them will not do as well in life as others, and even that some will not have as long a life. But how do we know that this is something that is social in nature rather than because of their individual abilities or talents?

We previously said that women in the UK do not, on average, earn the same as men. Statistics indicate that women earn around 80 per cent of what men earn. This is important in two ways. Firstly, it is important in terms of fairness. It would be unfair, wrong even, to pay two people different rates of pay for doing the same work. In the UK, before the introduction of equal pay legislation it was perfectly legal to pay a man more for doing the same job as a woman. The first Equal Pay Act in 1970 required that men and women get paid the same rate for the same job, but in 1975 equal pay legislation adopted the European Community principle of equal pay for work of equal value. In spite of this legislation, women still find that they earn less than men. Secondly, it is important because to get the things that we see as desirable we usually need money and for most of us we get money by working.

So, if income is a key factor in achieving what is desirable, we should be able to recognise that being female has an impact on life-chances. This is not about the individual abilities of women – it is simply about being female – so it would not be unreasonable to expect the state to intervene.

Of course, being female in the early 21st century is not the same as being female in the early 20th century. We can see that social values about gender have changed and, along with this, legislation has changed, which has made life fairer or more equal, though women still face discrimination and are still not equal with men. Changes to legislation, however, did not just happen; many women experienced real hardships, including being jailed, for offences which they carried out as part of their fight for equality in their attempt to get the state to act. What this demonstrates is that life-chances are not static; they are dynamic. It also demonstrates that sometimes the state is not so willing to make changes for the better.

What you might see is that life-chances reflect what can be called the fault lines of society: that is, those social divisions where being on one side gives an advantage and being on the other side gives a disadvantage. Gender is one of the fault lines. Gender inequalities in the UK may not seem as bad as they once were but they do still exist.

Similarly, in the 1950s and 1960s it was often the case that landlords who rented out rooms within a house of multiple occupation would have the legal right to display signs saying, for example, 'No Blacks'. In the same period it was still possible for men to be imprisoned if they were gay. When the law relating to homosexuality was changed in 1967 one prominent member of parliament, Roy Hattersley, argued that men should not be imprisoned for their disability (John and Furnish, 2017)! To suggest that being gay is a disability seems ludicrous now but historically being gay could lead to very serious consequences in the UK and still can in some countries.

So, when we think about life-chances, there are some things which are social and which disadvantage groups, not individuals. Personal ability can help but it cannot necessarily overcome discrimination that is experienced because of some characteristic over which you have no control, such as your sex, ethnicity, sexuality or the social class that you are born into.

What should be obvious is that society does not treat everyone equally, and because of this some of us find it easier to achieve what is socially desirable than others. However, as has been argued, society is dynamic. Things change constantly and some of these changes improve the situation for some groups while making it worse for others. That said, although there is still much to do to establish a truly equal society, it is far better to be female, belong to a minority ethnic group or be gay in 21st-century UK society than in the past.

This is because social pressures, especially the actions of groups such as trade unions and suffragettes, have fought for equal rights, which in turn has led to changes in legislation and social policy. At the same time the state may resist the ways in which some citizens seek to bring about changes within society. To that end it is worth noting that the police, crime, sentencing and courts bill which came into force in 2022 enables the state to restrict civil protests and to criminalise protestors. This bill will make it riskier, or harder, for groups to bring about social change in future. What the state does is important for all of us.

We have already indicated that poverty is often accepted as being something that can harm a child's life, and this is something which provides a further opportunity to consider how the state may shape the context of the lives of children and families. Some politicians have demonstrated concerns to tackle what is often referred to as child poverty. For example, the Child Poverty Act (2010) introduced by the Labour government under Gordon Brown required local authorities to report on the extent of child poverty and to explain what was being done both to tackle it and to reduce it. Governments were required to use this reporting to help them to combat child poverty and, ultimately, to eradicate it. If you are concerned about children who experience poverty, then you may see the Child Poverty Act 2010 positively. That does not mean that this concern is shared by all.

The Labour government that introduced the Child Poverty Act 2010 along with a commitment to eradicate child poverty was replaced in 2010 by the Conservative-led Coalition government and this in turn was replaced by a Conservative government in 2015. As was indicated within the chapter on political ideologies this change could reasonably be seen as leading to a change in the way that the government addresses child poverty.

### Note

In 2016 the Conservative government introduced the Welfare Reform and Work Act. This did two things in relation to tackling child poverty.

Firstly, it abolished legal targets in relation to reducing child poverty, and secondly, it stopped requiring local authorities to set up poverty reduction strategies.

A further issue in terms of the Welfare Reform and Work Act is important. From 2016, the Child Poverty Act (2010) was retrospectively renamed the Life Chances Act (2010).

By changing the name of the 2010 act in this way poverty was effectively removed from political consideration. Remember discourse?

It could be argued that in terms of the Welfare Reform and Work Act (2016) the Conservative government demonstrated that it was no longer concerned with discussing poverty in terms of what this means for children. Instead, the focus is now on who might be at risk of experiencing poverty (Dickerson and Popli, 2018). Calder (2018) provides a good account of what this change means for children. What it appears to do, though, is to work from the basis that poverty is a fact of life.

In some ways it may be; we have already seen that there are very often some families who experience poverty in any time period. The difference is that for the politicians who drew up the Welfare Reform and Work Act 2016, working to tackle poverty appears to have been scrapped as a political goal. Instead, the goal is to somehow identify who may be at risk of poverty in the future. Think of it as a snakes and ladders board where the ladders provide upward social mobility and the snakes can see us falling down, possibly into poverty. The Child Poverty Act (2010) can be understood as working to remove the snakes, or at least, removing those that drop us to the lowest levels. In comparison, the Welfare Reform and Work Act (2016) seems to be quite relaxed about poverty and is content to identify who might find it harder to climb a ladder. So in terms of what the state can do about inequality, we have to say whatever it wants, then we have to think about political ideologies to make sense of it.

## 12.5 Why is in-work poverty important?

It is not unreasonable to say that social inequality plays a large part in the problems that families experience. For example, what stands out in relation to troubled families as per the discussion in Chapter 3 is the extent to which these are poor families. This contributes to the overlap between troubled families and the underclass thesis. In terms of the underclass thesis, one thing that Mann (1992) argues is that when the economy is doing less well and more people find themselves without work the idea of an underclass, albeit sometimes given a different name, becomes a social concern. However, when the economy picks up we find that the underclass disappears as the unemployed find work.

However, Mann was writing at the start of the 1990s. Things are different now. What stands out in the early 2020s is that those individuals and families who can be said to be poor now are often in work. From 2011/2012 onwards, the majority of people experiencing poverty have been in working families (MacInnes et al, 2013; Hick and Lanau, 2018; McBride et al, 2018). The Child Poverty Action Group (2019) notes that the number of poor children who are living in working families increased to 70 per cent of the total number in poverty by 2017/2018. In 2018, one in eight workers was classified as being poor (Robb, 2018). This is partly as a consequence of a fall in the number of semi-skilled jobs alongside a rise in unskilled jobs but also it is because of low wages. This is in spite of the National Minimum Wage and moves to pay what is called a 'living' wage (Hirsch, 2018). Although the National Minimum Wage establishes a base line for wages it can be argued that it is not sufficiently high enough. The UK Poverty Report 2018 from the Joseph Rowntree Foundation noted that:

- In our society there are now almost 4 million workers in poverty, a rise of over half a million compared with five years ago and the highest number on record.
- The employment rate is also at a record high, but this has not delivered lower poverty.
- Since 2004/2005, the number of workers in poverty has increased at a faster rate than the total number of people in employment, resulting in workers being increasingly likely to find themselves in poverty.

The growth of poverty within the UK can also be evidenced in the growing number of families who rely on food banks (Lambie-Mumford and Green, 2017; O'Hara, 2020). As such, the issue of in-work poverty is important as is the role that the state has in addressing it in terms of strategies to alleviate poverty. For example, the National Minimum Wage has not always existed. The National Minimum Wage was introduced on 1 April 1999 by Blair's Labour government. At the time, proposals to introduce a minimum wage were resisted by some groups as unaffordable.

The National Minimum Wage should be seen as part of the Blair governments' aim to get more people into work alongside their claims that work is the route out of poverty. Twenty years after the introduction of a minimum wage, and in response to a claim by the Resolution Foundation predicting that child poverty will increase to its highest level for 60 years, a Conservative government spokesperson noted that 'we are committed to tackling child poverty and have made progress ... with 730,000 fewer children in workless households' (Mason et al, 2019: np). There is scope to adopt a critical lens to this claim. The problem should be obvious: if work is no longer a route out of poverty, then getting more parents into work will not be the solution to child poverty unless something changes with respect to wages.

For families with three or more children, child poverty fell from 2007–2008 but since then it has risen faster than for families with fewer children and is almost back to the level it was in 1996–1997 (48 per cent), just before the Labour government under Blair came to power. By 2024–2025 one in three children are forecast to be living in poverty (Brewer et al, 2021). As a student your task might be to discuss how we are able to explain this. We could point to the two-child limit on benefits and tax credits, but this only came into effect in April 2017, so it has to be something else. Think instead about what has happened to wages in recent decades.

---

**Study tip**

It is easy to find details about pay using data from the Office for National Statistics (ONS; visit www.ons.gov.uk).

However, we always have to be careful when we look at data. For example, the ONS illustrates that average weekly pay in January 2000 was £293.39. By December 2019 that had risen to £511.61. So, over 20 years average weekly pay had risen by £218.22. But as a student you always have to ask, 'So what?' We know that prices go up over time – this is what we call inflation – so what is this increase worth?

Fortunately, the ONS not only provides the figure for average weekly wages as they were in any given month since 2000; it also illustrates what this really means, what it calls real wages. This is a standardised figure.

For average wages: 'The figure in real terms (constant 2015 prices) is £474 per week, which is £1 (0.1%) higher than the pre-economic downturn peak of £473 per week for March 2008' (ONS, 2020). So, the value of wages by 2020 was £1 more than it was in March 2008.

---

A further problem for poorer workers is what can be called underemployment. This refers to a situation where a worker would work longer hours if possible: for example, those workers who are employed on part-time contracts but who want full-time contracts. Alongside this, and maybe more importantly, is the growth in precarious and insecure work. This has come to be referred to as the gig economy, as has been discussed (Gerrard, 2017; Gross et al, 2018; Choonara, 2019; MacDonald and Giazitzoglu, 2019). Such work is insecure and is not stable, with zero-hours contracts being common. As it is generally accepted that stability is important for children, consider what this means for a child in a family where wages are not stable. Workers on zero-hours contracts cannot be certain that they will have the same amount of work each week so they cannot trust that their income will be the same. This makes forward planning difficult.

Similar problems are experienced by workers who are compelled to be self-employed as this means that workers are denied benefits such as employment-related sick pay or pensions. Watch the film *Sorry We Missed You* by director Ken Loach to get an understanding of what this means for families (and justifiably say that you are studying!). For many insecure workers the welfare system provides some support; however, the value of welfare benefits in the UK has fallen as a consequence of policy changes introduced under the umbrella term austerity by the Conservative-led Coalition government from 2010.

What is evident is that many children and families experience hardship as a consequence of social inequalities. This is illustrated in a United Nations report. During November 2018 the United Nations sent a Special Rapporteur, Philip Alston, to the UK with the task of investigating and reporting on poverty (O'Hara, 2020). This report is relevant to understanding life-chances in terms of the disadvantages that are faced by many children. Alston notes that:

> Although the United Kingdom is the world's fifth largest economy, one fifth of its population (14 million people) live in poverty, and 1.5 million of them experienced destitution in 2017. Policies of austerity introduced in 2010 continue largely unabated, despite the tragic social

consequences. Close to 40 per cent of children are predicted to be living in poverty by 2021. Food banks have proliferated; homelessness and rough sleeping have increased greatly; tens of thousands of poor families must live in accommodation far from their schools, jobs and community networks; life expectancy is falling for certain groups; and the legal aid system has been decimated. The social safety net has been badly damaged by drastic cuts to local authorities' budgets, which have eliminated many social services, reduced policing services, closed libraries in record numbers, shrunk community and youth centres and sold off public spaces and buildings. The bottom line is that much of the glue that has held British society together since the Second World War has been deliberately removed and replaced with a harsh and uncaring ethos. A booming economy, high employment and a budget surplus have not reversed austerity, a policy pursued more as an ideological than an economic agenda. (Alston, 2019: 1)

We indicated above that the changes that have taken place within the UK are rarely by accident and that in general they are the consequences of political decisions and choices. It is useful to reiterate that neoliberal ideology underpins what came to be referred to as austerity. At the same time neoliberal policies since 1979 have made the position of workers weaker, such as by weakening the power of trade unions, and this has contributed to wages stagnating or falling. This is at the same time as the value of benefits has been reduced and that access to them was cut, also reflecting neoliberal ideas. In considering what this might mean for poorer children and families in particular, the United Nations report goes on to state:

After years of progress, child poverty has been rising since 2011–2012, almost entirely in working families. The Equality and Human Rights Commission forecasts that 1.5 million more children will fall into poverty between 2010 and 2021–2022, bringing the child poverty rate to a shocking 41 per cent. One in 10 girls in the United Kingdom has been unable to afford menstrual products, and many have missed school because of their period. Changes to benefits, and sanctions against parents, have unintended consequences on children and are driving the increase in child poverty. The Child Poverty Action Group found that Child Benefit will have lost 23 per cent of its real value between 2010 and 2020, due to sub-inflationary uprating and the current freeze. And low-paid jobs and stagnant wages have a direct effect on children, with families where two adults earn the minimum wage still falling 11 per cent short of the adequate income needed to raise a child. (Alston, 2019: 16)

Bear this in mind when considering that a child's family shapes their lived experiences and that this also influences their future. It is always important, however, to distinguish between the problems that a family experiences and the factors which contribute to it (Ridge, 2013). However, one important aspect of inequality is in terms of the ways in which it shapes access to one of the most fundamental aspects of our lives: housing. As such, Section 12.6 considers the landscape of housing within the UK in an attempt to critically assess how changes in housing may impact upon families and children.

## 12.6 Why housing matters to children

By this point it has been made clear that the state has concerns with respect to families and family life. In this section we will illustrate how housing policies can be seen as contributing to some of the problems which families encounter and how this can have a negative impact on children's lives.

It would be highly unusual for any political party not to claim that they support the family. The Conservative Party in particular have often sought to promote themselves as being pro-family (Royston, 2017; Gilbert, 2018); however, a distinction has to be made with respect to types of family as there is a clear sense that not all families are considered equally. Those families who rely on welfare benefits for income have often been seen in a negative light and do not appear to have been well supported since 2010 (CPAG, 2019).

One change to the benefit system relating to housing that has affected families is commonly referred to as the 'bedroom tax'. The spare-room subsidy, often called the bedroom tax, is a response to the idea that some individuals and/or families live in houses that are bigger than they need when measured in terms of a ratio of people to bedrooms. This is not to suggest that this policy applies to everyone; it does not. It only applies to those individuals or families who receive support from the state in the form of housing benefit and it includes a number of rules relating to the age and gender of children. It has the effect of reducing the housing benefit paid to a family by 14 per cent where they are deemed to have one spare bedroom and by 25 per cent where they have two (Bone, 2014). The policy aims to encourage individuals and families to move to housing which corresponds to their family structure, but note that this relies upon housing with fewer bedrooms being available to move into. Unfortunately, accommodation with fewer bedrooms is not always available, which means that there are harsh consequences for some families (Wright et al, 2020).

### Pause for reflection

Think about housing.

Try to list the features of housing that might be important to children and young people.

If you were describing the ideal home, what would it look like? Why?

In many ways it seems inconceivable to think about the family without also thinking about the living arrangements of that family and the way that a family home is central to this. Just consider how many television and newspaper or magazine adverts draw upon the idea of the ways in which we are able to 'turn a house into a home'. The relationship between housing and home is important. Think about your own experiences of school and consider how home–school relationships have come to be presented as being vital to promote children's academic success. In a similar vein, Murie (2016: 31) notes that from a neoconservative position the Right to Buy policy, as will be discussed later in this section, was presented as a means of 'supporting the family and providing stability'.

So, in terms of understanding children and families, the issue of housing is important because of the way in which it provides security and stability. As such, the state can shape the landscape of housing (no pun intended). The actions taken by the state shape the lives of children and families because of the ways in which the state can regulate our access to housing and in terms of establishing the standard of the housing that is available.

---

**Pause for reflection**

How times change ...

For the authors, growing up in the 1960s and 1970s, housing entailed either buying or renting. Renting was usually in the form of a council house, but many families rented a house related to an industry.

Growing up in South Yorkshire, as one of us did, meant that renting from the National Coal Board (NCB) was very common for families where someone worked for the NCB. Many villages in mining areas had extensive housing owned by the NCB.

At one time housing that was provided by employers was much more common and many towns would have housing originally built by companies for workers. Saltaire in Shipley and Bournville in Birmingham are examples of estates built for workers. Bournville is interesting in that there are no pubs in the community. This is because of the influence of the Quaker beliefs of the developers, the Cadbury family. Port Sunlight on the Wirral is a similar type of model village built for workers.

By the mid-1970s, though, renting from employers had declined significantly and the practice of employers building villages for workers does not exist today.

---

The growth in council housing can be understood as part of a process of municipalisation that was common in the mid-20th century. This refers to the way in which local authorities became much more involved in the provision of a range of social services (Child, 2018). During the 20th century housing became a political issue and it is interesting to compare the Labour Party's historical approach to housing with that of the Conservative Party by comparing the work of Child (2018) with that of Davies (2013). Today, however, the possibility of renting a house from a local authority (council housing) is much less likely.

After the Second World War the state aimed to ensure that decent-quality housing was available to all. This can be seen in concerns about replacing slums and with providing subsidised housing to meet the needs of groups who were less able to buy their own home. Housing costs can be high, so council housing was subsidised by the state so as to keep rents at an affordable level. This approach saw housing in Britain come to be dominated by either ownership or renting from local authorities, commonly referred to as council housing. Note that the term council housing has tended to be replaced with social housing, though this includes renting from housing associations also. Housing associations became more important as council housing declined.

Given that the state has had a long involvement with housing matters, it is reasonable to say that the contemporary landscape of housing within the UK is not accidental. It hasn't just happened. The state has been involved and this has had real consequences for children and families. Consider the points made by Bailey (2020: np) with respect to renting from a private landlord compared to social renting – that is, renting from a local authority or housing association – and think about what this means for children and families:

> private renting in the UK … is distinguished by high levels of insecurity, particularly in comparison with social renting. This insecurity was the direct goal of deregulation policies in the late 1980s as these were seen as a necessary pre-condition for attracting re-investment. It is potentially a more significant problem for lower income households for two reasons. First, frequent moves may disrupt social connections to family and friends which low-income households are particularly reliant on as a source of practical and emotional support. These connections are especially important for those with children, and lone parents most of all. For children, there is the additional concern that frequent moves may disrupt not only their social networks but also their schooling, with longer term impacts on educational attainment. Second, the subjective experience of insecurity may be more problematic for those in poverty. As their housing options are much more limited, the threat of loss of accommodation is likely to be a particular cause of stress.

Bailey paints a picture of a tenure of housing that is very insecure, and this cannot be good for either children or their families. How we access housing tends to be referred to as tenure. It is very important when it comes to assessing the degree of security that we have in our housing arrangements. It is therefore very important when we consider stability in children's lives.

In the early 20th century renting from a private landlord was very common but one reason for the decline in private renting after the Second World War was because both rents and tenancies were regulated by the government. What this meant was that landlords were restricted in terms of setting or increasing rents and there were controls on evicting tenants (Lund, 2016; Coulter, 2017). Regulating rents and making tenancies secure works in the favour of tenants in that it provides stability. Tenants can be secure with respect to the costs of their housing and know that landlords cannot evict them unless they have very good reasons to do so. It is important to recognise that such regulation is as a consequence of the actions of the state. Landlords had not created their own regulations or restrictions; these had been imposed by the state to make tenants more secure. As Coulter (2017) makes clear, though, during the 1980s and 1990s the state set about deregulating the private rental sector (PRS) with a view to removing this security. This was in line with neoliberal ideas about the provision of social services and was made possible by the Housing Act 1988 (Kemp, 2015).

Neoliberal ideology has led to two key changes in housing. Firstly, council housing was privatised through the sale of council houses to tenants. This led to the overall stock of council housing being reduced significantly. Secondly, the Housing Act 1988, along with the introduction of buy to let mortgages, saw a major increase in the availability of housing provided by private landlords. Following these developments what we see by the 2020s is a general consensus that housing, the thing that provides security and stability to families, is in crisis.

The Housing Act 1988 did two things that had a significant effect on renting. Firstly, it allowed landlords to charge market rents; secondly, it introduced assured shorthold tenancies. These are important because market rents mean that a landlord can charge whatever they want for a property and assured shorthold tenancies mean that tenants only have security for a short, fixed term, usually six months to one year. In this case the assurance is for the landlord rather than for the tenant.

It is worth noting that in cases of separation and/or divorce it is usual for a parent to be granted the right to remain in the home rather than having to sell it if there are children involved. This is based on putting the welfare of the child or children first and is often referred to as a Mesher Order. The children of a family who rent within the PRS are not provided for in the same way when it comes to their welfare. As was indicated above an assured shorthold tenancy in the UK is typically six months to one year. There are no rights for tenants beyond the period agreed to upon first renting in respect of staying in the property. Thinking about being critical, you have a very good example here of how children are not all treated equally.

Now, in itself, there is nothing wrong with the shift from renting properties from a local authority to renting from a private landlord. Across the world this type of tenure is very common, though this usually comes with much more security for tenants in terms of longer tenancy agreements and with restrictions on rent rises. As a student your task is to evaluate what housing means for children and families so you might argue that it is short-term assurances that are the problem, given that it is generally taken for granted that stability in a child's life is something that is good. In terms of health we can also accept that the quality of housing is important. We may also be concerned that the standard of comfort within a house is important. With that in mind, consider the following in terms of how Bailey (2020: np) makes it clear that the PRS is often associated with poor standards:

> the PRS is 'a demonstrably inferior tenure for low-income households' … The high costs of private rents can act as a barrier to employment or push working households into poverty. Poor PRS tenants are almost twice as likely to find it difficult to pay their rent as poor social tenants. In addition, the PRS has long been noted for its poor property standards and poor quality of management. As it has expanded recently, this has raised the average quality of properties but those in the PRS remain more likely to have substandard housing. Poor PRS tenants are as likely to struggle to keep their home warm in winter as poor social tenants, and both are worse off than poor owners and non-poor renters.

Given that our concerns in this book are with children's lives, the issue of housing is clearly very important. If properties in the PRS are often poor, as Bailey indicates, it is not surprising that such housing has the effect of being detrimental to some children (Bone, 2014). Given that council housing was seen as a solution to poor-quality housing that was typical before the Second World War, it is concerning, though maybe not surprising, that the growth of the PRS has also seen the return of poor-quality housing conditions. However, the privatising of council housing and promoting the expansion of the PRS was a political decision. It was done on purpose.

---

### Pause for reflection

Imagine that you are a government minister charged with creating a housing system that benefits children. It has to include private ownership as well as a rented sector.

What would it look like? What regulations would you want to set up so as to benefit children and families?

---

The decline of local authority housing, council housing, was made possible by the Housing Act 1980. This was introduced by the first Thatcher government and is often credited with resulting in significant working-class support for the Conservatives in the 1979 general election. The introduction of opportunities to buy council houses at a significant discount was very popular with many existing council tenants. Council tenants had previously been able to buy their council house only if the local authority was willing to sell it, and many local authorities were reluctant to do this because of the demand that existed for such housing. Note that although the Right to Buy policy is usually credited to Margaret Thatcher it actually pre-dated her time as prime minister (Jones, 2007; Davies, 2013; Murie, 2016). More importantly, what Thatcher did in introducing the 1980 Housing Act was to compel local authorities to sell council houses to tenants at a significant discount (up to 60 per cent for houses and 70 per cent for flats) and to restrict the further building of council housing (Jones, 2007; King, 2010; Disney and Luo, 2017).

Thatcher's stated aim was to increase the number of home owners in the UK. This did happen initially but it has since reduced and, ironically, many ex-council properties are now rented out by private landlords rather than by local authorities, usually at much higher rents and with far less security for tenants. One consequence is that the costs of housing benefit have increased significantly. Bone (2014: 4) points out that 'claimants in the PRS typically receive around 57% more per week in housing benefit than their counterparts in social housing'. What is also evident is that by 2020 the increasing cost of buying private housing is putting this out of reach of many young people unless they are able to be supported by their parents and that this is driving more people into the PRS. This acts as a sort of Catch-22 as the high cost of rent makes it even harder to save sufficient funds to buy a property and traps many families in insecure, poor-quality housing.

As has been demonstrated, the PRS within the UK is unable to provide the stability and security that we are often told that children require. As such, any consideration of children's lives and their futures should be assessed in a way which takes housing into account. If we are considering the extent to which children can thrive, most of us will readily acknowledge that children need a good base to work from. As such, we might consider that the housing that children experience will have some impact upon their ability to do well in later life. In this way we might consider that for some children, their experiences of poor housing may make it harder for them to escape the conditions of their childhood and result in them having an adulthood that is very similar to that of their parents.

## 12.7 Is social mobility important for children?

By now we have seen how the state does much to shape the lived experience of families, children and young people. The state has a significant role to play in shaping the social fabric within which we live, something that links back to Bronfenbrenner's socio-ecological model in terms of the different aspects of our lives. That is obvious in the discussion of how a government that was strongly influenced by neoliberalism acted to significantly change the nature of housing within the UK. What this has done is to make housing much less stable, and often of a very poor standard, for those families who are in the weakest economic position. We have also seen how inequalities are increasing and how more families are finding themselves in poverty.

Children who experience poverty are often seen as vulnerable and there is a general concern that they do less well at school, which in turn has a negative impact on their employment prospects and their adult lives. Maybe what we want to know at this stage then is the extent to which children can overcome the disadvantages that they may experience.

Some commentators are pessimistic about this. A key theme within cultural explanations of failing families and the underclass is the idea that poverty is reproduced as a consequence of children being socialised into a particular way of life which reflects characteristics exhibited by so-called failing families or the poor. One key weakness with this argument is that it adopts a deterministic position. As a student you should always be on your guard when it comes to being deterministic. We cannot say with confidence that growing up in poverty will mean that a child will remain in poverty as an adult. Some will, but equally, some will not.

Put simply, arguments which claim that growing up in a poor family will lead to a lifetime of poverty do not stand up to scrutiny. There are just too many factors involved. It is reasonable to argue that it may be harder for a child who has grown up in poverty to become wealthy in later life but it is by no means certain that they will not; some do. The fact that it is likely to be harder is the point that Marmot (2015) was making when he referred to inequality as a gradient: the steeper the gradient the harder it is to move upwards. This is not to say that we cannot move up. It is important to recognise the social influences on how our lives develop rather than falling into the trap of suggesting that both ability and inability are hereditary. Although we have to acknowledge that families provide the social and cultural context within which a child develops, at the same time a family does not establish the limits of that child's future.

---

### Study tip

We often believe things based on common sayings that we have grown up with but as a student you have to be critical and question both what you hear and what you read.

You will often hear people say 'like father, like son', or refer to families as being 'all like that in that family', but are they?

Are you a carbon copy of your parents (recognising also that not everyone lives with their parents)?

Now think about the ways in which the environment that you live in is different from that faced by your parents at the same age and even that your environment may be different from that of your siblings. For example, consider how your age position in a family can shape your experiences. This has brought us back to Bronfenbrenner.

---

This means that for a child living in poverty now, what they have to do to escape poverty will be different and the obstacles that they face will also differ from previous generations. So, if we want to consider the possibility of a child who has grown up in a failing family, or in poverty, of escaping and doing well for themselves, we also have to consider a number of other social and economic factors. Importantly, though, children can be socially mobile.

### Note

The idea of social mobility is really quite straightforward. It rests upon understanding society as unequal but where individuals can move up or down in terms of social position.

We typically characterise inequality on a vertical scale. Think of a ladder where each rung represents a socio-economic position. When we say socio-economic we mean that the economic assets, such as income or wealth, that we might have indicate our social position. This is often referred to as social class.

So, given that the social class of a child reflects the class of his or her parents, then a child who moves from one social class to another has been socially mobile.

Be aware that very often social mobility is spoken about as though it means moving upwards. That is not accurate. Social mobility can be up or down.

Ideas about how education can provide opportunities for social mobility can be seen to influence the ways in which education systems are established, though as was said in Chapter 5 cultural capital is also very important (Goldthorpe, 2016b; Munro, 2019). In the UK there is ongoing support for selection in schools and this is often associated with calls for grammar schools to be re-established nationally on the grounds that grammar schools provide opportunities for social mobility.

The evidence for this is not at all strong and what tends to happen is that in areas where grammar schools exist they manage to achieve better results than non-grammar schools as a consequence of the way in which they restrict who they admit, only admitting children who are academically stronger (Creasy, 2018). Universities are similar. Universities that are defined as good are overwhelmingly those universities which restrict entrance to students who have the highest entry qualifications. In general, children from poorer backgrounds are not well provided for by the existing grammar schools (Coe et al, 2008; Andrews et al, 2016). Grammar schools may offer advantages to those children who are admitted but the system operates in a way that means that this will always be a minority of children. What the grammar school system does then is to reinforce social inequalities, which is the very reason that most areas phased them out.

Be careful when reading this discussion, though; it is not that education is not important at all, rather it is that education cannot explain upward social mobility on its own, nor can it explain why less intelligent or less educated children from higher social classes do not experience downward social mobility to the extent that we might expect if class position reflected ability and merit. To explain why this is we need to consider the role of the family and to refer back to one of the concepts that was introduced earlier: cultural capital. For Goldthorpe, the actions of parents in higher social classes act to give advantages to children with respect to upward social mobility while also acting as a safety net which ensures that less intelligent children are less likely to experience downward mobility. It is also important to note that social mobility is more often a consequence of social and economic conditions in terms of opportunities than of ability or merit (Goldthorpe, 2016a, 2016b; Wilby, 2020).

Government ministers in particular often seem to equate evidence of social mobility as being positive and to promote it as being a valid goal. As a goal, evidence of social mobility can be held up as evidence to represent success in terms of the social policies that are in place and with respect to the type of society that we live in. However, social mobility is another one of those terms which can be described as seductive: who wouldn't want to have opportunities to be socially mobile, to be able to improve one's social position? The opposite of course is a society that is fixed, or rigid, a society where the class that you are born into is the class that you will remain in, and that is not at all attractive.

In considering social mobility we are inevitably drawn into a consideration of social inequality. Both Calder (2016) and Reay (2017) make the important point that social mobility is not a solution to inequality. Reay in particular notes that social mobility becomes more important as society becomes more unequal. There would be far less concern to be mobile if society was more equal. When we think about the life-chances of those who experience poverty we tend to see them as facing problems that are particular to being poor. This positions the poor as different and, although it can be acknowledged that the poor face certain specific problems, we have to be careful not to see inequality as representing a difference between those who are poor and those who are not poor in a way which sees the non-poor as experiencing the same social conditions.

---

**Pause for reflection**

An analogy that was often used after the 2008 financial crash was that we are all in this together, and during the COVID-19 pandemic of 2020 it was often said that we are all in the same boat.

These analogies only work though if we all share the same social position. We can start to see things more accurately when we consider that we are all in the same storm and then think about boats.

So, we may all be in the same storm but some of us are in ocean-ready luxury yachts and some of us are in open rowing boats and, even then, some of the boats are a bit leaky.

We may live in the same society, but we don't all experience it in the same way.

---

So, relating what Calder and Reay are saying to Marmot's gradient analogy, social mobility does not change the degree of incline; it just reports on those who manage to move up. As such, a focus on social mobility could be seen as simply a way of making inequality more acceptable by promoting the idea that those who are more capable will be able to avoid the worst consequences; that is to say that they will be able to escape poverty. If so, this sees society accepting poverty but becoming focused on how we can provide the means for some to escape poverty rather than working to tackle social inequalities, in spite of the problems that inequalities result in.

## 12.8 Using this chapter

At this point we have to think about how to use this chapter and in some ways this chapter has been a little less obvious in terms of structure. So, as we try to summarise each section we want you to think that you have to do the same when you write assignments. Chapter 12 started with a discussion of life-chances. This is certainly a term or concept that is used a lot with respect to children and young people and there will probably be a number of times when you can make good use of it in assignments. If you get the basics clear in your mind this is something that could be very useful for your studies as a whole. What might be needed to provide a good account of life-chances will include the following:

- Life-chances is a sociological concept rooted in the work of Max Weber. It relates to any individual's potential to achieve that which is seen as socially desirable.
- It is a concept which reflects the fact that society is unequal and that some children have advantages but some face obstacles to being successful in later life.
- Life-chances are shaped by social factors such as class, gender and ethnicity, each of which can lead to discrimination and disadvantage.
- A similar-sounding concept, life-choices, argues that success or failure in life is down to individual choices. This idea is individual in nature whereas life-chances is social.
- Life-choices is a weak argument.

In discussing life-chances you will probably end up establishing where the concept comes from and what it means before focusing on one particular issue which may help or hinder life-chances.

---

**Study tip**

It is always a good idea when writing assignments to explain what you mean by a key term or concept and then support it with a reference or two.

When it comes to referencing, one is always good but two or more are better. This is because two or more not only show that you have read widely; they also show that the point you are making is sound.

Be careful with what you choose to read, though. Take your cue from reading lists and always be very careful about what comes up on search engines such as Google or Bing. Choosing the first results from a general search engine often means that you end up with inappropriate reference sources. Your tutors will have put a lot of effort into finding good sources – use them.

---

Because life-chances can be seen to rest on the idea of social inequality we moved onto this topic next. Social inequalities are a key feature of life within the UK. There is much that you could do in terms of an assignment on inequality but there are some key points that we think are very likely to find a place within such an assignment:

- The Gini co-efficient is the usual method of illustrating how social inequality is changing.
- The UK is a very wealthy country, but it is very unequal when compared to similar countries and inequalities are getting wider.
- Functionalist theory has proposed that inequality has social benefits in that it acts to motivate people to take on additional education or training, or to work hard.
- Social inequalities can be seen to correlate with social class, gender and ethnicity.
- Some theorists have demonstrated that social inequality is detrimental to society.

Building on this discussion of inequality we noted that after 1997 Blair's Labour Party did much to help people enter the workplace on the basis that working was a way of helping people out of poverty. There has been a long-standing argument that poverty is the consequence of worklessness and therefore this seems a rational approach. However, we then demonstrated that during the 21st century the value of wages has declined for a number of reasons, such as the weakening of trade unions and the growth in insecure and precarious work. This means that within contemporary society there has been a growth in families that are poor but where one or both parents are working.

Having established that many families are experiencing poverty, including families where one or both parents work, we then drew on the idea that this inevitably impacts upon children. Arguments about poverty making children more vulnerable are quite common but, as we had discussed vulnerability earlier, we turned our attention to one of the issues that is said to be important in children's lives: stability. We then developed a discussion of how housing not only underpins stability, but also provides the basic conditions of a child's environment, and noted that for children from disadvantaged families housing is becoming dominated by the PRS.

We illustrated that in recent years the state has done things which have created problems such as promoting the growth of renting from private landlords. It is evident that this has pushed housing costs up and lowered standards at the same time. So, for us, it seemed that a discussion of housing is very relevant to studying children, families and the state. If you were to write an assignment which considered housing, then we think there are some key points that we would expect to be included:

- The home is central to family life, generally being seen as a source of stability in children's lives.
- The landscape of housing is shaped by the state.
- The last 30 years have seen a significant growth in the PRS; this is often poor-quality housing with a form of tenure which reduces stability because it is insecure.
- Changes to the welfare system such as the bedroom tax have made life harder for families where alternatives are unavailable.

Chapter 12 has also demonstrated that it is possible to escape poverty, that children are not destined to experience poverty just because their parents did. We refer to this as being upwardly socially mobile. If you are writing about social mobility then there are some key issues that were covered in this section:

- Social mobility is a consequence of social and economic conditions more than a consequence of ability or merit.
- Social mobility is not a solution to poverty at a societal level, only at a personal level.
- Social mobility is influenced by cultural capital.

Within this chapter we have set out an argument which was structured in a way that worked for us but you have to use the evidence from your reading to suit what you want to say. One thing that you really can't avoid, and really shouldn't scrimp on as a student, is reading. Read as much as you can.

---

**Further thoughts**

Think about your own future and what might be possible. Although anything *is* possible, give some more thought to what Marmot (2015) means when he says that the more unequal a society is, the harder it is for all of us.

Look for evidence of life-choices being used to motivate children and young people.

Consider also how in-work poverty undermines hard work. If work does not provide enough to live on, might that mean that there are few incentives to work?

---

## Further reading

Calder (2018) is useful with respect to children and life-chances. Ridge (2013) is useful in terms of understanding what poverty means for children. Rose and McAuley (2019) provide evidence from parents experiencing poverty in terms of their experiences. O'Hara (2020) draws upon lots of accounts of experiencing poverty, including the author's own experiences.

For further information about inequality look at the Equality Trust website at www.equalitytrust.org.uk/ and the Joseph Rowntree Foundation website at www.jrf.org.uk/. Both provide access to up-to-date information on inequalities in a range of areas.

For information on gender inequalities and how women are trying to tackle inequalities visit the Fawcett Society website at www.fawcettsociety.org.uk/.

# 13

# What, there's no conclusion?

## 13.1 So what?

At the end of any book, it is customary to have a conclusion. We aren't going to offer one. Typically, the conclusion sums up all the chapters and says where the book has been going. That means that there's always a short cut to reading academic books in that you can get quite a lot from reading the introduction and the conclusion. We think that we summarised each chapter as we went along so there's little to say other than to reiterate that to understand issues relating to children and young people you really do need to consider the social, cultural and political context that children and families exist within. That brings us back to the usefulness of Bronfenbrenner. It also returns us to making the point that theories relating to children that treat the child in isolation are rather weak.

That said, we want to end this book by raising a question that you can often put to good use, one that we introduced earlier: so what? This is a question that you can always usefully apply to both what you have read and what you have written. So, having read a book or a journal article you should ask, so what? What does this mean or what can you do with it?

So, what can you do with this book? We think that we have provided a broad introduction to the ways in which political ideologies underpin what the state does and have then shown how the state is able to shape the context of the lives of children and families through a consideration of a range of social policies. We also think that we have demonstrated why a consideration of politics and policy is important to understanding children and families. We are confident that many parts of the book will be useful to you within your assignments but you have to make the links; this is when you can be creative. We also want to reiterate a comment that we made quite early on in that your opinions are important, but only if they rest upon a lot of reading.

As such, we hope that you have followed our arguments and that you can see ways of using the discussions within this book to good effect. We also hope that we have helped in some way to improve the quality of your work. So, at this point there's only one further thing to say: good luck, and thank you for reading.

# References

ACRWC (1990) African Charter on the Rights and Welfare of the Child [online], Available from: www.unicef.org/esaro/African_Charter_articles_in_full.pdf [Accessed 7 April 2020].

Adams, R. (2020) 'Women "put careers on hold" to home school during UK COVID-19 lockdown', *The Guardian*, 30 July.

Albertson, K. and Stepney, P. (2019) '1979 and all that: a 40-year reassessment of Margaret Thatcher's legacy on her own terms', *Cambridge Journal of Economics*, 44(2): 319–342.

Allen, G. (2011) *Early Intervention: The Next Steps*, London: Cabinet Office.

Almond, B. (2008) *The Fragmenting Family*, Oxford: Oxford University Press.

Alston, P. (2019) *Visit to the United Kingdom of Great Britain and Northern Ireland: Report of the Special Rapporteur on Extreme Poverty and Human Rights*, Geneva: United Nations.

Anderson, D. L. and Graham, A. P. (2016) 'Improving student wellbeing: having a say at school', *School Effectiveness and School Improvement*, 27: 348–367.

Andrews, J., Hutchinson, J. and Johnes, R. (2016) *Grammar Schools and Social Mobility*, London: Education Policy Institute.

Anning, A. and Ball, M. (2008) *Improving Services for Young Children: From Sure Start to Children's Centres*, London: SAGE.

Ashley, L., Duberley, J., Sommerlad, H. and Scholarios, D. (2015) *A Qualitative Evaluation of Non-Educational Barriers to the Elite Professions*, London: Social Mobility and Child Poverty Commission.

Bagguley, P. and Mann, K. (1992) '"Idle thieving bastards"? Scholarly representations of the "underclass"', *Work, Employment and Society*, 6(1): 113–126.

Bailey, N. (2020). 'Poverty and the re-growth of private renting in the UK, 1994–2018', *PLoS ONE*, 15(2): e0228273.

Ball, E., Batty, E. and Flint, J. (2016) 'Intensive family intervention and the problem figuration of "troubled families"', *Social Policy and Society*, 15(2): 263–274.

Ball, S. J. (2016) 'Neoliberal education? Confronting the slouching beast', *Policy Futures in Education*, 14(8).

Baraldi, C. and Cockburn, T. (2018) 'Introduction: lived citizenship, rights and participation in contemporary Europe', in C. Baraldi and T. Cockburn (eds) *Theorising Childhood: Citizenship, Rights and Participation*, Cham: Springer International, pp 1–27.

Barlow, A. and Duncan, S. (2000) 'Supporting families? New Labour's communitarianism and the "rationality mistake": Part I', *Journal of Social Welfare and Family Law*, 22(1): 23–42.

Barnes, J., Belsky, J. and Melhuish, E. C. (2007) *The National Evaluation of Sure Start: Does Area-Based Early Intervention Work?*, Bristol: Policy Press.

Bates, L. (2014) *Everyday Sexism*, London: Simon & Schuster.

Bauman, Z. (2000) *Liquid Modernity*, Cambridge: Polity Press.

Bauman, Z. (2003) *Liquid Love: On the Frailty of Human Bonds*, Cambridge: Polity Press.

Beck, U. and Beck-Gernsheim, E. (1995) *The Normal Chaos of Love*, Cambridge: Polity Press.

Becker, S. (1997) *Responding to Poverty: The Politics of Cash and Care*, Harlow: Longman.

Belsey, A. (1986) 'The new Right, social order and civil liberties', in R. Levitas (ed) *The Ideology of the New Right*, Cambridge: Polity Press, pp 169–197.

Ben-Arieh, A. (2006) 'Is the study of the "state of our children" changing? Revisiting after 5 years', *Children and Youth Services Review*, 28(7): 799–812.

Beresford, P. and Alibhai-Brown, Y. (2016) *All Our Welfare: Towards Participatory Social Policy*, Bristol: Policy Press.

Bessant, J. (2014) 'A dangerous idea? Freedom, children and the capability approach to education', *Critical Studies in Education*, 55(2): 138–153.

Best, S. (2002) *Introduction to Politics and Society*, London: SAGE.

Beveridge, W. (1942) *Social Insurance and Allied Services*, London: HMSO.

Bom, I. van der, Paterson, L. L., Peplow, D. and Grainger, K. (2018) '"It's not the fact they claim benefits but their useless, lazy, drug taking lifestyles we despise": analysing audience responses to *Benefits Street* using live tweets', *Discourse, Context and Media*, 21(1): 36–45.

Bond, E. (2013). 'Mobile phones, risk and responsibility: understanding children's perceptions', *Cyberpsychology*, 7(1): 1–11.

Bone, J. (2014). 'Neoliberal nomads: housing insecurity and the revival of private renting in the UK', *Sociological Research Online*, 19(4): 1–14.

Bradshaw, J. (ed) (2016) *The Well-Being of Children in the UK*, Bristol: Policy Press.

Breen, R. (2022) *The Stubborn Persistence of Educational Inequality*, London: Institute for Fiscal Studies.

Brewer, M., Corlett, A., Handscomb, K. and Tomlinson, D. (2021) *The Living Standards Outlook 2021*, London: Resolution Foundation.

Bridge, G. (2020) 'Some infant formula milks contain more sugar than soda drinks – new research', The Conversation [online] 20 February, Available from: https://theconversation.com/some-infant-formula-milks-contain-more-sugar-than-soda-drinks-new-research-129655 [Accessed 11 October 2022].

Bronfenbrenner, U. (1979) *The Ecology of Human Development: Experiments by Nature and Design*, Cambridge, MA: Harvard University Press.

Brotherton, G. and Cronin, T. M. (2013) *Working with Vulnerable Children, Young People and Families*, London: Routledge.

Brown, K. J. (2017) *Vulnerability and Young People: Care and Social Control in Policy and Practice*, Bristol: Policy Press.

Brown, K. J. (2020) 'Punitive reform and the cultural life of punishment: moving from the ASBO to its successors', *Punishment and Society*, 22(1): 90–107.

Burkitt, I. (1993) 'Overcoming metaphysics: Elias and Foucault on power and freedom', *Philosophy of the Social Sciences*, 23(1): 50–72.

Cain, R. (2016) 'Responsibilising recovery: lone and low-paid parents, Universal Credit and the gendered contradictions of UK welfare reform', *British Politics*, 11(4): 488–508.

Calder, G. (2016) *How Inequality Runs in Families: Unfair Advantage and the Limits of Social Mobility*, Bristol: Policy Press.

Calder, G. (2018) 'What would a society look like where children's life chances were really fair?', *Local Economy*, 33(6): 655–666.

Calder, M. C. (2008) *Contemporary Risk Assessment in Safeguarding Children*, Lyme Regis: Russell House.

Casey, L. C. B. (2014) 'The National Troubled Families Programme', *Social Work and Social Sciences Review*, 17(2): 57–62.

Cassidy, C. (2012) 'Children's status, children's rights and "dealing with" children', *International Journal of Children's Rights*, 20(1): 57–71.

Chambers, D. (2001) *Representing the Family*, London: SAGE.

Charlesworth, S. J. (2000) *A Phenomenology of Working Class Experience*, Cambridge: Cambridge University Press.

Child, P. (2018) 'Landlordism, rent regulation and the Labour Party in mid-twentieth century Britain, 1950–64', *Twentieth Century British History*, 29(1): 79–104.

Children's Society (2018) *The Good Childhood Report 2018*, London: Children's Society.

Choonara, J. (2019) *Insecurity, Precarious Work and Labour Markets: Challenging the Orthodoxy*, Basingstoke: Palgrave Macmillan.

Churchill, H. (2013) 'Retrenchment and restructuring: family support and children's services reform under the coalition', *Journal of Children's Services*, 8(3): 209–223.

Clark, D. (2021) 'Gini index of the United Kingdom from 1977 to 2020', [online], Available from: www.statista.com/statistics/872472/gini-index-of-the-united-kingdom/ [Accessed 8 December 2021].

Clarke, J. (2010) 'After neo-liberalism?', *Cultural Studies*, 24(3): 375–394.

Coates, D. (1984) *The Context of British Politics*, London: Hutchinson.

Cockcroft, T., Bryant, R. and Keval, H. (2016) 'The impact of dispersal powers on congregating youth', *Safer Communities*, 15(4): 213–223.

Coe, R., Jones, K., Searle, J., Kokotsaki, D., Mohd Kosnin, A. and Skinner, P. (2008) *Evidence on the Effects of Selective Educational Systems*, Durham: CEM Centre, Durham University.

Coleman, J. and Hagell, A. (2007) *Adolescence, Risk and Resilience: Against the Odds*, Chichester: John Wiley.

Cooper, M. (2017) *Family Values: Between Neoliberalism and the New Social Conservatism*, New York: Zone Books.

Coote, A. and Lyall, S. (2013) 'Strivers v skivers: real life's not like that at all', *The Guardian*, 11 April.

Coram and Coram International (2017) *Constructing a Definition of Vulnerability: Attempts to Define and Measure*, London: Coram and Coram International.

Corby, F. H. (2015) 'Parenting support: how failing parents understand the experience', *Journal of Education and Social Policy*, 2(2): 38–46.

Coulter, R. (2017) 'Social disparities in private renting amongst young families in England and Wales, 2001–2011', *Housing, Theory and Society*, 34(3): 297–322.

CPAG (2019) Child Poverty in Working Families on the Rise [online], Available from: https://cpag.org.uk/news-blogs/news-listings/child-poverty-working-families-rise [Accessed 20 March 2020].

Creasy, R. (2018) *The Taming of Education*, Basingstoke: Palgrave Macmillan.

Creasy, R. and Corby, F. (2019) *Taming Childhood? A Critical Perspective on Policy, Practice and Parenting*, Basingstoke: Palgrave Macmillan.

Cronin, J. E. and Radtke, T. G. (1987) 'The old and the new politics of taxation: Thatcher and Reagan in historical perspective', *Socialist Register*, 23(1): 263–296.

Crossley, S. (2015) *The Troubled Families Programme: The Perfect Social Policy?*, CCJS Briefing paper 13, London: Centre for Crime and Justice Studies.

Crossley, S. (2017) *In Their Place: Imagined Geographies of Poverty*, London: Pluto Press.

Crossley, S. (2018a) *Troublemakers: The Construction of 'Troubled Families' as a Social Problem*, Bristol: Bristol University Press.

Crossley, S. (2018b) 'The UK government's Troubled Families Programme: delivering social justice?', *Social Inclusion*, 6(3): 301–309.

D'Cruz, H., Gillingham, P. and Melendez, S. (2007) 'Reflexivity, its meanings and relevance for social work: a critical review of the literature', *British Journal of Social Work*, 37(1): 73–90.

Dauda, C. L. (2010a) 'Childhood, age of consent and moral regulation in Canada and the UK', *Contemporary Politics*, 16(3): 227–247.

Dauda, C. L. (2010b) 'Sex, gender, and generation: age of consent and moral regulation in Canada', *Politics and Policy*, 38(6): 1159–1185.

Davey, C. and Lundy, L. (2011) 'Towards greater recognition of the right to play: an analysis of Article 31 of the UNCRC', *Children and Society*, 25(1): 3–15.

David, M. E. (1986) 'Moral and maternal: the family in the right', in R. Levitas (ed) *The Ideology of the New Right*, Cambridge: Polity Press, pp 136–166.

David, M. E. (2016) *Reclaiming Feminism: Challenging Everyday Misogyny*, Bristol: Policy Press.

Davies, A. (2013) '"Right to Buy": the development of a Conservative housing policy, 1945–1980', *Contemporary British History*, 27(4): 24.

Davies, W. (2014) *The Limits of Neoliberalism: Authority, Sovereignty and the Logic of Competition*, London: SAGE.

Davis, K. and Moore, W. E. (1945) 'Some principles of stratification', *American Sociological Review*, 10(2): 242–249.

Deacon, A. (2002) *Perspectives on Welfare: Ideas, Ideologies and Policy Debates*, Buckingham: Open University Press.

Dean, H. (1991) 'In search of the underclass', in P. Brown and R. Scase (eds) *Poor Work: Disadvantage and the Division of Labour*, Milton Keynes: Open University Press, pp 23–39.

Dean, M. (2014) 'Rethinking neoliberalism', *Journal of Sociology*, 50(2): 150–163.

Dermott, E. and Pomati, M. (2017) 'The cost of children: parents, poverty and social support', in G. Main and E. Dermott (eds) *Poverty and Social Exclusion in the UK, Volume 1: The Nature and Extent of the Problem*, Bristol: Policy Press, pp 155–172.

DfE and Ford, V. (2021) *£20m to Provide More Early Help for Vulnerable Families*, London: HM Government.

DfES (2006) *What to Do if You're Worried a Child Is Being Abused*, Nottingham: DfES.

Dickerson, A. and Popli, G. (2018) 'The many dimensions of child poverty: evidence from the UK Millennium Cohort Study', *Fiscal Studies*, 39(2): 265–298.

Disney, R. and Luo, G. (2017) 'The Right to Buy public housing in Britain: a welfare analysis', *Journal of Housing Economics*, 35: 51–68.

Donetto, S. and Maben, J. (2015) '"These places are like a godsend": a qualitative analysis of parents' experiences of health visiting outside the home and of Children's Centres services', *Health Expectations*, 18: 2559–2570.

Dorey, P. (2015) 'A farewell to alms: Thatcherism's legacy of inequality', *British Politics*, 10: 79–98.

Dorling, D. and Tomlinson, S. (2019) *Rule Britannia: Brexit and the End of Empire*, London: Bite Back Publishing.

Douglas, G. (1990) 'Family law under the Thatcher government', *Journal of Law and Society*, 17(4): 411–426.

Dowden, R. (1978) 'Margaret Thatcher: interview for Catholic Herald' [online], Available from: www.margaretthatcher.org/document/103793 [Accessed 9 December 2021].

Driver, S. and Martell, L. (1998) *New Labour: Politics after Thatcherism*, Cambridge: Polity Press.

Duffy, B., Hewlett, K., Murkin, G., Benson, R., Hesketh, R., Page, B., Skinner, G. and Gottfried, G. (2021) *Culture Wars in the UK: Political Correctness and Free Speech*, London: The Policy Institute.

Eatwell, R. and Goodwin, M. (2018) *National Populism: The Revolt against Liberal Democracy*, London: Pelican.

Ecclestone, K. and Hayes, D. (2009) *The Dangerous Rise of Therapeutic Education*, London: Routledge.

Ecclestone, K. and Lewis, L. (2014) 'Interventions for resilience in educational settings: challenging policy discourses of risk and vulnerability', *Journal of Education Policy*, 29: 195–217.

Edwards, P. (2015) 'New ASBOs for old?', *Journal of Criminal Law*, 79(4): 257–269.

Edwards, R. (2003) 'Introduction: themed section on social capital, families and welfare policy', *Social Policy and Society*, 2(4): 305–308.

Electoral Commission (2022) Results and Turnout at the EU Referendum [online], Available from: www.electoralcommission.org.uk/who-we-are-and-what-we-do/elections-and-referendums/past-elections-and-referendums/eu-referendum/results-and-turnout-eu-referendum [Accessed 19 July 2022].

Elliott, A. and Lemert, C. (2014) *Introduction to Contemporary Social Theory*, Abingdon: Routledge.

Elliott, B. and McCrone, D. (1987) 'Class, culture and morality: a sociological analysis of neo-conservatism', *Sociological Review*, 35(3): 485–515.

Emmerson, C., Frayne, C., McNally, S. and Silva, O. (2006) Aimhigher: Excellence Challenge: A Policy Evaluation Using the Labour Force Survey [online], Available from: https://ifs.org.uk/publications/3801 [Accessed 7 February 2022].

Etzioni, A. (2005) 'Response to Simon Prideaux's "From Organisational Theory to the New Communitarianism of Amitai Etzioni"', *Canadian Journal of Sociology/Cahiers canadiens de sociologie*, 30(2): 215–217.

Fairclough, N. (2000). *New Labour, New Language?*, London: Routledge.

Farquharson, C., McNally, S. and Tahir, I. (2022) *Education Inequalities*, London: Institute for Fiscal Studies.

Farr, J. (2004) 'Social capital: a conceptual history', *Political Theory*, 32(1): 6–33.

Fattore, T., Mason, J. and Watson, E. (2007) 'Children's conceptualisation(s) of their well-being', *Social Indicators Research*, 80: 5–29.

Fava, N. M., Li, T., Burke, S. L. and Wagner, E. F. (2017) 'Resilience in the context of fragility: development of a multidimensional measure of child wellbeing within the Fragile Families dataset', *Children and Youth Services Review*, 81(Supplement C): 358–367.

Featherstone, B., Gupta, A. and Morris, K. (2017) 'Bringing back the social: the way forward for children's social work?', *Journal of Children's Services*, 12(2/3): 190–196.

Ferguson, H. (2003) 'Welfare, social exclusion and reflexivity: the case of child and woman protection', *Journal of Social Policy*, 2: 199–216.

Fergusson, D. M. and Horwood, L. J. (2003) 'Resilience to childhood adversity: results of a 21-year study', in S. S. Luthar (ed) *Resilience and Vulnerability: Adaptation in the Context of Childhood Adversities*, Cambridge: Cambridge University Press, pp 130–155.

Field, F. (2010) *The Foundation Years: Preventing Poor Children Becoming Poor Adults*, London: Cabinet Office.

Field, J. (2017) *Social Capital*, London: Routledge.

Fine, B. (2010) *Theories of Social Capital: Researchers Behaving Badly*, London: Pluto Press.

Finlayson, L. (2016) *An Introduction to Feminism*, Cambridge: Cambridge University Press.

Fives, A. (2008) *Political and Philosophical Debates in Welfare*, Basingstoke: Palgrave Macmillan.

Fletcher, A., Gardner, F., McKee, M. and Bonell, C. (2012) 'The British government's Troubled Families Programme: a flawed response to riots and youth offending', *British Medical Journal*, 344(7860): np.

Fletcher, D. and Sarkar, M. (2013) 'Psychological resilience: a review and critique of definitions, concepts, and theory', *European Psychologist*, 18: 12–24.

# References

Fletcher, D. R. and Wright, S. (2018) 'A hand up or a slap down? Criminalising benefit claimants in Britain via strategies of surveillance, sanctions and deterrence', *Critical Social Policy*, 38(2): 22.

Fontes, L. A. (2005) *Child Abuse and Culture: Working with Diverse Families*, London: Guilford.

Foucault, M. (1989) *The Birth of the Clinic: An Archaeology of Medical Perception*, London: Routledge.

Fraser, D. (2009) *The Evolution of the British Welfare State: A History of Social Policy since the Industrial Revolution*, Basingstoke: Palgrave Macmillan.

Freedman, J. (2001) *Feminism*, Buckingham: Open University Press.

Frost, N. (2011) *Rethinking Children and Families: The Relationship between Childhood, Families and the State*, London: Continuum.

Frost, N. and Parton, N. (2009) *Understanding Children's Social Care: Politics, Policy and Practice*, London: SAGE.

Frydenberg, E. (2008) *Adolescent Coping: Advances in Theory, Research, and Practice*, London: Routledge.

Furedi, F. (2001) 'Paranoid parenting', *The Guardian*, 26 April.

Furedi, F. (2004) *Therapy Culture: Cultivating Vulnerability in an Uncertain Age*, London: Routledge.

Gamble, A. (1988) *The Free Economy and the Strong State: The Politics of Thatcherism*, Basingstoke: Macmillan.

Gandesha, S. (2018) 'Understanding Right and Left populism', in J. Morelock (ed) *Critical Theory and Authoritarian Populism*, London: University of Westminster Press, pp 49–70.

Garrett, P. B. (2018) *Welfare Words: Critical Social Work and Social Policy*, London: SAGE.

Garrett, P. M. (2007) ' "Sinbin" solutions: the "pioneer" projects for "problem families" and the forgetfulness of social policy research', *Critical Social Policy*, 27(2): 203–230.

Gentleman, A. (2022) 'Windrush scandal caused by "30 years of racist immigration laws" – report', *The Guardian*, 29 May.

George, V. and Wilding, P. (1994) *Welfare and Ideology*, New York: Harvester Wheatsheaf.

Gerrard, J. (2017) *Precarious Enterprise on the Margins: Work, Poverty, and Homelessness in the City*, New York: Palgrave Macmillan.

Gibb, J., Jelicic, H. and La Valle, I. (2011) *Rolling Out Free Early Education for Disadvantaged Two Year Olds: An Implementation Study for Local Authorities and Providers*, London: National Children's Bureau.

Gilbert, A. (2018) *British Conservatism and the Legal Regulation of Intimate Relationships*, Oxford: Hart Publishing.

Gillies, V., Horsley, N. and Edwards, R. (2017) *Challenging the Politics of Early Intervention: Who's 'Saving' Children and Why*, Bristol: Policy Press.

Goldthorpe, J. H. (2016a) 'Social class mobility in modern Britain: changing structure, constant process', *Journal of the British Academy*, 4(2): 89–111.

Goldthorpe, J. H. (2016b) 'Decades of investment in education have not improved social mobility', *The Guardian*, 12 May.

Greenstein, J. (2019) 'Development without industrialization? Household well-being and premature deindustrialization', *Journal of Economic Issues*, 53(3): 612–633.

Gregg, D. (2010) *Family Intervention Projects: A Classic Case of Policy-Based Evidence*, London: Centre for Crime and Justice Studies.

Grieve, D. (2020) *Conservatives and the European Convention on Human Rights*, Conservative Group for Europe.

Griffith, R. (2009) 'Safeguarding children: key concepts and principles', *British Journal of School Nursing*, 4(7): 335–340.

Griffiths, R. (2017) 'No love on the dole: the influence of the UK means-tested welfare system on partnering and family structure', *Journal of Social Policy*, 46(3): 543–561.

Gross, S.-A., Musgrave, G. and Janciute, L. (2018) *Well-Being and Mental Health in the Gig Economy: Policy Perspectives on Precarity*, London: University of Westminster Press.

*Guardian* (2002) 'Full text of Tony Blair's speech on welfare reform', *The Guardian*, 10 June.

*Guardian* (2014) 'Teenagers who share "sexts" could face prosecution, police warn', *The Guardian*, 22 July.

Guldberg, H. (2009) *Reclaiming Childhood: Freedom and Play in an Age of Fear*, London: Routledge.

Habib, S., Peacock, C., Ramsden-Karelse, R. and Tinsley, M. (2021) *The Changing Shape of Cultural Activism: Legislating Statues in the Context of the Black Lives Matter Movement*, Runnymede Trust, Runnymede/CoDE COVID 19 Briefings.

Hall, J., Eisenstadt, N., Sylva, K., Smith, T., Sammons, P., Smith, G., Evangelou, M., Goff, J., Tanner, E., Agur, M. and Hussey, D. (2015) 'A review of the services offered by English Sure Start Children's Centres in 2011 and 2012', *Oxford Review of Education*, 41: 89–105.

Hamilton, W. (2011) 'Young people and mental health: resilience and models of practice', in L. O'Dell and S. Leverett (eds) *Working with Children and Young People: Co-constructing Practice*, Basingstoke: Palgrave Macmillan, pp 92–105.

Hannam, J. (2012) *Feminism*, Harlow: Longman.

Harris, J. and White, V. (2018) *Undeserving Poor*, Oxford: Oxford University Press.

Hart, H. L. A. (1997) 'Are there any natural rights?', in R. E. Goodin and P. Pettit (eds) *Contemporary Political Philosophy: An Anthology*, Oxford: Blackwell, pp 281–288.

Hatt, S., Baxter, A. and Tate, J. (2008) ' "The best government initiative in recent years": teachers' perceptions of the Aimhigher programme in the south west of England', *Journal of Further and Higher Education*, 32(2): 129–138.

Hauhart, R. C. (2003) 'The Davis–Moore theory of stratification: the life course of a socially constructed classic', *The American Sociologist*, 34(4): 5–24.

Hay, C. (2014) 'Neither real nor fictitious but "as if real"? A political ontology of the state', *British Journal of Sociology*, 65(3): 459–480.

# References

Hayek, F. v. (2013 [1973, 1976, 1979]) *Law, Legislation and Liberty*, Abingdon: Routledge.

Heap, V. and Dickinson, J. (2018) 'Public Spaces Protection Orders: a critical policy analysis', *Safer Communities*, 17(3): 182–192.

Hegewisch, A. and Gornick, J. C. (2011) 'The impact of work-family policies on women's employment: a review of research from OECD countries', *Community, Work and Family*, 14(2): 119–139.

Hewitt, M. (1992) *Welfare, Ideology and Need: Developing Perspectives on the Welfare State*, Hemel Hempstead: Harvester Wheatsheaf.

Heywood, A. (2021) *Political Ideologies: An Introduction*, London: Bloomsbury.

Hick, R. O. D. and Lanau, A. (2018) 'Moving in and out of in-work poverty in the UK: an analysis of transitions, trajectories and trigger events', *Journal of Social Policy*, 47(4): 661–682.

Hirsch, D. (2018) 'The "living wage" and low income: can adequate pay contribute to adequate family living standards?', *Critical Social Policy*, 38(2): 367–386.

HM Government (2020) 'Government confirms extra support for Troubled Families to succeed', Press release.

HM Government (2021) *Supporting Families – 2021 and Beyond*, London: Ministry of Housing.

Hoggett, J. and Frost, E. (2018) 'The Troubled Families Programme and the problems of success', *Social Policy and Society*, 17(4): 523–524.

Hoghughi, M. and Long, N. (2004) *Handbook of Parenting: Theory and Research for Practice*, London: SAGE.

Holt, A. (2010) *Managing 'Spoiled Identities': Parents' Experiences of Compulsory Parenting Support Programmes*, London: John Wiley & Sons.

Holt, K. (2014) *Child Protection*, Basingstoke: Palgrave Macmillan.

Hood, C. (1991) 'A public administration for all seasons?', *Public Administration*, 69 (Spring): 3–19.

Hughes, M., Wikely, F. and Nash, T. (1994) *Parents and Their Children's Schools*, Oxford: Blackwell.

Inglis, D. and Thorpe, C. (2019) *An Invitation to Social Theory*, Cambridge: Polity Press.

Ireland, S. (2011) 'ASBOs are dead, long live ASBOs', *Criminal Justice Matters*, 86(1): 26–27.

James, A. (2009) 'Childhood matters: is children's wellbeing a high enough priority', *Mental Health Today*: June, 18–20.

James, A. and Prout, A. (1997) *Constructing and Reconstructing Childhood: Contemporary Issues in the Sociological Study of Childhood*, London: Falmer Press.

Jay, Z. (2021) 'A tale of two Europes: how conflating the European Court of Human Rights with the European Union exacerbates Euroscepticism', *British Journal of Politics and International Relations*, 24(4): 563–581.

Jenkins, N. E. (2006) ' "You can't wrap them up in cotton wool!" Constructing risk in young people's access to outdoor play', *Health, Risk and Society*, 8(4): 379–394.

Jenkins, S. (2006) *Thatcher & Sons: A Revolution in Three Acts*, London: Allen Lane.

Jensen, T. (2018) *The Cultural Industry of Parent-Blame: Parenting the Crisis*, Bristol: Bristol University Press.

Jochelson, K. (2005) *Nanny or Steward? The Role of Government in Public Health*, London: The King's Fund.

John, E. and Furnish, D. (2017) 'Elton John: "We want to raise children who accept our choices"', *The Daily Telegraph*, 4 July.

Johnston, G. and Percy-Smith, J. (2003) 'In search of social capital', *Policy and Politics*, 31(3): 321–334.

Jones, G. (2007) 'Assessing the success of the sale of social housing in the UK', *Journal of Social Welfare and Family Law*, 29(2): 135–150.

Jones, K. (1991) *The Making of Social Policy in Britain 1830–1990*, London: Athlone.

Jones, O. (2016) *Chavs: The Demonization of the Working Class*, London: Verso.

Jones, P. and Bradbury, L. (2018) *Introducing Social Theory*, Cambridge: Polity Press.

Jordan, B. (1973) *Paupers: The Making of the New Claiming Class*, London: Routledge and Kegan Paul.

Jordan, B. (1987) *Rethinking Welfare*, Oxford: Basil Blackwell.

Joseph Rowntree Foundation (2018) UK Poverty 2018 [online], Available from: www.jrf.org.uk/report/uk-poverty-2018 [Accessed 20 March 2020].

Joseph-Salisbury, R., Connelly, L. and Wangari-Jones, P. (2021) '"The UK is not innocent": Black Lives Matter, policing and abolition in the UK', *Equality, Diversity and Inclusion: An International Journal*, 40(1): 21–28.

Joyce, R. and Sibieta, L. (2013) Labour's Record on Poverty and Inequality [online], Available from: www.ifs.org.uk/publications/6738 [Accessed 27 July 2020].

Jupp, E. (2017) 'Families, policy and place in times of austerity', *Area*, 49(3): 266–273.

Kaltwasser, C. R., Taggart, P., Espejo, P. O. and Ostiguy, P. (2017) *Populism: An Overview of the Concept and the State of the Art*, Oxford: Oxford University Press.

Kemp, P. A. (2015) 'Private renting after the Global Financial Crisis', *Housing Studies*, 30(4): 601–620.

King, P. (2010) *Housing Policy Transformed: The Right to Buy and the Desire to Own*, Bristol: Policy Press.

Knight, A., La Placa, V. and McNaught, A. (eds) (2014) *Wellbeing: Policy and Practice*, Banbury: Lantern Publishing.

Knowles, G. (2009) *Ensuring Every Child Matters*, London: SAGE.

Knowles, G. and Holmstrom, R. (2013) *Understanding Family Diversity and Home–School Relations: A Guide for Students and Practitioners in Early Years and Primary Settings*, London: Routledge.

Koch, I. (2017) 'What's in a vote? Brexit beyond culture wars', *American Ethnologist*, 44(2): 225–230.

La Placa, V. and Knight, A. (2014) 'Wellbeing: a new policy phenomenon?', in A. McNaught, V. La Placa and A. Knight (eds) *Wellbeing: Policy and Practice*, Branbury: Lantern Publishing, pp 17–26.

Lambert, M. (2019) 'Between "families in trouble" and "children at risk": historicising "troubled family" policy in England since 1945', *Children and Society*, 33(1): 82–91.

# References

Lambie-Mumford, H. and Green, M. A. (2017) 'Austerity, welfare reform and the rising use of food banks by children in England and Wales', *Area*, 49(3): 273–280.

Lareau, A. (2011) *Unequal Childhoods: Class, Race, and Family Life*, London: University of California Press.

Larner, W. (2000) 'Neo-liberalism: policy, ideology, governmentality', *Studies in Political Economy*, 63(1): 5–25.

Layard, R. (2011) *Happiness: Lessons from a New Science*, London: Penguin.

Lee, S. and Beech, M. (2008) *Ten Years of New Labour*, Basingstoke: Palgrave Macmillan.

Lehtonen, A. (2018) '"Helping workless families": cultural poverty and the family in austerity and anti-welfare discourse', *Sociological Research Online*, 23(1): 84.

LeMoyne, T. and Buchanan, T. (2011) 'Does "hovering" matter? Helicopter parenting and its effect on well-being', *Sociological Spectrum*, 31(4): 399–419.

Levitas, R. (1998) *The Inclusive Society? Social Exclusion and New Labour*, Basingstoke: Palgrave.

Levitas, R. (2012) There May be 'Trouble' Ahead: What We Know about Those 120,000 'Troubled' Families, Poverty and Social Exclusion [online], Available from: www.poverty.ac.uk/policy-response-working-papers-famil ies-social-policy-life-chances-children-parenting-uk-government [Accessed 11 October 2022].

Lewis, J. (2011) 'Parenting programmes in England: policy development and implementation issues, 2005–2010', *Journal of Social Welfare and Family Law*, 33(2): 107–122.

Lewis, J., Cuthbert, R. and Sarre, S. (2011) 'What are Children's Centres? The development of CC services, 2004–2008', *Social Policy and Administration*, 45(1): 35–54.

Lin, N. (2001) *Social Capital: A Theory of Social Structure and Action*, Cambridge: Cambridge University Press.

Lindon, J., Webb, J. and Lindon, J. (2016) *Safeguarding and Child Protection*, London: Hodder Education.

Lindsay, G., Strand, S. and Davis, H. (2011) 'A comparison of the effectiveness of three parenting programmes in improving parenting skills, parent mental-well being and children's behaviour when implemented on a large scale in community settings in 18 English local authorities: the parenting early intervention pathfinder (PEIP)', *BMC Public Health*, 1: 962.

Lindsay, G., Totsika, V. and Thomas, R. (2019) 'Evaluating Parent Gym: a community implemented universal parenting programme', *Journal of Children's Services*, 14(1): 1–15.

Longfield, A. (2020) *Best Beginnings: A Proposal for a New Early Years Guarantee to Give All Children in England the Best Start in Life*, London: Children's Commissioner for England.

Lowe, R. (2005) *The Welfare State in Britain since 1945*, Basingstoke: Palgrave Macmillan.

Lund, B. (2016) *Housing Politics in the United Kingdom: Power, Planning and Protest*, Bristol: Policy Press.

Lupton, D. (1999) *Risk*, London: Routledge.

Lyndon, S. (2019) 'Troubling discourses of poverty in early childhood in the UK', *Children and Society*, 33(6): 602–609.

Lyon, C. M. (2007) 'Interrogating the concentration on the UNCRC instead of the ECHR in the development of children's rights in England?', *Children and Society*, 21(2): 147–154.

MacDonald, R. and Giazitzoglu, A. (2019) 'Youth, enterprise and precarity: or, what is, and what is wrong with, the "gig economy"?', *Journal of Sociology*, 55(4): 724–740.

Macdonald, R., Shildrick, T. and Furlong, A. (2014) 'In search of "intergenerational cultures of worklessness": hunting the yeti and shooting zombies', *Critical Social Policy*, 34: 199–220.

MacInnes, T., Aldridge, H., Bushe, S., Kenway, P. and Tinson, A. (2013) *Monitoring Poverty and Social Exclusion 2013*, York: Joseph Rowntree Foundation.

Mann, K. (1992) *The Making of an English 'Underclass'? The Social Divisions of Welfare and Labour*, Milton Keynes: Open University Press.

Marmot, M. (2015) 'The richer you are, the better your health – and how this can be changed', *The Guardian*, 11 September.

Martínez-Martí, M. L. and Ruch, W. (2017) 'Character strengths predict resilience over and above positive affect, self-efficacy, optimism, social support, self-esteem, and life satisfaction', *Journal of Positive Psychology*, 12(2): 110–120.

Mason, R., Proctor, K. and Elliott, L. (2019) 'Fears child poverty may rise to record 60-year high under Tories', *The Guardian*, 26 November.

May-Chahal, C. and Coleman, S. (2003) *Safeguarding Children and Young People*, London: Routledge.

McBride, J., Smith, A. and Mbala, M. (2018) '"You end up with nothing": the experience of being a statistic of "in-work poverty" in the UK', *Work, Employment and Society*, 32(1): 210–218.

McDermott, S. (2017) 'I lost my job over a Facebook post – was that fair?', BBC [online], Available from: https://www.bbc.co.uk/news/stories-41851771 [Accessed 3 November 2019].

McElwee, N. (2007) 'Chapter 1: Snowflake children', *Child and Youth Services*, 29(1/2): 1–27.

McNamee, S. (2016) *The Social Study of Childhood*, London: Palgrave.

McNaught, A. (2011) 'Defining wellbeing', in A. Knight and A. McNaught (eds) *Understanding Wellbeing: An Introduction for Students and Practitioners of Health and Social Care*, Cheltenham: Lantern Publishing, pp 30–45.

Megele, C. and Buzzi, P. (2018) *Safeguarding Children and Young People Online: A Short Guide for Social Workers*, Bristol: Policy Press.

Mende, M., Scott, M. L., Garvey, A. M. and Bolton, L. E. (2019) 'The marketing of love: how attachment styles affect romantic consumption journeys', *Journal of the Academy of Marketing Science*, 47(2): 255–273.

Miller, L. and Hevey, D. (2012) *Policy Issues in the Early Years*, London, SAGE.

# References

Mirowski, P. (2014) *The Political Movement That Dared Not Speak Its Own Name: The Neoliberal Thought Collective under Erasure*, New York: Institute for New Economic Thinking.

Mirowski, P. and Plehwe, D. (eds) (2009) *The Road from Mont Pèlerin: The Making of the Neoliberal Thought Collective*, Cambridge, MA: Harvard University Press.

Moore, A. and Reynolds, P. (2018) 'Sex, sexuality and social media: a new and pressing danger?', in A. Moore and P. Reynolds (eds) *Childhood and Sexuality: Contemporary Issues and Debates*, London: Palgrave Macmillan, pp 225–246.

Moore, K. (2019) *Wellbeing and Aspirational Culture*, Cham: Springer International.

Morgan, D. H. J. (2011) *Rethinking Family Practices*, Basingstoke: Palgrave Macmillan.

Morgan, D. H. J., McCarthy, J. R., Gillies, V. and Hooper, C.-A. (2019) 'Family troubles, troubling families, and family practices', *Journal of Family Issues*, 40(16): 2225–2238.

Morgan, P. (2007) *The War between the Family and the State: How Government Divides and Impoverishes*, London: Institute for Economic Affairs.

Morris, K., Mason, W., Bywaters, P., Featherstone, B., Daniel, B., Brady, G., Bunting, L., Hooper, J., Mirza, N., Scourfield, J. and Webb, C. (2018) 'Social work, poverty, and child welfare interventions', *Child and Family Social Work*, 23(3): 364–372.

Moss, P., Dillon, J. and Statham, J. (2000) 'The "child in need" and "the rich child": discourses, constructions and practice', *Critical Social Policy*, 20(2): 233–255.

Mount, F. (1982) *The Subversive Family*, New York: The Free Press.

Mudde, C. and Kaltwasser, R. (2017) *Populism: A Very Short Introduction*, Oxford: Oxford University Press.

Mullin, A. (2012) 'The ethical and social significance of parenting: a philosophical approach', *Parenting: Science and Practice*, 12(2/3): 134–143.

Munro, L. (2019) *Life Chances, Education and Social Movements*, London: Anthem Press.

Murie, A. (2016) *The Right to Buy? Selling off Public and Social Housing*, Bristol: Policy Press.

Murray, C. (1984) *Losing Ground: American Social Policy, 1950–1980*, New York: Basic Books.

Murray, C., Lister, R., Institute of Economic Affairs and Health and Welfare Unit (1996) *Charles Murray and the Underclass: The Developing Debate*, London: Institute of Economic Affairs, Health and Welfare Unit.

Neckerman, K. M. (1993) 'The emergence of "underclass" family patterns, 1900–1940', in M. B. Katz (ed) *The 'Underclass' Debate*, Princeton, NJ: Princeton University Press, pp 194–219.

NESS (2012) *The Impact of Sure Start Local Programmes on Seven Year Olds and Their Families*, London: Institute for the Study of Children, Families and Social Issues, University of London.

Nettleingham, D. (2019) 'Beyond the heartlands: deindustrialization, naturalization and the meaning of an "industrial" tradition', *British Journal of Sociology*, 70(2): 610–626.

Nicolson, P. (2014) *A Critical Approach to Human Growth and Development*, Basingstoke: Palgrave Macmillan.

Nixon, J. (2007) 'Deconstructing "problem" researchers and "problem" families: a rejoinder to Garrett', *Critical Social Policy*, 27(4): 546–556.

O'Brien, B. (2016) 'Public spaces protection orders: an "attack of vagueness"', *Safer Communities*, 15(4): 183–189.

O'Brien, M. and Kyprianou, P. (2017) *Just Managing? What It Means for the Families of Austerity Britain*, Cambridge, Open Book Publishers.

O'Byrne, D. J. (2019) 'The rise of populism, the demise of the neoliberal and neoconservative globalist projects, and the war on human rights', *International Critical Thought*, 9(2): 254–268.

O'Hara, G. (2018) *New Labour's Domestic Policies: Neoliberal, Social Democratic or a Unique Blend?*, London: Tony Blair Institute for Global Change.

O'Hara, M. (2020) *The Shame Game: Overturning the Toxic Narrative of Poverty*, Bristol: Policy Press.

O'Hara, M. and Thomas, M. (2014) *Austerity Bites: A Journey to the Sharp End of Cuts in the UK*, Bristol: Policy Press.

OBR (2022) Brexit Analysis [online], Available from: https://obr.uk/foreca sts-in-depth/the-economy-forecast/brexit-analysis/#assumptions [Accessed 19 July 2022].

Olssen, M. (2016) 'Neoliberal competition in higher education today: research, accountability and impact', *British Journal of Sociology of Education*, 37(1): 129–148.

Olsson, C. A., Bond, L., Burns, J. M., Vella-Brodrick, D. A. and Sawyer, S. M. (2003) 'Adolescent resilience: a concept analysis', *Journal of Adolescence*, 26(1): 1–12.

ONS (2018) *Statistical Bulletin: UK Labour Market: February 2018 Estimates of Employment, Unemployment, Economic Inactivity and Other Employment-Related Statistics for the UK*, London: Office for National Statistics.

ONS (2019) Families and Households in the UK: 2019 [online], Available from: www.ons.gov.uk/peoplepopulationandcommunity/birthsdeathsandmarria ges/families/bulletins/familiesandhouseholds/2019 [Accessed 3 August 2020].

ONS (2020) Average Weekly Earnings in Great Britain: February 2020 [online], Available from: www.ons.gov.uk/employmentandlabourmarket/peopleinwork/ employmentandemployeetypes/bulletins/averageweeklyearningsingreatbritain/ february2020 [Accessed 20 March 2020].

Page, R. M. (2015) *Clear Blue Water? The Conservative Party and the Welfare State since 1940*, Bristol: Policy Press.

Parr, S. (2017) Explaining and understanding state intervention into the lives of "troubled" families', *Social Policy and Society*, 16(4): 577.

Parton, N. (2004) 'From Maria Colwell to Victoria Climbié: reflections on public inquiries into child abuse a generation apart', *Child Abuse Review*, 13(2): 80–94.

Parton, N. (2006) *Safeguarding Childhood: Early Intervention and Surveillance in a Late Modern Society*, Basingstoke: Palgrave Macmillan.

Paterson, L. L., Coffey-Glover, L. and Peplow, D. (2016) 'Negotiating stance within discourses of class: reactions to *Benefits Street*', *Discourse and Society*, 27(2): 195–214.

Peck, J. (2010) *Constructions of Neoliberal Reason*, Oxford: Oxford University Press.

Perraudin, F. (2019) 'Yorkshire schools will not get back millions lost in trust's collapse: Wakefield City Academies Trust centralised schools' reserves and then went bust', *The Guardian*, 18 November.

Pinto, S. (2017) 'Researching romantic love', *Rethinking History*, 21(4): 567–585.

Portes, J. (2021) 'Now it's official: Brexit will damage the economy long into the future', *The Guardian*, 28 October.

Powell, M. A. (ed) (1999) *New Labour, New Welfare State? The 'Third Way' in British Social Policy*, Bristol: Policy Press.

Powell, M. A. (2000) 'New Labour and the Third Way in the British welfare state: a new and distinctive approach?', *Critical Social Policy*, 20(1): 39–60.

Prendergast, L. M., Hill, D. and Jones, S. (2017) 'Social exclusion, education and precarity: neoliberalism, neoconservatism and class war from above', *Journal for Critical Education Policy Studies*, 15(2): 23–58.

Prideaux, S. (2005) *Not So New Labour: A Sociological Critique of New Labour's Policy and Practice*, Bristol: Policy Press.

Putnam, R. D. (2001) *Bowling Alone: The Collapse and Revival of American Community*, London: Touchstone.

Putnam, R. D. and Goss, K. A. (2002) 'Introduction', in R. D. Putnam (ed) *Democracies in Flux: The Evolution of Social Capital in Contemporary Society*, Oxford: Oxford University Press, pp 3–20.

Rawlinson, K., Badshah, N. and Weaver, M. (2022) 'Windrush scandal: timeline of key events', *The Guardian*, 16 April.

Reay, D. (2017) *Miseducation: Inequality, Education and the Working Classes*, Bristol: Policy Press.

Reay, D., Davies, J., David, M. and Ball, S. J. (2001) 'Choices of degree or degrees of choice? Class, "race" and the higher education choice process', *Sociology*, 35(4): 855–874.

Reay, D., David, M. E. and Ball, S. (2005) *Degrees of Choice: Social Class, Race and Gender in Higher Education*, Stoke on Trent: Trentham Books.

Ridge, T. (2013) '"We are all in this together"? The hidden costs of poverty, recession and austerity policies on Britain's poorest children', *Children and Society*, 27(5): 406–417.

Robb, C. (2018) *More People in Work, But Many Still Trapped in Poverty*, York: Joseph Rowntree Foundation.

Roberts, R. (2010) *Wellbeing from Birth*, London: SAGE.

Robson, S. (2011) 'Internationalization: a transformative agenda for higher education?', *Teachers and Teaching*, 17(6): 619–630.

Romano, S. (2018) *Moralising Poverty: The 'Undeserving' Poor in the Public Gaze*, London: Routledge.

Rönkä, A., Malinen, K., Metsäpelto, R.-L., Laakso, M.-L., Sevón, E. and Verhoef-van Dorp, M. (2017) 'Parental working time patterns and children's socioemotional wellbeing: comparing working parents in Finland, the United Kingdom, and the Netherlands', *Children and Youth Services Review*, 76: 133–141.

Rose, W. and McAuley, C. (2019) 'Poverty and its impact on parenting in the UK: re-defining the critical nature of the relationship through examining lived experiences in times of austerity', *Children and Youth Services Review*, 97: 134–141.

Royston, S. (2017), Welfare reform and the "family test", in *Broken Benefits*, Bristol: Bristol University Press, pp 122–133.

Runciman, W. G. (1990) 'How many classes are there in contemporary British society?', *Sociology*, 24(3): 377–396.

Ryan, F. (2019) 'Young people like Jess need the safety net. But austerity has destroyed it; councils are buckling under the strain of families in crisis, thanks to catastrophic cuts to children and young people's services', *The Guardian*, 28 February.

Sage, D. (2012) 'A challenge to liberalism? The communitarianism of the Big Society and Blue Labour', *Critical Social Policy*, 32(3): 365–382.

Saltiel, D. (2013) 'Understanding complexity in families' lives: the usefulness of family practices as an aid to decision-making', *Rediscovering Family and Kinship: New Directions for Social Work Theory, Policy and Practice*, 18: 15–24.

Sayer, T. (2008) *Critical Practice in Working with Children*, Basingstoke: Palgrave Macmillan.

Scholz, S. J. (2010) *Feminism: A Beginner's Guide*, Richmond: Oneworld.

Shaw, B., Watson, B., Frauendienst, B., Redecker, A., Jones, T. and Hillman, M. (2013) *Children's Independent Mobility: A Comparative Study in England and Germany (1971–2010)*, London: Policy Studies Institute.

Shildrick, T. (2018) 'Lessons from Grenfell: poverty propaganda, stigma and class power', *Sociological Review*, 66(4): 783–798.

Simpson, D., Lumsden, E. and McDowall Clark, R. (2015) 'Neoliberalism, global poverty policy and early childhood education and care: a critique of local uptake in England', *Early Years*, 35(1): 96–109.

Siraj, I. and Mayo, A. (2014) *Social Class and Educational Inequality: The Impact of Parents and Schools*, Cambridge: Cambridge University Press.

Siraj-Blatchford, I., Mayo, A., Melhuish, E., Taggart, B., Sammons, P. and Sylva, K. (2013) 'The learning life course of at "risk" children aged 3–16: perceptions of students and parents about "succeeding against the odds"', *Scottish Educational Review*, 42(2): 5–17.

Sixsmith, J., Gabhainn, S. N., Fleming, C. and O'Higgins, S. (2007) 'Children's, parents' and teachers' perceptions of child wellbeing', *Health Education*, 107(6): 511–524.

Skinner, Q. (1997) 'The state', in R. E. Goodin and P. Pettit (eds) *Contemporary Political Philosophy: An Anthology*, Oxford: Blackwell, pp 3–25.

Smart, C. (2007) *Personal Life*, Oxford: Wiley.

Smith, F. (2013) 'Parents and policy under New Labour: a case study of the United Kingdom's new deal for lone parents', *Children's Geographies*, 11(2): 160–173.

Smith, J. (1997) 'The ideology of "family and community": New Labour abandons the welfare state', *Socialist Register*, 33(1): 176–197.

Smith, K. M. (2014) *The Government of Childhood: Discourse, Power and Subjectivity*, Basingstoke: Palgrave Macmillan.

Smith, M. J. (1998) *Social Science in Question*, London: SAGE.

Spratt, J. (2016) 'Childhood wellbeing: what role for education?', *British Educational Research Journal*, 42(2): 223–239.

Steel, L., Kidd, W. and Brown, A. (2012) *The Family*, Basingstoke: Palgrave Macmillan.

Stepney, P., Lynch, R. and Jordan, B. (1999) 'Poverty, exclusion and New Labour', *Critical Social Policy*, 19(1): 109–127.

Stollznow, K. (2021) 'Why is it so offensive to say "all lives matter"?', *The Conversation*, 13 January.

Storey, J. (2018) *Cultural Theory and Popular Culture: An Introduction*, Abingdon: Routledge.

Strangleman, T. (2018) 'Mining a productive seam? The coal industry, community and sociology', *Contemporary British History*, 32(1): 18–38.

Street, M. (2021) 'Theorising child well-being: towards a framework for analysing early childhood education policy in England', *Journal of Early Childhood Research*, 19(2): 211–224.

Taket, A. R., Nolan, A. and Stagnitti, K. (2014) 'Family strategies to support and develop resilience in early childhood', *Early Years: An International Journal of Research and Development*, 34: 289–301.

Taylor, D. (2011) 'Wellbeing and welfare: a psychosocial analysis of being well and doing well enough', *Journal of Social Policy*, 40(4): 777–795.

Taylor, G. (2007) *Ideology and Welfare*, Basingstoke: Palgrave Macmillan.

Taylor, Z. E., Eisenberg, N., Spinrad, T. L. and Widaman, K. F. (2013) 'Longitudinal relations of intrusive parenting and effortful control to ego-resiliency during early childhood', *Child Development*, 84(4): 1145–1152.

Taylor-Gooby, P. (1991) *Social Change, Social Welfare and Social Science*, London: Harvester/Wheatsheaf.

Thane, P. (1996) *Foundations of the Welfare State*, Harlow: Longman.

Thatcher, M. T. F. (1987) 'Interview for *Woman's Own* ("no such thing as society")' [online], Available from: www.margaretthatcher.org/document/106689 [Accessed 17 September 2019].

Thompson, N. (2017) *Social Problems and Social Justice*, London: Palgrave.

Tisdall, L. (2017) 'Education, parenting and concepts of childhood in England, c. 1945 to c. 1979', *Contemporary British History*, 31(1): 24–46.

Trussell, T. (2019) End of Year Statistics [online], Available from: www.trusselltrust.org/news-and-blog/latest-stats/end-year-stats/ [Accessed 21 July 2020].

Tunstill, J. and Willow, C. (2017) 'Professional social work and the defence of children's and their families' rights in a period of austerity: a case study', *Social Work and Social Sciences Review*, 19(1): 40–66.

Turnbull, G. (2016) 'The price of youth: commodification of young people through malleable risk practices', *Journal of Youth Studies*, 19(8): 1007–1022.

Turnbull, G. and Spence, J. (2011) 'What's at risk? The proliferation of risk across child and youth policy in England', *Journal of Youth Studies*, 14(8): 939–960.

Turner, R. S. (2011) *Neo-Liberal Ideology: History, Concepts and Policies*, Edinburgh: Edinburgh University Press.

UNICEF (1989) UN Convention of the Rights of the Child [online], Available from: www.unicef.org/rightsite/237.htm [Accessed 12 March 2018].

Uprichard, E. (2008) 'Children as "being and becomings": children, childhood and temporality', *Children and Society*, 22(4): 303–313.

Valentine, G. and Harris, C. (2014) 'Strivers vs skivers: class prejudice and the demonisation of dependency in everyday life', *Geoforum*, 53: 84–92.

Vincent, C. D. and Maxwell, C. (2016) 'Parenting priorities and pressures: furthering understanding of "concerted cultivation"', *Discourse: Studies in the Cultural Politics of Education*, 37(2): 269–282.

Vincent, C. D. and Neis, B. L. (2011) 'Work and family life: parental work schedules and child academic achievement', *Community, Work and Family*, 14(4): 449–469.

Waites, M. (2001) 'Regulation of sexuality: age of consent, section 28 and sex education', *Parliamentary Affairs*, 54(3): 495–508.

Walker, S. (2020) ' "Baby machines": Eastern Europe's answer to depopulation', *The Guardian*, 4 March.

Walkerdine, V. (2009) 'Developmental psychology and the study of childhood', in M. J. Kehily (ed) *An Introduction to Childhood*, Maidenhead: Open University Press, pp 112–123.

Warner, J. (2013) 'Social work, class politics and risk in the moral panic over Baby P', *Health, Risk and Society*, 15(3): 217–233.

Weaver, M. (2015) ' "Poshness tests" block working-class applicants at top companies', *The Guardian*, 16 June.

Wellard, I. and Secker, M. (2017) ' "Visions" for children's health and wellbeing: exploring the complex and arbitrary processes of putting theory into practice', *Sport, Education and Society*, 22(5): 586–601.

Wells, K. (2018) *Childhood Studies*, Cambridge: Polity Press.

Welshman, J. (1999) 'The social history of social work: the issue of the "problem family", 1940–70', *British Journal of Social Work*, 29(3): 457–476.

Welshman, J. (2013) *Underclass: A History of the Excluded since 1880*, London: Bloomsbury Academic.

Whalley, M. (2007) *Involving Parents in Their Children's Learning*, London: Paul Chapman.

Wheeler, S. (2018) ' "Essential assistance" versus "concerted cultivation": theorising class-based patterns of parenting in Britain', *Pedagogy, Culture and Society*, 26(3), 327–344.

Wheway, R. (2007) *Not a Risk Averse Society: Fair Play for Children*, Bognor Regis: Fair Play for Children.

# References

Whitaker, R. (1987) 'Neo-conservatism and the State', *Socialist Register*, 23(1): 1–31.

Whittaker, K. A. and Cowley, S. (2012) 'An effective programme is not enough: a review of factors associated with poor attendance and engagement with parenting support programmes', *Children and Society*, 26(2): 138–149.

Wilby, P. (2020) 'The expert in social mobility who says education cannot make it happen', *The Guardian*, 17 March.

Wilding, R. (2017) *Families, Intimacy and Globalization: Floating Ties*, Basingstoke: Palgrave Macmillan.

Wilkinson, R. G. and Pickett, K. (2010) *The Spirit Level: Why Equality Is Better for Everyone*, London: Penguin.

Wilkinson, R. G. and Pickett, K. (2018) *The Inner Level: How More Equal Societies Reduce Stress, Restore Sanity and Improve Everyone's Wellbeing*, London: Allen Lane.

Williams, F. (1989) *Social Policy: A Critical Introduction: Issues of Race, Gender and Class*, Cambridge: Polity Press.

Wilson, A. (2001) 'Social policy and sexuality', in M. Lavalette and A. Pratt (eds) *Social Policy: A Conceptual and Theoretical Introduction*, London: SAGE, pp 121–140.

Wilson, E. (1977) *Women and the Welfare State*, London: Tavistock.

Wright, S., Fletcher, D. R. and Stewart, A. B. R. (2020) 'Punitive benefit sanctions, welfare conditionality, and the social abuse of unemployed people in Britain: transforming claimants into offenders?', *Social Policy and Administration*, 54(2): 278–294.

Wrong, D. H. (1999) 'Inequality and the division of labor: the Davis–Moore theory reexamined', *European Journal of Sociology*, 40(2): 233–256.

Wyness, M. G. (2012) *Childhood and Society*, Basingstoke: Palgrave Macmillan.

# Index

**A**

abuse  71, 157–9
adverse childhood experiences  142
African Charter on the Rights and Welfare
    of the Child  72
agency  6, 10, 142, 154–5, 173
ages and stages  24
AimHigher project  175
anti-social behaviour  30
    Anti-Social Behaviour Order
      (ASBO)  67
    Criminal Behaviour Order  68
    Civil Injunctions  68
aspiration  35, 86, 101, 175, 89, 187
    aspirational  33, 44
    see also life-choices
austerity  7, 83, 105, 127–8, 183–4

**B**

being critical  2, 47, 111, 147
Beveridge report  111–12, 121
Black Lives Matter  48, 66
Bourdieu, Pierre  100
Brexit  74–5
Bronfenbrenner, Urie  3–6, 154

**C**

child abuse  157–8
child protection  157, 160–1, 166
child's voice  24
childcare
    costs and subsidies  115–17
    gender  113
childhood  19, 22, 32, 60, 120
children
    as becomings  23–4, 34, 120
    as beings  23–4, 71
Children's Centres  103
    see also Sure Start
Civil Injunctions  see anti-social behaviour
Clause 28  55
Communitarianism  36, 96–8
    and parenting  97
consumerism  13
Criminal Behaviour Order  see anti-social
    behaviour
cultural capital  98, 100–2
culture wars  54, 90–2

**D**

deindustrialisation  7–8
democracy  73
deregulation  119
    in housing  187–8
discourse  12–13, 17–20, 132
    as power  21–2, 24, 110
domestic violence  18
    see also smacking children

**E**

early intervention  33, 37
Effective Provision of Pre-school, Primary and
      Secondary Education Project EPPE  34
equal pay legislation  174–9
European Court of Human Rights  58, 65–6
Every Child Matters  103, 161–2

**F**

failing families  6, 21, 37, 104
    cultural differences  91–2
    poverty  104, 191
family  9–10
    discourse  19–20
    family practices,  10, 15, 33
    fluid family  11, 17
feminist concerns  113–14
food banks  104, 182
Foucault, Michel  17, 65, 124
Functionalism  97, 175
    social inequality  175

**G**

gig economy  127, 172, 183
Gini co-efficient  176

**H**

happiness  127–8
Head Start  5
health and safety  148, 154
hegemony  81
housing
    bedroom tax  185
    benefits  190
    council housing  186–7, 189–90
    housing associations  187
    Mesher orders  188
    private rented sector (PRS)  187–9

regulation and deregulation 188
right to buy 189–90
social housing 187
human capital 96

**I**

ideology 79–81
indecent images 164
individualism
anti-social behaviour 68
communitarianism 96
Piaget 4
responsibility 32, 84
inequality 33, 83, 104, 175–7, 195
Black Lives Matter 66
neoconservatism 91
neoliberalism 86
'New Labour' 94
social mobility 193–4
wellbeing 128

**L**

Lareau, Annette 34–5
life-chances 32, 94, 171–2, 194–5
gender 179
inequality 177, 183–4
Life Chances Act (2010) 172
Sure Start 120
life-choices 173–4
love 12–13
tough love 33
*Love Island* 14

**M**

managerialism 166
Marriage (Same Sex Couples) Act (2013) 55
milestones 24
morals 21, 91, 97

**N**

nanny state 63–4
need 31, 114–16, 133–4
children in need 132–3
neoconservatism 89–93, 105
sexuality 55–6
*see also* culture wars
neoliberalism 32–3, 84–9, 105
Conservative Party 83
Every Child Matters 103
housing 190
*see also* deregulation; managerialism
New Labour 83–4, 93–6, 106
Every Child Matters 167

Third Way 93, 95
*see also* communitarianism
New Poor Law 117–18
nude selfies *see* sexting

**O**

obesity 19, 52–3, 156

**P**

parenting 19, 31–5
'good enough' 160
helicopter parents 126, 142
parenting orders 31
parenting programmes 32
parenting styles 34–5
risk 19, 145, 149
support 36–7
Piaget, Jean 4
politics
left-wing and right-wing 43, 81–4
*see also* Third Way
populism 74–5
potential 23–4
poverty 183–4, 191
Child Poverty Act (2010) 180–2, 184
intergenerational 44
in-work poverty 181–2
Marmot, Michael 177
poverty progaganda 114
Thatcher, Margaret 46
underclass 41–2
Welfare Reform and Work Act (2016) 180–1
*see also* austerity; food banks

**R**

reflective practice 16, 151
reflexivity 16–17, 151–2
Reggio Emilia 20
regulation
of family life 29–31, 49, 60–1, 112
in housing 188
of sex 56
resilience 136, 139–42
and adversity 142–3
role of parents 142
as trait or process 140–1
rhetoric 47, 107
rights 48, 59, 65–6
children 70–2
communitarianism 96–7
culture wars 91–2
denial or restrictions 68–9
ideology 80

personal freedoms 62–3, 67
the state 72, 77, 180
*see also* African Charter on the Rights and
    Welfare of the Child; European Court
    of Human Rights; United Nations
    Convention on the Rights of the Child
risk 148, 155–6
    children at risk or as risk 149
    development 147
    exploratory risk 151
    mobile phones 151, 164–5
    parenting 19, 149
    resilience 151
    restricted lives 154
    *see also* toxic trio

**S**
safeguarding 157–8, 168
    age of consent 163
    Children Act (1989) 158
    Criminal Records Bureau (CRB) 161
    Every Child Matters 162
    New Labour 161, 167
    *see also* child protection; toxic trio
school uniform 70–1
self-esteem 147–8
sexting 164
    Sexual Offences Act (2003) 164
    *see also* indecent images
smacking children 18, 71
snowflakes 136, 143, 154
social capital 98–100
social democracy 93–4
social inclusion 80, 96
social justice 48, 95, 104
    Commission for Social Justice 95
social mobility 100, 102, 192, 196
    cultural capital 100–1, 192–3
    grammar schools 192
    polish, and poshness tests 101
    *see also* life-chances
social networks 165
socio-ecological model *see* Bronfenbrenner
state, the 57–9
structure 10, 43, 86, 154
Sure Start 5, 103, 120

**T**
the definite article 11
therapy 135–6
toxic trio 158–9
troubled families 38–41, 47–8, 104
    discourse 22

rhetoric 47
social justice 48, 104
Supporting Families 41
*see also* failing families; underclass

**U**
underclass 41–6, 181
United Nations Convention on the Rights
    of the Child (UNCRC) 72

**V**
values 17, 50, 54–5, 75, 160
    Beveridge Report 111–12
    Children's Centres 103
    ideologies 80
    moral values 91
    neoconservatism 92–3
*verstehen* 14–15
vulnerability 23, 131–7, 148
    age of consent 163
    developing resilience 136
    discourse 132, 135
    parenting 154
    poverty 134
Vygotsky, Lev 4–5

**W**
wanting it 173–4
welfare 85, 88, 95, 110, 134, 183
    child benefit 61
    dependency 42
    deserving/undeserving 114
    discourse 96, 110
    ideology 110
    need 115
    reflexivity 17
    *see also* New Poor Law
Welfare Reform and Work Act
    (2016) 180–1
Welfare State 110–12
    family roles/gender 111–13, 118
    feminist critiques 113–14
    underclass 42–3
    *see also* Beveridge Report
wellbeing 123–30
    as dynamic 125
    inequality 128
    mental health 128
    subjective wellbeing 124
    *see also* happiness
Windrush 59–60
woke 54, 82, 92
workhouse *see* New Poor Law

www.ingramcontent.com/pod-product-compliance
Lightning Source LLC
Chambersburg PA
CBHW080557030426
42336CB00019B/3218